certain solitudes

certain solitudes

On the Poetry
of Donald Justice

EDITED BY

DANA GIOIA AND WILLIAM LOGAN

The University of Arkansas Press
Fayetteville ■ 1997

01 00 99 98 97   5 4 3 2 1

Designed by Liz Lester

⊛ The paper used in this publication meets the mini-
mum requirements of the American National Standard
for Permanence of Paper for Printed Library Materials
Z39.48-1984.

Library of Congress cataloging-in-publication data

Certain solitudes : on the poetry of Donald Justice /
    edited by Dana Gioia and William Logan.
        p.   cm.
    Includes bibliographical references and index.
    ISBN 1-55728-475-X (alk. paper)
        1. Justice, Donald Rodney, 1925–   —Criticism
    and interpretation. I. Gioia, Dana. II. Logan,
    William, 1950–   .
    PS3519.U825Z65   1997
    811'.54—dc21   97–40809
                                                CIP

for Jean Ross Justice

ACKNOWLEDGMENTS

Grateful acknowledgment is made for permission to print the following:

Bruce Bawer. "'Avec une élégance grave et lente': The Poetry of Donald Justice," copyright © 1992 by Bruce Bawer. Originally published in *Verse*, winter/spring 1992. Reprinted by permission of the author. "The Poetry in Things Past and Passing," copyright © 1988 by Bruce Bawer. Originally published in *Washington Post Book World*, January 3, 1988. Reprinted by permission of the author.

Philip Booth. "Syracuse Years: 1966–1970," copyright © 1997 by Philip Booth. Published here, for the first time, by permission of the author.

Edgar Bowers. "With Don and Jean Justice at Chapel Hill," copyright © 1997 by Edgar Bowers. Published here, for the first time, by permission of the author.

Witter Bynner. "A Note on Donald Justice," copyright © 1960 by Witter Bynner. Originally published in *Poetry*, October 1960. Reprinted by permission of the Witter Bynner Foundation for Poetry.

Joel O. Conarroe. "Five Poets," copyright © 1967 by Joel O. Conarroe. Originally published in *Shenandoah*, summer 1967. Reprinted by permission of the author.

Joseph Di Prisco. "Departures: The Poetry of Donald Justice," copyright © 1976 by Joseph Di Prisco. Originally published in *San Francisco Review of Books*, July/August 1976. Reprinted by permission of the author.

Laurence Donovan. "Donald Justice's Miami," copyright © 1992 by Laurence Donovan. Originally published in *Verse*, winter/spring 1992. Reprinted by permission of the author. "Review," copyright © 1988 by Laurence Donovan. Originally published in *South Florida Poetry Review*, winter 1988. Reprinted by permission of the author.

Irvin Ehrenpreis. "Poetry by the Yard?" copyright © 1974 by Irvin Ehrenpreis (writing an unsigned review). Originally published in *TLS*, March 29, 1974. Reprinted by permission of the estate of Irvin Ehrenpreis. "Boysenberry Sherbet," copyright © 1975 by Irvin Ehrenpreis. Originally published in *New York Review of Books*, October 16, 1975. Reprinted by permission of the estate of Irvin Ehrenpreis.

David Galler. "Four Poets," copyright © 1961 by David Galler. Originally published in *Sewanee Review*, winter 1961. Reprinted by permission of the author.

Dana Gioia. "Tradition and an Individual Talent," copyright © 1992 by Dana Gioia, from *Can Poetry Matter?: Essays on Poetry and American Culture* (Graywolf, 1992). Originally published in *Verse*, winter/spring 1992. Reprinted by permission of the author. "An Interview with Donald Justice," copyright © 1996 by Dana Gioia. Originally published in *American Poetry Review*, March/April 1996. Reprinted by permission of the author. "A Poet's Poet," copyright © 1992 by Dana Gioia. Originally published in *New Criterion*, May 1992. Reprinted by permission of the author.

Jorie Graham. "Iowa City, 1976," copyright © 1992 by Jorie Graham. Originally published in *Verse*, winter/spring 1992. Reprinted by permission of the author.

Emily Grosholz. "Poetry Chronicle," copyright © 1980 by Emily Grosholz. Originally published in *Hudson Review*, summer 1980. Reprinted by permission of the author.

David Hartnett. "Mythical Childhoods," copyright © 1988 by David Hartnett. Originally published in *TLS*, April 15–21, 1988. Reprinted by permission of the author.

Edward Hirsch. "Heroes and Villanelles," copyright © 1987 by Edward Hirsch. Originally published in *New York Times Book Review*, August 23, 1987. Reprinted by permission of the author.

Alan Hollinghurst. "Good for Nothing?" copyright © 1980 by Alan Hollinghurst. Originally published in *New Statesman*, August 22, 1980. Reprinted by permission of the author.

Richard Howard. "'As the Butterfly Longs for the Cocoon or the Looping Net,'" from *Alone with America* (Atheneum, 1971), copyright © 1971 by Richard Howard. Reprinted by permission of the author. "New Work from Three Poets," copyright © 1974 by Richard Howard. Originally published in *North American Review,* spring 1974. Reprinted by permission of the author.

William Hunt. "The Poems of Donald Justice," copyright © 1968 by the Modern Poetry Association. Originally published in *Poetry,* July 1968. Reprinted by permission of the editor of *Poetry* and the author.

David Kirby. "Refined Craftsman," copyright © 1993 by David Kirby. Originally published in *American Book Review,* April/May 1993. Reprinted by permission of the author.

William Logan. "The Present Bought on the Terms of the Past," copyright © 1980 by William Logan. Originally published in *Crazyhorse,* spring 1980. Reprinted by permission of the author. "The Midnight of Nostalgia," copyright © 1992 by William Logan. Originally published as "The Force of Nostalgia" in *Verse,* winter/ spring 1992. Reprinted by permission of the author. "Justice in Florida" appears in this collection for the first time.

Edwin London. "Justice and *The Death of Lincoln,*" copyright © 1997 by Edwin London. Published here, for the first time, by permission of the author.

John Lucas. "Best Rhymes with Zest," copyright © 1988 by John Lucas. Originally published in *New Statesman,* April 8, 1988. Reprinted by permission of the author.

Derek Mahon. "Men at Forty," copyright © 1980 by Derek Mahon. Originally published in *London Review of Books,* August 21–September 3, 1980. Reprinted by permission of the author.

Walter Martin. "Arts of Departure," copyright © 1997 by Walter Martin. Published here, for the first time, by permission of the author.

Brian McCrea. "'It Figured': Donald Justice at the Racetrack," copyright © 1997 by Brian McCrea. Published here, for the first time, by permission of the author.

Jerome J. McGann. "The Importance of Being Ordinary," copyright © 1974 by Jerome J. McGann. Originally published in *Poetry*, October 1974. Reprinted by permission of the author.

James McMichael. "Justice," copyright © 1967 by James McMichael. Originally published in *North American Review*, November 1967. Reprinted by permission of the author.

Robert Mezey. "Of Donald Justice's Ear," copyright © 1992 by Robert Mezey. Originally published in *Verse*, winter/spring 1992. Reprinted by permission of the author.

Charles Molesworth. "Anniversary Portraits," copyright © 1980 by Charles Molesworth. Originally published in *New York Times Book Review*, March 9, 1980. Reprinted by permission of the author.

Howard Nemerov. Untitled review, copyright © 1960 by Howard Nemerov. Originally published in *The American Scholar*, autumn 1960. Reprinted by permission of Margaret Nemerov.

Robert Pawlowski. Untitled review, copyright © 1967 by Robert Pawlowski. Originally published in *Denver Quarterly*, summer 1967. Reprinted by permission of the author.

Michael Peich and Jeffrey Cobb. "Donald Justice: A Bibliographical Checklist," copyright © 1997 by Michael Peich and Jeffrey Cobb. Published here, for the first time, by permission of the authors.

William H. Pritchard. "Poetry Chronicle," copyright © 1967 by William H. Pritchard. Originally published in *Hudson Review*, summer 1967. Reprinted by permission of the author.

Robert Richman. "Intimations of Inadequacy," copyright © 1993 by Robert Richman. Originally published in *Poetry*, June 1993. Reprinted by permission of the author.

Jean Ross. "Graduate School: The Thin Young Man," copyright © 1992 by Jean Ross. Originally published in *Verse*, winter/spring 1992. Reprinted by permission of the author.

Michael Ryan. "Flaubert in Florida," copyright © 1984 by Michael Ryan. Originally published in *NER/BLQ*, winter 1984. Reprinted by permission of the author.

Greg Simon. "'My Still to Be Escaped From': The Intentions of Invisible Forms," by Greg Simon, from *American Poetry Review*, March/April 1976. Reprinted by permission of *American Poetry Review*.

W. D. Snodgrass. "Justice as Classmate," copyright © 1992 by W. D. Snodgrass. Originally published in *Verse*, winter/spring 1992. Reprinted by permission of the author.

Richard Stern. "A Very Few Memories of Don Justice," copyright © 1997 by Richard Stern. Published here, for the first time, by permission of the author.

Mark Strand. "A Reminiscence," copyright © 1992 by Mark Strand. Originally published in *Verse*, winter/spring 1992. Reprinted by permission of the author.

Richard Wertime. "Poets' Prose," copyright © 1985 by Richard Wertime. First published in *Yale Review*, summer 1985. Reprinted by permission of the author and *Yale Review*.

Charles Wright. "Jump Hog or Die" from *Quarter Notes* by Charles Wright (University of Michigan Press, 1995), copyright © 1995. First published in *Verse*, winter/spring 1992. Reprinted by permission of the author.

Alan Young. "Identifying Marks," copyright © 1980 by Alan Young. Originally published in *TLS*, May 30, 1980. Reprinted by permission of the estate of Alan Young.

Vernon Young. "Two Hedgehogs and a Fox." Reprinted from *Parnassus: Poetry in Review*, 8, no. 1 (fall/winter 1979), courtesy of Poetry in Review Foundation.

The Department of English of the University of Florida made it possible to include the photographs of Donald Justice.

CONTENTS

essays

memoirs

interview

reviews

bibliography

INTRODUCTION

Since the late fifties, few American poets have had the quiet but marked influence of Donald Justice. Among the poets of his generation, no teacher has set the standards for so many younger poets—or, more importantly, so many different poets. The great temptation for a teacher is to submit to the flattery of imitation—few of Robert Lowell's students at Harvard escaped his subject matter or style. It would be more difficult to identify, among poets as divergent as Mark Strand and Charles Wright and Jorie Graham, the common application learned in workshop from Donald Justice. They have inherited not a language but a conscience about language.

As the most distinguished teacher at the Iowa Writers' Workshop for two long periods of his career, Justice worked with a vast number of younger poets, many of whom have had distinguished careers as teachers themselves. Justice's influence as a teacher, however, has obscured his influence as a poet. Though his poetry has earned a Pulitzer Prize and the Bollingen Prize, he has rarely figured seriously in academic criticism. Literary culture, for all its whims and sudden moods, loves nothing more than a settled judgment and is slow to appreciate a poet whose gains and attractions are cumulative, whose work has never suffered, or contrived, a radical breach. It is only in the past decade that Elizabeth Bishop, long considered a poet's poet, a sly and delightful artificer of surfaces, has begun to seem as profound and as disturbing a poet as Robert Lowell. Donald Justice is another poet's poet whose grace and determinations are likely to wear longer than some of the styles currently in fashion.

Justice belongs to a generation of American poets of remarkable depth and variety. The poets born in the twenties were too young to remember the publication of Auden's early work, but reached maturity in his shadow. Poets a decade older (like Berryman and Jarrell) had wrestled with Yeats, but Auden set the arguments of style for poets beginning to publish in the late forties and early fifties, even when the result was a radical reaction. As editor from 1947 to 1959 of the Yale Series of Younger Poets, he introduced the first books of many of the best poets of that generation, including W. S. Merwin, Adrienne Rich, John Ashbery, James Wright, and John Hollander.

If Justice stood a little aside from these poets, it was partly because he was born in the South. Before the Fugitives, American poets began their careers at Harvard (Eliot, Stevens, Frost, Cummings), and even Justice's generation was crowded with Ivy League educations. The Fugitives were crucial in defending—even finally in creating—not just a regional art, but a regional art with more than regional effect; their best students, however, like Randall Jarrell and Robert Lowell, turned to other models (one might say that they too learned, from Ransom in this case, a conscience about language). The Fugitives were outsiders within—within a tradition—and that might be a close definition of Justice's inheritance.

As a college student Justice had received encouragement from a now forgotten second-generation Agrarian, George Marion O'Donnell, a rival of Jarrell's; and Justice's M.A. thesis at North Carolina took the movement as its subject. His later year at Stanford, on the outer edge of Yvor Winters's circle, was another sign of his position slightly to one side of fashion, though he shared many of the formal and classical concerns of the poets of the fifties.

Justice was fortunate to arrive at the Iowa Writers' Workshop at a remarkable time, as part of perhaps the most remarkable classes the Workshop has ever had. The poets he met there in 1952 and 1953 included W. D. Snodgrass, William Stafford, Philip Levine, Jane Cooper, William Dickey, Donald Petersen, and Henri Coulette. Among the teachers during his two years were Lowell, Berryman, and Karl Shapiro. The

Workshop was still intimate, housed as it was for years afterward in metal-roofed barracks (sometimes called Quonsets, a little inaccurately, in the memoirs here). When Justice returned to teach at Iowa in 1957, it was at the beginning of the period of expansion that formed the Workshop's present character. Iowa's later reputation in poetry came largely through Justice's weekly workshops—his close and even finicky attention to texts, his love of competition and argument, his broad knowledge of American and British poetry, his openness to challenge and experiment.

Justice as a teacher, however, must not overshadow Justice as a poet. He was perhaps fortunate to publish his first book late, at thirty-five, a year after the sea change of Lowell's *Life Studies* and Snodgrass's *Heart's Needle,* whose brilliance worked such disasters in the styles of Justice's generation. Justice withstood the hurricanes of the sixties, the slavish imitations of manner and the now too-easily-mocked confessional poems. He had set himself different tasks, so different (and so traditional) that the development of his work was scarcely noticed, or noticed with hostility. His reticence, his deceptively light touch, and his guarded control meant that even when he did publish a book like *Departures,* a departure into experiments with free verse, his inner toils received little regard.

In 1980, the award of the Pulitzer Prize for *Selected Poems* confirmed the private judgment of many poets, that Justice had gradually become a central conscience of the period. Poets whose work issues from the modesty of intelligence do not always find any but a posthumous accord. After all, we are still condescending to Hardy, a poet very similar to Justice in temperament.

In 1981, Justice was hired by the University of Florida to revive a moribund writing program originally founded by Andrew Lytle. The only writer of reputation on the faculty was the novelist Harry Crews. Justice was attracted by Gainesville's proximity to his childhood home in Miami and his parents' former home in Georgia; and he was followed to

Florida by William Logan and Debora Greger, and then Padgett Powell. During a decade in Florida, Justice was a major influence on the design and temperament of the program, which in some aspects reproduced the small Writers' Workshop he had found at Iowa in 1952.

Despite his ironic temper and cynical eye, Justice has shared with the Fugitives a love for a then vanishing, now almost vanished Southern landscape: some of his poems have the cool monochrome of Walker Evans' photographs. Justice's late work has been deeply entangled with the past, the past when it was the present. His recent poems have an emotional force that the mere confession of sins could not attain (if such a past could be confessed, it would no longer be a sin). Justice's sweetness, his beautiful portraiture, his near silence on the matter of love, have concealed the darkness of his melancholy, the terrible costs that have led to such thorough consideration of the missing.

It is too early to say, about a poet whose work is still in progress, what the eventual judgments of critics will be. These reminiscences and essays are presented as a partial balance to, a partial recovery from, the neglect of Donald Justice's poetry. Though he has escaped the consideration of academic critics, he has often had the attention of intelligent reviewers. A long section of contemporary reviews records the terms of his reception, both favorable and unfavorable. In this section the reader will find, apart from the understandings, some of the misunderstandings from which understandings are made. This book, offered in homage to a talent rare and unusual, as well as unusually American, contains early contributions toward a literary biography and a criticism in some measure equal to Donald Justice's achievement.

A NOTE ON THE TEXT

This volume began as a special feature of *Verse,* for which the editors commissioned a group of essays and memoirs from Donald Justice's critics, friends, and former students. Most of those pieces, some of them revised, appear here; but they have been supplemented by further essays and memoirs, and by a large selection of contemporary reviews. The book reviews have been printed with only minor editorial interference. Typographical errors and misquotations have been silently corrected, book titles uniformly placed in italics, and poem titles in quotations. Oddities of spelling and punctuation have otherwise been left intact, except that the American style of punctuation at the end of quotations has been adopted. Most such pieces come from omnibus reviews, as the reader will deduce from the occasional odd transitions and comparisons such a format forces reviewers to make. Justice revised some of his work for *Selected Poems* and made other revisions for the reissue of his first two books as well as further revisions for *A Donald Justice Reader.* He also made changes in interviews for *Platonic Scripts.* The texts used by the essayists and reviewers here are therefore heterodox; but the editors have allowed the slight confusion or slippage of the text of the poems because particular texts have often meant particular readings.

DONALD JUSTICE:
A CHRONOLOGY

1925

August 12: Born in Miami, Florida, to Vascoe and Mary Ethel (Cook) Justice.

1930

Began piano lessons, age five.

1931

Fall: Entered Allapattah Elementary School, Miami, Florida.

1935

Summer: Diagnosed with osteomyelitis. Missed one year of school.

1936

Fall: Entered Andrew Jackson High School, Miami, Florida. Played clarinet in band and orchestra during junior high and high school.

1941

Fall: Entered Miami Senior High School.

1942

Spring: Graduated from high school.

Fall: Entered University of Miami. Began to study musical composition with Carl Ruggles, who wintered in Miami, continuing until 1945.

1945

Spring: Graduated with B.A. in English from University of Miami.

Fall: Spent a year working in New York at odd jobs.

1946

Fall: Began graduate work at University of North Carolina (later University of North Carolina, Chapel Hill). Met Jean Catherine Ross in Chaucer class.

1947

Spring: Graduated with M.A. in English from University of North Carolina. Thesis on the Fugitive-Agrarian poets.

August 22: Married Jean Catherine Ross.

Fall: Instructor in English, University of Miami. One-year appointment.

1948

Fall: Began graduate work at Stanford University, where he intended to study with Yvor Winters. Forced to audit Winters's classes when the head of the department decided that such study was not appropriate in the first year of work toward the Ph.D.

1949

Spring: Left Stanford without taking degree.

Fall: Instructor in English at University of Miami (through 1951).

1951

The Old Bachelor and Other Poems (Pandanus Press), published by Preston Dettman, a young printer who worked in a Miami record shop.

1952

Spring: Entered Ph.D. program in creative writing (the Writers' Workshop) at University of Iowa. Studied with Paul Engle, Karl Shapiro, Robert Lowell, and John Berryman. Thought Berryman the best teacher.

1954

Spring: Graduated with Ph.D. from University of Iowa.

Fall: Rockefeller Foundation fellow in poetry. Traveled in Europe (first trip abroad).

1955

Fall: Visiting assistant professor, University of Missouri at Columbia. Two-year appointment, but quit after one year when the school broke a promise about salary.

1956

Fall: Assistant professor, Hamline University, St. Paul, Minnesota.

1957

Fall: Lecturer, program in creative writing (the Writers' Workshop), University of Iowa.

1960

Fall: Assistant professor, University of Iowa.

The Summer Anniversaries (Wesleyan University Press), winner of the Lamont Award for 1959.

Editor, *The Collected Poems of Weldon Kees* (Stone Wall Press), limited edition.

1961

August 10: Son, Nathaniel Ross Justice, born.

1962

Fall: Visiting assistant professor, Reed College, Portland, Oregon. One-semester appointment.

Editor, *The Collected Poems of Weldon Kees* (University of Nebraska Press), trade edition.

1963

Fall: Associate professor, University of Iowa.

A Local Storm (Stone Wall Press/Finial Press), limited edition.

1964

Ford Foundation fellow in theater. On leave from the University of Iowa, worked with the Actors' Workshop in San Francisco (1964–1965).

1965

Co-editor with Alexander Aspel, *Contemporary French Poetry* (University of Michigan Press).

1966

Fall: Associate professor, Syracuse University, Syracuse, New York.

Three Poems (Virginia Piersol), limited edition.

1967

Spring: National Endowment for the Arts fellowship in poetry.
Fall: Professor, Syracuse University.

Took the fall term off, using the NEA grant, and gave the Elliston lectures at the University of Cincinnati.

Night Light (Wesleyan University Press).

1970

Fall: Visiting professor, University of California at Irvine. One-year appointment.

Sixteen Poems (Stone Wall Press), limited edition.

1971

Fall: Professor, University of Iowa.

1972

From a Notebook (Seamark Press), limited edition.

1973

National Endowment for the Arts fellowship for a libretto.

L'Homme qui se ferme / The Man Closing Up (Stone Wall Press), limited edition.

Departures (Atheneum).

1976

Spring: Bain-Swiggett lecturer, Princeton University.

Guggenheim Foundation fellow in poetry.

1979

Selected Poems (Atheneum).

1980

April: Received Pulitzer Prize in Poetry for *Selected Poems*.

Fall: Visiting professor, University of Virginia, Charlottesville, Virginia. One-semester appointment.

National Endowment for the Arts fellowship in poetry.

In the Attic (Toothpaste Press), limited edition.

1981

Spring: Hired at the University of Florida on a delayed appointment.

Fall: Returned to the University of Iowa for a final year.

1982

Fall: Professor, University of Florida, Gainesville, Florida.

1984

Platonic Scripts (University of Michigan Press), criticism.
Tremayne (Windhover Press), limited edition.

1987

The Sunset Maker (Atheneum).

1988

American Academy of Poets fellow.
The Death of Lincoln (W. Thomas Taylor), opera libretto.

1989

National Endowment for the Arts fellowship in poetry.

1990

Co-editor with Robert Mezey, *The Collected Poems of Henri Coulette* (University of Arkansas Press).

1991

Co-winner (with Laura Riding) of Bollingen Prize.

1992

Elected a member of the American Academy and Institute of Arts and Letters.
May: Retired from the University of Florida.
Returned to Iowa City.
A Donald Justice Reader (Middlebury College Press/University Press of New England).

1994

Editor, *The Comma after Love: Selected Poems of Raeburn Miller* (University of Akron Press).

1995

New and Selected Poems (Alfred A. Knopf).
Banjo Dog (Thaumotrope Press), limited edition.

1997

Spring: Elected a chancellor of the Academy of American Poets.

essays

Of Donald Justice's Ear

Robert Mezey

In an essay written in the early eighties, Donald Justice wrote,
"Words sometimes, through likeness of sound, become
bound to one another by ties remotely like those of human
kinship. This is not to propose that any *meaning* attaches to
the sounds independent of the words. But the interlocking
sounds do seem to reinforce and in some curious way to
authenticate the meanings of the words, perhaps indirectly to
deepen and enlarge them. A part of the very nature of poetry
lies in this fact."

For at least one reader, perhaps the essential part. One
can think of poets who have written beautifully without
metaphor, without sensuous or concrete diction, without
subject or drama, even without intelligence, but none who
has done so without an ear. And I would go further: I would
say that the poet who has the requisite power not only discloses the very nature of poetry but seems to penetrate to the
very nature of experience. I am not speaking now of ono-
matopoeia or the various kinds of mimicry, crude and sophisticated, that ingenious poets are capable of. Any poet of
sufficient skill can slow down his tempo and articulation,
"When Ajax strives, some rock's vast weight to throw," or
contrive the flashy magic of Tennyson's moaning doves and
murmuring bees. Justice's skill is more than sufficient for such
professional illusions as in

> To stand, braced in a swaying vestibule,

or, at somewhat greater length,

> And then a
> Slow blacksnake, lazy with long sunning, slides

> Down from its slab, and through the thick grass, and hides
> Somewhere among the purpling wild verbena.

(We shall save the delights of that characteristic rhyme for another occasion.) No, I am thinking rather of something like Wordsworth's "Or the unimaginable touch of Time," something that cannot quite properly be called imitative form but thrills us all the same with its power to evoke, by means of little more, apparently, than a couple of very light accents and a diction almost entirely abstract, an intense, almost physical apprehension of the slow, soundless crumbling of the centuries. Wordsworth calls it unimaginable even as he makes us imagine it. In such lines we have the sensation that words have somehow slipped free from their characters, their shadowy life in the world of signs, and come down, as Yeats implored his sages to do, to participate in the world of experience. It is as if we are touching, through the medium of language, that constantly receding wonder, reality. We feel that the poem is creating truth itself. Perhaps that is why we cannot do without it, those of us who cannot.

It is not always easy to distinguish between the obvious sorts of verbal mimesis, however fine, and this deeper thing I have been trying to describe. One mark of the distinction may be that the former is likely to be susceptible of analysis and the latter not. For example, in this lovely quatrain about a sofa in a dance teacher's parlor (her "makeshift ballroom"):

> At lesson time, pushed back, it used to be
> The thing we managed somehow just to miss
> With our last-second dips and twirls—all this
> While the Victrola wound down gradually.

I would say that the last line is a particularly beautiful instance of imitation. One could lead a reasonably sensitive student to see how the third line with its vivid lexicon, fluid cadence, and short vowels speeds to the dash, to be pulled up short as the last line, beginning with the long "while," almost a syllable and a half, descends to the long vowels in midline, the insistent nasals, the juncture that enforces a slight pause between "wound" and the unaccented but long, heavy "down," the faded rhyme, and the limpness, the dying fall, of the adverb with its feeble final accent. (Of course it goes without saying that all such effects depend utterly on the meanings of the words; meters and tropes of sound mean nothing in themselves. So I began my brief analysis by indicating the lexicon, and so Justice was careful to include a similar stipulation in the paragraph I quoted earlier, for there are still many simple souls in the textbooks and classrooms who think that every trochee expresses conflict or resistance and that sibilance in a line of verse signifies evil. One would think that Ransom had laughed such readers off the stage forever; alas, apparently not.)

But how, I wonder, would I analyze the effect of these two lines from an elegy for a friend kicked to death in an alley (a poem, by the way, that has my nomination for the best villanelle in the language)?

> I picture the snow as falling without hurry
> To cover the cobbles and the toppled ashcans completely.

How does he do it, and so effortlessly, or so it seems? That calm, steady, almost nerveless line; that dry, cruel phrase, "without hurry"; the infinitive that suggests intention without in the least asserting it; the intricate pattern of sound in the second line, subtler than any chiasmus, flakes of vowel and consonant that bond together to cover the fifteen syllables of the five-beater completely—I am waxing impressionistic because I am at a loss to account for the haunting power of these cold-eyed and heartbreaking lines.

Or take the ending of his exquisite version of Rilke's "Letzer Abend," where the doomed officer's jacket hangs across the chair:

Like the coats scarecrows wear

And which the birdshadows flee and scatter from;
Or like the skin of some great battle-drum.

It is elementary to suggest that the static quality of the trim-
eter derives partly from the heavy ionic foot, the thick jam of
consonants, especially the *s* juncture, and the internal rhyme,
assonance, and alliteration; but it is impossible, at least to me,
to tell clearly how the extra syllable of "birdshadows" and the
lighter assonance of "shadows" and "scatter" seem to embody
the wild and panicky movement the line describes. It has
something to do, surely, with the dramatic preposition that
ends the clause and the ominous semi-colon, not to mention
the odd force of our realization that we are following not the
fleeing birds but their shadows; but now we are trying to
explain the inexplicable. And that great last line—yes, only a
dullard would fail to feel the reverberation of the internal
rhyme (another one!)—but what could account for the power
of the final word, a power that lies to some extent in its near-
ness to and its distance from being a triple rhyme and seems
almost to summon up the much more dreadful scattering to
come? I don't know.

This is state-of-the-art, as they say. I wish it were truly
representative of the state of the art. But, still, it gives some
cheer to remember that at the end of the twentieth century,
when American poetry is drearier and more amateurish than
it has been at any time since the end of the nineteenth, a few
writers are "saying the thing once for all and perfectly." The
gratitude I feel for "Last Evening" and for so many of Donald
Justice's poems is the gratitude I feel for any act or gesture of
love and loving care. That is, no doubt, "a love that masquerades as pure technique." But it *is* love.

"Avec une élégance grave et lente": The Poetry of Donald Justice

Bruce Bawer

On the American poetry scene these days, the only thing rarer than a fine poem is a negative review. Yet reviewers of Donald Justice, who has written some of the finest poems of our time, have often been not only negative but surprisingly hostile. Calvin Bedient, assessing Justice's 1979 *Selected Poems* in the *Sewanee Review,* described him as "an uncertain talent that has not been turned to much account." Wrote Gerald Burns: "*Selected Poems* reads like a very thin Tennessee Williams— little poems about obscure Florida people and architecture. . . . As a *career* his, though honest, does not quite make the ascent to poet from racket." And Alan Hollinghurst, apprais- ing the same volume for *The New Statesman,* complained that Justice's poems lacked "vitality . . . urgency . . . colour and surprise," that they suffered from "lassitude," "a weary pas- sivity," and "a habit of elegance which cushions meaning," and that the poems, "formal but *fatigués* . . . create the impres- sion of getting great job-satisfaction without actually doing much work."

What has Justice done to deserve such attacks? Well, he was imprudent enough to publish his first book at a time when the Beats were at the height of their popularity and when many readers were unable to see, in his low-decibel traditional verses, anything but an absence of the "vitality" and "urgency" that they admired in the Beats and in the recognized non-Beat camps of the day: the Black Mountain poets, the New York poets, the confessionalists. Nor did Justice necessarily appeal to the academic admirers of his fellow traditionalists Richard

Wilbur and Anthony Hecht; for it was, and is, in the nature of a certain kind of postwar academic critic to feel very much at home with the poems of a Wilbur or a Hecht—many of which seem, by their intricacy and impersonality, to solicit critical attention—while feeling uncomfortable with a plainer and more personal poet such as Justice, to whose sublime and delicate music such a critic may well be deaf and to whose conspicuous and compassionate interest in people's lives and feelings he may be constitutionally incapable of responding except by reflexively and defensively dismissing the poet as sentimental.

Nor has Justice gone out of his way to endear himself to the poetry world. While many poets of his generation have distributed enthusiastic blurbs like Halloween candy, Justice has committed the grave error of saying what he really thinks about his contemporaries. In the interviews collected in *Platonic Scripts,* he scorns the vapid, glibly romantic *idées reçues*— *"Nature is good . . .* government is *bad . . .* [poetry is] *good for the Soul"*—that form the contemporary Poets' Code; in a time when poets pay more attention to politics than to aesthetics, Justice declares that poems should not be didactic; in a time when one of the major prerequisites for an American poet seems to be an endless capacity for self-righteousness about his vocation, Justice observes stingingly that poets today "act as if they believed there were something almost sacred in the name of *poet.*" While other poets hesitate to step on toes, he refers bluntly to the "so-called poetry of the Beats," dismisses terms like Olson's "organic form" as so much pretentious blather, and is "appalled" by poets who brag about moving young people to tears, saying that such things are "morally wrong" and that poems should properly be "objects of contemplation." Ultimately, the dismissive reviews of Justice's *Selected Poems* are a reflection not of any failing in the work itself but of the manifold moral and cultural failures of an age in which it has been Justice's peculiar honor to be the apotheosis of the unfashionable poet.

Justice's poetry is, it must be said, understated. (He once agreed with an interviewer who remarked that "understatement is to you, practically, a religious principle.") But it does not lack vitality and urgency. What it lacks, rather, are the vulgarity, hysteria, conceit, anarchism, and morbid fixation on madness, drug abuse, grubby sex, and the like that characterize the most extreme Beat and confessional verses and that some readers, alas, equate with vitality and urgency. The urgency of Justice's finest verse is of a thoroughly different order. It is the urgency of deeply controlled feeling about loss and mortality, about the inevitable passing of time and the irrevocable pastness of the past. And while a table of contents that includes such titles as "Sonnet to My Father" and "Tales from a Family Album" and "On the Death of Friends in Childhood" might well strike many a critic as a firm guarantee of a poet's sentimental leanings, Justice's poems are delivered from sentimentality by honest feeling, careful observation, and fresh expression—and by a seemingly stoical resistance to grief. In an age of emotional exhibitionism, Justice rises, time and again, beyond his particular circumstances toward the level of tragic myth. To be sure, many a line from a Justice poem might indeed sound maudlin in other contexts, such as the closing line of one poem: "But already the silent world is lost forever." Yet such a line is maudlin only if it strikes one as false and easy, as having been forced onto a poem rather than having grown out of it. Such is not the case here. On the contrary, the poem positions the reader perfectly for the line, so that it seems true and heartfelt, the inevitable terminus of a very real emotional journey; the poem, in other words, captures with extraordinary precision the tenor of a mind and the rhythms of its thought, and the concluding line comes as the natural reflection on all that has gone before.

It is, to be sure, misleading to speak of Justice's poetry as if it were all of an ilk. His first book, *The Summer Anniversaries* (1960), established the intelligent, composed, and pensive voice with which he is most frequently identified—and established, too, his independence from the accepted poetic modes of the day. For many of his contemporaries, notably his teacher Robert Lowell (whose pivotal *Life Studies* had appeared a year earlier), the breakthrough to using autobiographical material in poetry was coupled with a break with form, a rejection of virtuosity as the ultimate poetic value in favor of sincerity; but though many of the poems of *The Summer Anniversaries* patently concern people and places that are of great personal significance for the poet, none of the poems is in free verse; Justice refuses to join Lowell, Snodgrass, Sexton, et al., in emphasizing sincerity at the expense of formal artistry ("Now that is simply not the kind of poetry I write," he once told an interviewer apropos of Snodgrass). Justice distinguishes between writing about himself, which he tries not to do ("I've always felt it was an author's privilege to leave himself out if he chose," he has said, citing with approval Eliot's now-unfashionable theory of the impersonality of the poet), and writing about people and places that have been important to him. Indeed, though his family and friends proliferate in *The Summer Anniversaries,* Justice attempts to restrict himself to the role of the observer and chronicler, and when he *is* present (or, more accurately, when there is an *I* in the poem that one tends to identify with the poet), he does his best to objectify his experience, to place mythic elements in the foreground, and to exclude the irrelevantly personal.

Justice has said that poems, at their best, transform a subjective experience into an object not unlike a treasured family photograph, an object that preserves a precious moment for readers of present and future generations as well as for the later refreshment of one's own memory, and he has expressed the hope that "some of the poems I've tried to write were treasurable in the sense that I *know* a photograph can be treasurable. Treasured." ("I like it," he has said of his poem "First Death," "because it records something otherwise lost.") Rather than write subjective, anti-literary, free-verse effusions in the manner of the Beats or the confessional poets, then, he seeks to create timeless, unapologetically literary objects—*made* objects ("I think of poetry as making things")—that preserve selected encounters, observations, and reflections. More than one interviewer has seemed bemused by Justice's traditional bent, by his habit of constant revision and his devotion to established forms; one interlocutor even asked if he ever felt the need to "free yourself from this restraint or control?" Justice's reply: "I don't think I feel the need to let go. Nowadays people may think of that as a flaw. I don't." Critics routinely praise the "courage" of an Allen Ginsberg; but there is more pluck in Justice's firm "I don't" than in all of Ginsberg's *Collected Poems*.

Formal though they are, though, Justice's poems do not recall what he has called the "hard, thuddy iambic pentameter line" of Lowell's dense, formal verses in *Lord Weary's Castle* any more than they recall the more relaxed free-verse rhythms of *Life Studies* and after. Rather, his poems exhibit a limpid lyricism, a gracefully flowing music. Trained in his early years as a pianist, Justice himself makes reference to the musicality of his poems, prefacing his volume *The Sunset Maker* with several tempo markings from major modern composers: "Sec et musclé" (Milhaud), "Avec une élégance grave et lente" (Debussy), "broadly singing" (Carl Ruggles). Justice's most representative poems do tend to display these characteristics: they are dry, muscular, elegant, grave, and slow (one might mark them *piano* and *andante*), with a fine, smooth, and austere melodic line, as it were, reminiscent of many a modern French composer.

Justice is, moreover, a poet who, even as he pays tribute to the radiant possibilities of human experience and the natural world, associates unalloyed wonder and joy at these things with the innocence of childhood, characterizing life, in "To a Ten-Months' Child," as a state that one enters from a "remote . . . kingdom" and, in "Song," describing a glorious dawn with awe and saying that "all that day / Was a fairy tale / Told once in a while / To a good child." To Justice,

growing up is a matter of recognizing that life is not the perfectly sublime affair that one may have believed it to be in
one's early years: in "The Snowfall," he refers to the "terrible
whispers of our elders / Falling softly about our ears / In childhood, never believed till now." The innocence of joy and the
terror of knowledge are also themes of the memorable
"Sonnet," in which the innocents are not children but Adam
and Eve:

> The walls surrounding them they never saw;
> The angels, often. Angels were as common
> As birds or butterflies, but looked more human.
> As long as the wings were furled, they felt no awe.
> Beasts, too, were friendly. They could find no flaw
> In all of Eden: this was the first omen.
> The second was the dream which woke the woman:
> She dreamed she saw the lion sharpen his claw.
> As for the fruit, it had no taste at all.
> They had been warned of what was bound to happen;
> They had been told of something called the world;
> They had been told and told about the wall.
> They saw it now; the gate was standing open.
> As they advanced, the giant wings unfurled.

Both in its vision of man and his world and in its means of
imparting that vision, this poem is vintage Justice. With one
stunning final image—an image that is all the more effective
for the quiet simplicity with which it is presented and for the
omission of any reference to Adam and Eve's reaction to it—
Justice makes one feel the terror of the knowledge that comes
to all of us when we move beyond the complacent bliss of
childhood: the knowledge of our mortality, of the world's
imperfection, and of our separation from the awful, winged
majesty of God and His angels. The irony here, a familiar one
in Justice's poetry, is that though the happiness of a child, or
of Adam and Eve in Eden, is untainted by the adult's bitter

knowledge, it is only in that state of knowledge, born of loss, that the irreclaimable joys of creation can be fully appreciated.

A reader of "Sonnet"—and of the numerous poems in which Justice refers to saints and angels and heaven—might be excused for concluding that he is a religious man. Yet though he was raised as a Southern Baptist, Justice has said that he lost his faith as a young man. "I don't believe in the spiritual," he declared flatly in a 1975 interview. "You know, there is a power in the obvious. That which is hidden I can't see." Yet in these secular times, Justice has a remarkable sense of what one cannot describe as anything other than the sanctity of the quotidian (he writes in "Unflushed Urinals" of "The acceptingness of the washbowls, in which we absolve ourselves!"); to him, sin and grace manifestly remain vital concepts, and life, for all its deficiencies, has its moments of sublime radiance.

His second and third collections find Justice in territory that one doesn't necessarily think of as his own. These are books of experiment, in which Justice wanders afield from the disciplined forms and elegant musicality of his debut volume to try his hand at blank verse, syllabic verse, and free verse. Both books also contain a number of verses inspired not by personal experience but by the work of other poets; since such poems as "The Telephone Number of the Muse" suggest that Justice felt abandoned by the Muse, one presumes that imitation and experiment were his way of keeping busy at his craft during her supposed absence. And indeed, though they are far from unaccomplished, the poems of *Night Light* (1967, revised 1981) and *Departures* (1973) represent something of a loosening, a thinning out, a descent into the fine but familiar from the serene and singular music of *The Summer Anniversaries*.

The models for the poems in these two volumes come from all over the map. There is a pair of "American Sketches" written in imitation of William Carlos Williams (to whom they are dedicated); there is a poem entitled "After a Phrase

Abandoned by Wallace Stevens"; and there are several elliptical, portentous poems, with wildly different line lengths and
short, clipped sentences, in imitation of Lorca and Vallejo.
These poems, surreal and often deliberately disjointed and frag-
mentary, are quite admirable of their kind, but they strike one
as being very much against the grain of Justice's own native
music, which typically casts its spell by means of clear and
coherent imagery, elegant and supple language, and delicate
variations on the iambic line. Justice's Lorcaesque poems, by
contrast, tend to be too metrically varied, too expressionistic,
and too loosely conversational in tone and rhythm to satisfy a
lover of Justice's best work; conversely, there may well be too
much in these poems of Justice's to satisfy an ardent admirer
of Vallejo or Lorca. The bottom line is that Justice's gently
responsive sensibility and strong sense of control don't really
lend themselves to the jagged rhythms and erratic thought patterns of a Lorca-type poem; to read Justice's Lorcaesque poems,
in fact, is a bit like hearing an opera singer do *Showboat:* it's not
great opera and it's not great Kern. Nonetheless, both books
show a side of Justice that one cannot but admire: namely,
Justice the astute and sensitive student of his art, who has never
lost the essential humility, and the willingness to learn, of the
earnest young painter copying an Old Master canvas in a
museum.

In the new poems included in the Pulitzer Prize–winning
Selected Poems (1979), Justice leaves Lorca and company behind
and writes in what might be described as a sharper, more
seasoned version of his *Summer Anniversaries* voice. Indeed,
one of the finest poems in *Selected Poems* is "The Summer
Anniversaries," an alternate version of "Anniversaries," the
opening poem in his debut volume. The poem charts the
speaker's growth from a ten-year-old who, though wheelchair-
bound, glories in the bounties of the earth—

> I thought it absurd
> For anyone to have quarreled

Ever with such a world—
O brave new planet!—
And with such music in it.

—to a twenty-one-year-old who sees a balloon "veer crazily
off" and compares it to himself, "All sense of direction gone,"
to a thirty-year-old who watches

Through the window beside my desk
Boys deep in the summer dusk
Of Iowa, at catch,
Toss, back and forth, their ball.
Shadows begin to fall.
The colors of the day
Resolve into one dull,
Unremarkable gray,
And I watch them go in from their play[,]
Small figures of some myth
Now, vanishing up the path.

With extraordinary concision and effectiveness, the poem
captures in turn the child's naive enthusiasm about life, the
adolescent's confusion and romantic self-pity, and the adult's
preoccupation with the prosaic business of existence, which,
when he notices young people at all, causes him to think of
them—and of his own younger self—as if they were part
of some half-remembered legend. The poem is a splendid
example, too, of Justice's genius for distancing: as much as
any sonnet of Donne, it represents not an indulgence in personality but an escape from personality's restrictions; the
specifics take on a symbolic weight, and one does not find
oneself wondering (as one does with much confessional verse)
about the poem's degree of autobiographical accuracy. (The
poem is reminiscent, in particular, of Donne's "A Valediction:
Of Weeping," in which three round objects—a ball, a tear,
and the earth—are connected imagistically; here, similarly,

Justice connects three round objects—a wheelchair wheel, a balloon, a ball—all emblems of the cycle of life.)

The Sunset Maker (1987) displays the music of Justice's poetry at its most elevated and austerely beautiful. In this volume, which contains not only twenty-five poems but two stories and a prose memoir, Justice is more than ever a poet of things past and passing, lamenting his incalculable losses and tendering his most cherished memories—mostly of his parents and of his childhood piano teachers—in language replete with allusions to the fragile beauty of music, to the ever-shifting light and shadow of nature ("The sun seems not to move at all, / Till it has moved on"), and to the tenets and typology of Christianity, with its assurance of an eternal and omnipresent deity (after rain, Justice writes in "Mule Team and Poster," the sun returns, "Invisible, but everywhere present, / and of a special brightness, like God"). The echoes of Stevens are more multitudinous than ever: if a line like "Mordancies of the armchair!" (in "Tremayne") brings to mind "Sunday Morning," a reference to "the last shade perhaps in all of Alabama" (in "Mule Team and Poster") recalls "Anecdote of the Jar." As in earlier volumes, Justice takes somber note of the contrast between the real world and childhood's fanciful view of it, noting that the world a child dreams "is the world we run to from the world."

For the Justice of *The Sunset Maker,* the chief function of art is to preserve what little it can of life. Perhaps the book's two most idiosyncratic items are the poem "The Sunset Maker" and its pendant, a story entitled "Little Elegy for Cello and Piano"; both works concern the speaker's friendship with a recently deceased and largely forgotten composer named Eugene Bestor, who survives only in a six-note phrase remembered by the speaker:

> The hard early years of study, those still,
> Sequestered mornings in the studio,
> The perfect ear, the technique, the great gift

All have come down to this one ghostly phrase.

And soon nobody will recall the sound

These six notes made once or that there were six.

It is to be hoped—not only for his sake, but for that of American poetry—that Justice's work will be more widely remembered than that of the fictional Bestor. Certainly there is more than one phrase in Justice's verse—plain, unaffected, and gently apocalyptic—that haunts the memory: "Darkness they rise from, darkness they sink back towards," "It is the lurch and slur the world makes, turning," "To shine is to be surrounded by the dark." Justice is the poet of a world in which loss is ubiquitous, sorrow inevitable, and adult joy always bittersweet, a world in which the genuinely heroic act, for a literary artist, is not to thrash about uncontrollably, raising a manic and ugly din, but to fashion a body of work whose beauty and poise and gravity in the face of life's abomination may, one trusts, help it to endure.

Flaubert in Florida

Michael Ryan

The unusual technical variety of Donald Justice's poetry issues from his consistent refusal to repeat himself, though such "rich refusals" are indicative of an invariable temperament woven into the fabric of the poetry like "God in the universe, present everywhere and visible nowhere," a temperament as relentless as Flaubert's in its insistence on perfect objectivity. Since his first poems, the unmistakable impression of that famous signature has been just underneath Justice's own: the painstaking search for *le mot juste*, that particular mixture of razor intelligence, cold eye, disaffection, and hermeticism. Justice would agree with Flaubert that "Poetry is as precise as geometry," but would probably note with irony that we now know that even basic axioms can only be proved within closed systems. Each of Justice's poems is a closed system. Formal limits, conventional or invented, are in his view connected to the nature of language. Only by means of such limits can a world which is always threatening to dissolve be focused and "fixed"—as he says of the effect of meter—by achieving form (it would be characteristic if he chose the word "fixed" in this context for both of its meanings: "stabilized" *and* "rectified"). At the same time, a formal exercise is sterile unless it uncovers some rich, unavoidable secret. Flaubert kept a stuffed, green parrot on his writing desk to remind himself of the irrational—the same writing desk on which he composed the sentence "Poetry is as precise as geometry." For both Flaubert and Justice, the work does not resolve this paradox so much as embody it, as if concurrent, conflicting desires for the wholly mysterious and the wholly comprehensible can be satisfied only in and by the work itself.

Justice's green parrot appears in "Tales from a Family Album," caged but alive—fed by an "aunt" who, the speaker says, never "overcame her fears, yet missed no feeding, / Thrust in the crumbs with thimbles on her fingers." This is the sort of elaborate literary joke Justice delights in, and it sometimes generates lines and even whole poems. In "The Mild Despair of Tremayne," "mordancies of the armchair" is obviously a take-off from Stevens's "complacencies of the peignoir"; in "Variations on a Text by Vallejo," Donald Justice dies in Miami on a sunny Sunday, instead of César Vallejo in Paris on a rainy Thursday. And in "The Summer Anniversaries" (recast completely in Justice's *Selected Poems* from the opening poem in his first volume), when the poet-at-age-ten exclaims "O brave new planet!— / And with such music in it," we are probably expected to understand that, in contrast to Miranda in *The Tempest* ("O brave new world, / That hath such people in't!"), this particular child *prefers* music.

But the allusiveness pervading Justice's poems is less an act of criticism (as it was for Pound) or a structural principle (as it was for Eliot), than simply a way of working, of getting the poem onto the page, for a writer who is "loaded down with self-consciousness." This description of Justice is his own, from an interview that appeared in the spring 1975 issue of *The Ohio Review;* he talks there about this way of working as "borrowing the voice":

> Borrowing the voice allows me, it seems, to speak of myself more directly, more objectively because the voice is not mine. Not simply mine. Probably more than other poets I know, I play games in my poems (as I do in my life), and one of the unwritten rules of the game for me, as I like it played, is that you can risk this much personality or that much confession if the voice is promised to be that of someone else to start with. Even without my recognizing it at the time of writing, that may be one of the reasons I can get pretty literary in choice of subjects, in taking off from

other people's texts. There is something in the works
of others, I suppose, that gets to me personally, that
affords me another perspective, the objectivity and
distance I like, so that it is as if I could say to myself,
let me use his experience as an image of my own, and
I won't have to use mine. But using his turns out to
be another experience for me, so it really *will* be mine
in the end.

This doesn't account for all, or nearly all, of Justice's
poems—since 1975, he has written most often about private
experiences, past and present, with his usual detachment yet
without "borrowing the voice." But the passage illustrates the
paradoxical cast of mind ("the objectivity and distance *I like"*)
that determines how his poems are made. And they are, above
all, *made,* whether from their external forms inward or from
their emotional centers outward (as in the poems Justice starts
with another poet's "experience as an image of my own").
The hazards and limitations of this way of working are obvious, but if as a consequence we rarely feel that "he *had* to
write about the subject he took, and in that way" (one of
Eliot's main criteria for "a great writer"), the poet's distance
may be compensated by the poem's immediacy. Given ideal
skill, a poet certainly argues implicitly for a particular kind of
poetry by writing his own poems the way he does, but he also
writes the way he does simply because he hasn't any other
choice. Stevens put it better when he said, "I write the way
I do not because it pleases me, but because no other way
pleases me." The particular character of Justice's style—its
unusual lucidity and perfect decorum—may be his response
to his temperament as well as a reflection of it. How can a
person for whom "emotion tends to disappear when much
show is made of it" (another self-description) still write
poetry? Justice's style is his answer to this question.

This, then, is Justice's signature, too: the poet's emotion
is withheld while the poem's material is presented. The opposite has often been true in American poetry since 1959, the

annus mirabilis of confessional poetry with Lowell's *Life Studies* and Snodgrass's *Heart's Needle.* Justice and Snodgrass were students at Iowa during the fifties, and Lowell taught there briefly. *Heart's Needle,* Snodgrass's first volume, won the Pulitzer Prize in 1960; Justice's first volume, *The Summer Anniversaries,* appeared the same year. It shows Justice writing, if anything, *against* the confessional impulse, as he has ever since. The passion animating Justice's work has always been a passionate restraint, even a passion *for* restraint. In this way, it resembles Elizabeth Bishop's, but Justice tends much more to irony which can in one mood turn bitter (see "Sonatina in Green") and, in his dominant mood, he is more attracted to possibilities for menace. Like Bishop for most of her life, Justice has been known as a "craftsman" and "a poet's poet." His poems invite this, as if, like some people, they would rather be respected than loved. At first glance, they may appear "cold," "traditional," or, as an acquaintance of mine described them, "sturdy"—to prefer modest accomplishment to ambitious failure. This is not endearing to a Romantic age. Like *Madame Bovary,* Justice's poetry goes to a great deal of trouble not to ask the reader to complete it. He tells us, twice, in "Poem": "This poem is not addressed to you," and, moreover, "Nor does it matter what you think" (there is a negation in almost every line). Not exactly a Whitmanian embrace.

Yet Justice's relentless insistence on clarity, on realizing the subject within the borders of the poem, amounts to a consideration of the reader which to my mind is the greatest consideration. In a literary atmosphere which has indulged obscurity as "brilliance," Justice's style, were it a matter of choice, would represent an act of moral courage. If this style proceeds from traditional assumptions about language, it nonetheless may make new poetry by going deeper into old, rich veins and by fusing alloys of old and new, of English and European traditions.

Ingmar Bergman, whose films were a springboard for one

of Justice's poems ("A Dancer's Life"), once said in an interview that the best camera angle is usually the one where the audience doesn't notice the camera. Justice certainly aims for such transparency, to present the subject seemingly without his intervention in "the best words in the best order." As a consequence, each word is required to have a fresh, rational use and placement, and decorum and wit are therefore elevated to major poetic virtues.

So the worst of Justice's poetry suffers from "virtuosity," never from other common contemporary maladies of sloppiness, overwriting, sentimentality, opacity, or tin ear. When Justice's poems fail, it is usually because they are eviscerated by self-conscious irony, mannerism, and literary poses of spiritual exhaustion that derive ultimately from the poetry of Flaubert's contemporaries and that have already resurfaced in every possible guise in English poetry over the last hundred years. As the graffito says, ennui is boring. And as Eudora Welty says in her beautiful essay on Henry Green, "Virtuosity, unless it move the heart, goes at the head of the whole parade to dust." Adding immediately, "With Henry Green we always come back to this: this work is so moving." The extraordinary distillation that can be the main virtue of Justice's style leaves nothing for us to care about when the subject is too removed or attenuated or literary to begin with.

Consequently, Justice's poems are best when it does seem that "*he* had to write about the subject he took, and in that way" (changing Eliot's emphasis from *had* to *he*), when his style seems a discipline to contain his urgency, a way to make the subject pervade the poem, as if (as in Eliot's poetry) such powerful emotion had to be powerfully muted in order to be objectively realized. These subjects, invariably, are a challenge to Justice's control, because of their richness or mystery, or—perhaps "despite" the writer—his personal investment in them.

Here is one of the earliest (and shortest) of these poems, from *The Summer Anniversaries,* dating from about 1959:

A Map of Love

Your face more than others' faces
Maps the half-remembered places
I have come to while I slept—
Continents a dream had kept
Secret from all waking folk
Till to your face I awoke,
And remembered then the shore,
And the dark interior.

This is the closest thing to a love poem in Justice's *Selected Poems*—the only other "beloved" addressed directly is a dressmaker's dummy—although there are other poems about sexual love, most often treated ironically. There's no irony in "A Map of Love," even if the poem begins with a characteristic qualification or deflation ("more than others' faces") that will be the business of this particular poem to overcome. This sort of deflation is the given when Justice picks up his pen; here it is explicit rather than assumed, which may account in part for this poem's effectiveness. The beloved's presence is barely felt, but the poem is not about her—it's about what she provokes, what takes place in the internal territory of the speaker's psyche. Thus the title (revised—and improved—from "Love's Map"), which is the governing trope.

Though this conceit is inventive enough, and its handling graceful enough, the main pleasure of the poem comes, at least to me, from how it presents its information in one sentence draped across trochaic tetrameter couplets. The poetry is more in this, the poem's enactment—the relationship of syntax, rhythm, and content—than in its paraphrasable ideas. "Your face" in the sixth line, for example, causes one of the few disjunctions between metrical and rhetorical stress in the poem, and we feel it as a slight dissonance, a subconscious emphasis, at an important moment in the drama. Marvell showed how the tetrameter couplet could be used in a serious poem by enjambing frequently; Justice does this, and in addition truncates the last six lines to seven syllables each, so that he's not locked into using feminine rhymes (e.g., *faces / places*), which in couplets tend after a while to become comic. The two middle rhyming pairs (*slept / kept, folk / awoke*) have a hard, clipped sound, which sets us up for another variation at the end (*shore / interior*), a soft, half-rhyme on the final, weakly stressed syllable. This is Justice's main currency: subtle effects solidly based in the arrangement of the language, the organization of the poem. Metrically, the last line consists of two weaker stresses flanking two strong ones, again a *slight* variation within the established pattern of a four-stress line in which the first and last stresses are at least as strong as the others. The syntax of the sentence, besides organizing the elements of the plot, acquires a clarity and ease at the end which is in contrast with the knots and inversion in the middle. The last line "comes right with a click like a closing box" (as Yeats put it); it wants to gather and culminate all that has preceded it, and it does. The speaker's shock of recognition is dramatized by the syntax; what is discovered (in the Platonic sense, "remembered") comes last: "the dark interior." We not only understand this shock, we feel it, literally, because of the variations in the sound, rhythm, and syntax.

This feeling, of course, is fused by the words of the poem to our understanding, our "memory" of having discovered "the dark interior" through another. Such effects may be most easily traced in poems in fixed forms because the pattern of rhythm and rhyme is roughly identifiable, but the sound and syntax of free verse must work analogously or it probably isn't verse at all. The extraordinary palpability of Justice's poems derives as much from the clarity of their shapes as of their subjects, but subject and shape are of course inextricable in language that simultaneously has sound, syntax, and meaning. Since we pay attention primarily to meaning, the sound and syntax subliminally influence the way we receive it, but the sound and syntax—separately and in combination—also make complicated, protean shapes of their own that the reader may not attend to, but which work on him nonetheless. For Justice, however, at least in 1964, a poem by its nature calls for "a different sort of attention on the part of both writer and reader":

> If in a novel the great event is likely to be a death or
> wedding, in a poem it may well be a sentence, a line,
> a phrase, or just possibly a single word.

This was the sort of attention encouraged by New Criticism; if current academic criticism is any indication, such attention has almost disappeared from the reading, if not the writing, of poetry. The poets included in *New Poets of England and America* (1957), most of them born in the twenties, were brought up on the assumptions of New Criticism, but almost all of them discarded these assumptions as "academic" within a few years of the anthology's publication. Though Justice was also influenced by the proliferation of translation in the sixties and himself edited an anthology of *Contemporary French Poetry*, he never underwent the complete turnaround of a Merwin or Rich. Reading Justice's *Selected Poems* in chronological sequence, as it's happily arranged, no careful reader would confuse a poem from the late sixties with one written ten years earlier or ten years later; the volume as a whole presents even Justice's poetic development with unusual clarity. Yet the attention to "a sentence, a line, a paragraph, or just possibly a single word," which he could have learned from Yvor Winters at Stanford in 1948, is the constant in Justice's *Selected Poems* from the oldest poems to the most recent.

What makes the book interesting as a volume, however, is the sense of Justice's testing his assumptions and experimenting with them, from poem to poem. So, if in 1964 (in an essay called "The Writing of Poetry," also quoted above) he wrote

In a good short poem a fine sense of relations among
its parts is felt, word connecting with word, line with
line: as with a spider web, touch it at any part and the
whole structure responds.

—which could be an excerpt from the most orthodox New
Critical text (and is surely behind the writing of "A Map of
Love")—at about the same time he could also write a poem
which challenges such structural ideas:

The Suicides

If we recall your voices
As softer now, it's only
That they must have drifted back

A long way to have reached us
Here, and upon such a wind
As crosses the high passes.

Nor does the blue of your eyes
(Remembered) cast much light on
The page ripped from the tablet.

■ ■ ■

Once there in the labyrinth,
You were safe from your reasons.
We stand, now, at the threshold,

Peering in, but the passage,
For us, remains obscure; the
Corridors are still bloody.

■ ■ ■

What you meant to prove you have
Proved—we did not care for you
Nearly enough. Meanwhile the

Bay was preparing herself
To receive you, the for once
Wholly adequate female

To your dark inclinations;
Under your care the pistol
Was slowly learning to flower

In the desired explosion,
Disturbing the careful part
And the briefly recovered

Fixed smile of a forgotten
Triumph; deep within the black
Forest of childhood that tree

Was already rising which,
With the length of your body,
Would cast the double shadow.

■ ■ ■

The masks by which we knew you
Have been torn from you. Even
Those mirrors, to which always

You must have turned to confide,
Cannot have recognized you,
Stripped, as you were, finally.

At the end of your shadow
There sat another, waiting,
Whose back was always to us.

■ ■ ■

When the last door had been closed,
You watched, inwardly raging,
For the first glimpse of your selves
Approaching, jangling their keys.

Musicians of the black keys,
At last you compose yourselves.
We hear the music raging
Under the lids we have closed.

If the overall structure of "The Suicides" does not seem much like a spider web, the poem nonetheless makes as much sense as "A Map of Love," even if sense does derive largely from the "relations among its parts." The conceit of "A Map of Love" causes the sequence of images to acquire a kind of momentum like that in problem-solving, and, in retrospect, we see that their order and relationship are fixed and necessary (map-shore-interior). In "The Suicides," the sections seem to be in an appropriate order, and we especially feel the "lastness" of the last section, but the images from section to section don't lock into a connecting logic of their own. The high passes of section one, for example, have nothing to do with the mirrors of section four, and, in fact, a main source of pleasure in the poem is the multiplicity and variety of its figures.

Then how does the poem hold together? There are "spider webs" in "The Suicides," but they are within the sections and not among them, so this represents only what might be called the poem's "secondary" structure. The effect of this sectioning is to let in more air, which is—and this indicates Justice's expertise—sorely needed because of the nature of the subject. And the subject, as it turns out, is less the suicides, the people who died, than the reaction of the living, the opacity of self-destruction. In spite of their differences, "The Suicides" and "A Map of Love" are identical in this one way: just as the presence of the beloved is distilled in the earlier poem, the suicides are barely felt because the poem is not about them but about the connection of their act of self-destruction to the living.

This is also the connection that holds the poem together. The grace and ingenuity of "The Suicides" become apparent when one notices the placement of the we-you pronouns, and the variety of ways they are yoked, syntactically and dramatically. This address—of a kind of representative "we" to an equally, if oppositely, representative "you"—pervades the poem, but Justice modulates it continuously, causing it to be absorbed into little dramas, putting a little more weight now upon the "we" (as in the second section), now upon the "you" (as in the third). As a structuring device, this allows much more range than the development of a single conceit. The poem seems at once various and unified, fluid and solid.

Each section of "The Suicides" begins with the we-you address, cast in terms of drama or statement or some combination of the two. This is necessary structural work, but never seems obtrusive or repetitious:

> If *we* recall *your* voices
> As softer now . . .
>
> . . . .
>
> Once there in the labyrinth,
> *You* were safe from your reasons.
> *We* stand, now, at the threshold . . .
>
> . . . .
>
> What *you* meant to prove *you* have
> Proved—*we* did not care for *you*
> Nearly enough.
>
> . . . .
>
> The masks by which *we* knew *you*
> Have been torn from *you*.

Probably part of our pleasure in the poem comes from the variety, efficiency, and inventiveness with which this structural work is accomplished, whether we are aware of its being accomplished or not. We're reminded at the beginning of each section that the poem is addressed to the suicides, and this focuses each section's elaboration of its figures, while these elaborations keep the focus on the suicides from being unbearably constricted. The result is a pattern of departure and return, a movement in the mind thinking about the suicides, away and back, the response preferred and the one compelled.

The last section is a kind of coda to this movement. It's a formal tour de force, the end words of the first stanza mirrored in the second: "closed," "raging," "yourselves," "keys"; "keys," "yourselves," "raging," "closed." The form mimics the balance and opposition of the "we" and "you" throughout the poem. The first stanza is given to the suicides and is a wholly dramatic rendering of their first moments after death. And the second stanza belongs to the "we," the living, once again addressing the suicides (though for the first time with an epithet: "Musicians of the black keys"). Drama and direct address, the representative "you" and the representative "we," departure and return—the opposites previously combined in the poem are here isolated, presented in separate stanzas. Yet they are linked through the form, the end words locking into place a closure that the previous sections avoid. The connection between the "we" and the "you," the living and the dead—as in "A Map of Love"—is more felt than spoken, and felt primarily through the poem's form and structure. And of course it's no accident that the emotional climax of the poem occurs at a moment when the form is most disciplined.

"The Suicides" is one of Justice's earliest poems in syllabics, which he used frequently in the mid-sixties, and in which he did some of his best work ("The Suicides," "The Tourist from Syracuse," "Hands") and, curiously, some of his worst ("In the Greenroom," "At a Rehearsal of *Uncle Vanya*," "To the Hawks"). The former group are in seven-syllable lines, and the latter in five, and it's as if the shorter line is too constricted. But the syllabic line, even as Justice uses it, has no prosodic identity in English; it doesn't provide a measure (since the duration of each syllable is variable) but simply an arbitrary restriction to an otherwise free verse. Justice no doubt became interested in syllabics through his translation of French—in which the syllable *is* the measure—and it may have given him a way to write a line that is closer to speech than did his earlier metrical line on his way to writing free verse with its own rhythmical identity.

A good book could be written on how Justice uses free verse that would also be a manual of prosody for contemporary poetry. Invariably, the line acts as a tensioning device against the syntax of the sentence, which both discloses its prose rhythm and makes it into something else. One of the best examples, "Men at Forty," also dates from the mid-sixties, when Justice was working primarily with the syllabic line. The poem consists of five stanzas and five sentences, and it gives me great pleasure to watch how the sentences fall into the stanzas and across them and how the sentence is cut on the phrase to uncover its rhythm and cut against the phrase for the sake of the poetry.

Men at Forty

Men at forty
Learn to close softly
The doors to rooms they will not be
Coming back to.

At rest on a stair landing,
They feel it
Moving beneath them now like the deck of a ship,
Though the swell is gentle.

And deep in mirrors
They rediscover
The face of the boy as he practices tying
His father's tie there in secret

And the face of that father,
Still warm with the mystery of lather.
They are more fathers than sons themselves now.
Something is filling them, something

That is like the twilight sound
Of the crickets, immense,

> Filling the woods at the foot of the slope
> Behind their mortgaged houses.

The basic prosodic principle at work here is one Justice learned from his lifetime study of meter: the establishment of a pattern and variation on it. The first two lines must be cut on the phrase in order for the third to have any effect cut against the phrase (reinforced by the triplet rhyme: *forty* / *softly* / *be*). And this applies to the first two sentences each snugly fitting a stanza, a pattern varied by the last three sentences in the last three stanzas. The breaks between stanzas three and four and stanzas four and five also seem articulate, almost part of the content, as does the fact that the statement embedded in the fourth stanza is one sentence and one line.

"Men at Forty" has all the clarity of shape of the most formal poem because it *is* a most formal poem. Justice's most effective writing has often taken the form of free verse because it has caused an even greater fidelity to the subject. This is what I mean by "palpability": it is as if the thing itself were given to us to hold in our hands; it is a quality of lucidity in the choice of words and their organization, the language honed to a fine transparency.

> And the sun will be bright then on the dark glasses of
>   strangers
> And in the eyes of a few friends from my childhood
> And of the surviving cousins by the graveside,
> While the diggers, standing apart, in the still shade of the
>   palms,
> Rest on their shovels, and smoke,
> Speaking in Spanish softly, out of respect.
> . . . .
> The breast of Mary Something, freed from a white
>   swimsuit,
> Damp, sandy, warm; or Margery's, a small caught bird—
> . . . .
> And here comes one to repair himself at the mirror,

> Patting down damp, sparse hairs, suspiciously still black,
> Poor bantam cock of a man, jaunty at one a.m., perfumed,
>   undiscourageable . . .

The tone, of course, varies, and the kinds of "things" presented, and the uses made of them. But, as in "Men at Forty," this quality of Justice's style seems to be what allows him to bring over into language something which we did not have before.

Like so many of Justice's poems, the donnée of "Men at Forty" can be traced to a literary source; in this case, to Wallace Stevens's "Le Monocle de Mon Oncle":

> If men at forty will be painting lakes
> The ephemeral blues must merge for them in one,
> The basic slate, the universal hue.
> There is a substance in us that prevails.

The figure of Flaubert probably shades into the large figure of Wallace Stevens in the background of Justice's work, and it would be hard not to be overshadowed by it. Justice shares many of Stevens's beliefs, and lack of them; poetry is certainly "a conscious activity" for Justice, and he probably learned from Stevens that poems can conceal as well as reveal. But one does not feel in Justice's work that it is "a sanction of life," except perhaps a life in memory. The "Supreme Fiction," the "magnificent fury," the "blessed rage for order" that animates Stevens's poetry at its best—in short, the ambition in his work to encompass life and even to replace it—is not part of Justice's temperament or intention. This may be only Justice's reading of history or literary history, but it informs the poems he has written. As he says in "Homage to the Memory of Wallace Stevens": "The *the* has become an *a*." However, those who have read Justice as a Stevens epigone have read him badly.

"Men at Forty" is also illuminated by what Justice does

not take from "Le Monocle de Mon Oncle," namely, the subject of a sexual relationship in middle age. This absence is an undercurrent in Justice's poem, the absence of anyone else except in memory, the absence of connection.

And this, I think, is Justice's main subject, though most often it appears only implicitly—characteristically enough—in poems about memory, about an almost Edenic childhood. Though the child is "happily ignored" and knows "the pleasures of certain solitudes," Justice's myth of childhood is pervaded by a sense of community, of a proper, workable, social role not available to the adult *poète maudit*, even a tenured *poète maudit*. What the childhood actually was—and a number of Justice's poems refer to a serious childhood disease—is less important than the fact of its being remembered, because the very act of remembering is a gesture of identity in a dissolving world.

"How hard it is to live with what you know and nothing else"—this line is Camus's, and one from which Justice would certainly excise the first two words. But it begins to describe the stark discipline of Justice's poetry and the boundaries of its spirit and tells me why I sometimes find it moving even if, as he has said, he would not have it so. It is a poetry of isolation, composed in exile, most often—not so paradoxically—with the help of other poems, knowingly, sometimes even "rationally" (while employing "chance methods"), always moving toward the consolations of memory and form. I think my favorite poem of Justice's is my favorite because this implicit condition is made explicit and is written about directly. It is, in this sense, both uncharacteristic and, for me at least, central to his work. The poem was composed as one of a pair of companion pieces (the other is entitled "Absences"), and it "borrows the voice" of Cesar Vallejo's "Ágape." Both of these contexts may enrich our reading of the poem, but I think I begin to see the heart of Justice's work when it is stripped of them:

Presences

Everyone, everyone went away today.
They left without a word, and I think
I did not hear a single goodbye today.

And all that I saw was someone's hand, I think,
Thrown up out there like the hand of someone drowning,
But far away, too far to be sure what it was or meant.

No, but I saw how everything had changed
Later, just as the light had; and at night
I saw that from dream to dream everything changed.

And those who might have come to me in the night,
The ones who did come back but without a word,
All those I remembered passed through my hands like
       clouds—

Clouds out of the south, familiar clouds—
But I could not hold onto them, they were drifting away,
Everything going away in the night again and again.

Arts of Departure

Walter Martin

". . . it should be remembered that the author was several different persons during the course of writing, which covered many years."

I

In one of several modestly revealing comments about translation scattered through the interviews in *Platonic Scripts,* Donald Justice says, "Certainly you don't want to imitate. I don't want to imitate poets who write in other languages any more than I would want to imitate poets who write in my language; but I can perhaps learn something intangible from them." Only a poet who had spent much of his life teaching and learning from teachers—Winters, Berryman, Lowell—would put it that way, perhaps. Justice is a man for whom translation, difficult as it is, is never enough. Poets of original and genuine inspiration, driven to express themselves, incapable of holding back from doing so, have seldom been content to find equivalents for other men's verses, even when that was their honest and only intention.

II ▪ *Tain't what a man sez, but wot he* means *that the traducer has got to bring over.*

"I am not unaware, of course, that there are many readers who take persistent pleasure in deprecating everything and that they will vent their spleen on this work too," said Saint Jerome.

"It is difficult when you are following another man's footsteps, to keep from going astray somewhere. . . . If I translate word for word, the result is ludicrous; if I am forced to change the words or rearrange them, it will look as though I had failed in my duty as a translator." This is where the trouble starts, and the treason in the well-known equation, *traduttore traditore*.

The ideal translator is not traitor but arbitrator, bent on reconciling the conflicting claims of two languages, each competing for the reader's attention. In the business of settling differences by give-and-take, by trade-off, by compromise, he is a go-between who must make the ever-more-delicate decisions upon which the life of the text depends. There are many good reasons why the translation of poetry should not be attempted, many reasonable explanations for why the attempt is bound to fail. " 'Tis much like dancing on ropes with fettered legs: a man may shun a fall by using caution; but the gracefulness of motion is not to be expected; and when we have said the best of it, 'tis but a foolish task; for no sober man would put himself into danger for the applause of escaping without breaking his neck." Thus Dryden, chiding Ben Jonson for adopting the metaphrastic method in his version of the *Art of Poetry* (1640). The metaphrast turns his author from one tongue to another, word by word and line for line, and to Dryden such a method was self-defeating. Had not Horace himself cautioned, *Nec verbum verbo curabis reddere fidus / Interpres*?

Paraphrase, as exemplified by Waller in his fourth book of the *Aeneid* (1658), seemed a more sensible solution to the ancient dualism of Beauty versus Fidelity. Such a translation, "with latitude, where the author is kept in view . . . so as never to be lost, but his words are not so strictly followed as his sense; and that too is admitted to be amplified, but not altered," became Dryden's own ideal and the modus operandi for his transformations of Horace, Ovid, Juvenal, and Virgil. The method of the paraphrast was not the opposite of metaphrastic procedure. It was seen as the common-sense compromise between hard-line Jonsonian literalism and the dreaded excesses of Mr. Cowley in his eccentric and extravagant versions, or perversions, of Pindar. His *imitations,* that is, of Pindar in the *Pindarique Odes* (1656).

In an *imitation,* the translator "(if now he has not lost that name) assumes the liberty, not only to vary the words and sense, but to forsake them both as he sees occasion; and taking only some general hints from the original, to run division on the groundwork as he pleases." Cowley in his own preface justifies having "taken, left out, and added what I please" by asserting that a man would be thought mad if he translated Pindar literally, assuring us that "it does not at all trouble me that the Grammarians [pedants] perhaps will not suffer this libertine way of rend'ring foreign Authors, to be called Translation; for I am not so much enamour'd of the Name Translator, as not to wish rather to be Something Better, tho' it want yet a Name." To which Dryden's reply was that *imitation*, so-called, was nothing less than profanation of the dead.

III ■ *That servile path thou nobly dost decline,*
   Of tracing word for word and line for line.

We take a more generous attitude to the outrage of *imitation* nowadays, thanks to some notable successes by modern practitioners. *"Qui n'est successivement ravi et outré, s'il garde un œil pour le latin, par ce que VALÉRY a fait des Bucoliques?"* asks Pierre Leyris, himself a distinguished translator of Hopkins and Eliot. Exasperation and delight—are they not what we have come to expect from the great imitators, whether a Pope or a Pound? The squawking that greeted Pound's *Propertius* and Lowell's *Imitations* were one and the same. Now they are taught in the classroom; the alert learn something intangible from them, as we know from the example of Justice.

At Iowa in the fall of 1953 he took a translation course from Lowell: "We as a class, went through about two-thirds of those poems [in *Imitations*] . . . I was surprised to see them show up later in his book. It was his work; his own voice is all too recognizable in those versions, but we had been privileged to have a sort of preview." When the book appeared eight years later, its dust jacket carried this disclosure: "Mr. Lowell calls this unusual collection of poetry 'a book of versions and free translations.' His intention is not to make a literal rendering of a poem written in another tongue, but to try to create from the original a poem which is successful *in English*. At times there are wide departures from the originals, yet he usually stays quite close. Though they are 'imitations,' the imitator is unmistakably Robert Lowell."

Lowell's own introduction continues the apologia by suggesting that the reader set aside prior notions of these particular foreign poets altogether, at least on first reading, and listen instead to the *sequence,* "one voice running through many personalities," which he hopes will have "something equivalent to the fire and finish" of the originals. He confesses that he has been "reckless with literal meaning, and labored hard to get the tone," which "is of course everything." Or rather—backpedaling here—he has labored to get "*a* tone, for *the* tone is something that will always more or less escape transference to another language and cultural moment. I have tried to write live English and to do what my authors might have done if they were writing their poems now and in America." Then the credo: *I believe that poetic translation . . . must be expert and inspired, and needs at least as much technique, luck and rightness of hand as an original poem.* Expertise and inspiration having licensed him to make new poems based on Sappho, to strip Villon, take Hebel out of dialect, cut Hugo's "Gautier" in half, unclot Mallarmé, lop a third off Rimbaud's "Drunken Boat," add stanzas to Rilke, shift lines by Villon, move sections, change images, alter meter and intent—"And so forth!"

This was *running division on the ground-work* with a vengeance, and to modern "Grammarians" an act of cavalier insouciance and indecency. Perverse as translation and unpalatable as poetry.

IV ■ *The idea of translation in general embodied here—it is an idea only and by no means intended to achieve the status of a theory—is that meaningful versions of poems in one language can exist in another. These are neither word-for-word prose versions nor "imitations," though each of these kinds of translation can serve a useful purpose.*

Contemporary French Poetry, coedited by Alexander Aspel and Donald Justice, appeared in 1965. Aspel chose the poets to be translated; Justice, the twenty-four young translators— Edmund Keeley, Charles Wright, Mark Strand, and W. D. Snodgrass among them. Justice wrote a "Note on the Translations" from which the above is extracted.

The book was further evidence of America's fascination with an ideal of French verse. (A lopsided affair, one might add, since, apart from the awkward piety toward Poe, the French have never shown any enthusiasm for American poetry.) It contains straightforward renditions of work by members of the so-called "middle generation," survivors of surrealism, the great-great-grandchildren of Rimbaud and Baudelaire. What seemed daring in its day now seems outdated. This goes for much of the English as well, a mild-mannered Esperanto that rarely gets out of line, the translatorese that smothered all too many poems in the sixties and beyond. One exception, a poem by Philippe Jaccottet entitled *"La Traversée,"* is worth quoting in full to show what Justice could accomplish when fettered by the triple constraints of rhythm, rhyme, and syllable count.

La Traversée

Ce n'est pas la Beauté que j'ai trouvée ici,
ayant loué cette cabine de seconde,
débarqué à Palerme, oublié mes soucis,
mais celle qui s'enfuit, la beauté de ce monde.

L'autre, je l'ai peut-être vue en ton visage,
mais notre cours aura ressemblé à ces eaux

qui tracent leurs grands hiéroglyphes sur les plages
au sud de Naples, et que l'été boit aussitôt,

signes légers que l'on récrit sur les portières . . .
Elle n'est pas donnée à nous qui la forçons,
pareils à des aventuriers sur les frontières,
à des avares qui ont peur de la rançon.

Elle n'est pas non plus donnée aux lieux étranges,
mais peut-être à l'attente, au silence discret,
à celui qui est oublié dans les louanges
et simplement accroît son amour en secret.

The Crossing

It is not Beauty I've discovered here—
having reserved this cabin, second-class,
landed at Palermo, forgot my care—
but the world's beauty only, which will pass.

I may have seen that other in your face,
but we are like these waters moving on,
that on the beaches south of Naples trace
great hieroglyphs, and are by summer gone,

faint signs, inscribed again on portières . . .
She is not given us who force our way,
who would adventure out on her frontiers,
misers, who fear the ransom we must pay.

She is not given to any foreign place,
although to waiting and to silence she may be,
to one forgotten in the midst of praise,
who simply tends his love, and secretly.

Elective affinity is the one indispensable element in the art
of translation. If the poet is beguiled by the features he finds

reflected in his original, he may do a good job. If not, not. This particular example—Justice as metaphrast—is about as far from the notion of *imitatio* as one could get. Lowell himself had come to the conclusion that meter had something to do with fidelity in translation, that a metrical version may well "turn out to be more accurate, for some queer reason," and that theory is tested here. The result is a poem, metrical, accurate, that would not have seemed out of place in *The Summer Anniversaries*. (Indeed, Alexander Aspel's assessment of the poems of Jaccottet—also born in 1925—sounds oddly clairvoyant when read with Justice's own later work in mind: "A feeling of frailty, shadow, and void in a secretly threatened reality underlies Jaccottet's reaction to the world. His diction has a limpid quality, an ease in motion and a light grace producing effects of transparency and discreet serenity. . . . Jaccottet is not a poet of self-confession or mere self-assertion.")

V ■ *French and English constitute the same tongue.*

In 1973 the Stone Wall Press published a letterpress edition of 150 copies of *The Man Closing Up*, which included both a "translation" and an "improvisation." This curious amalgam takes off in two directions from a long French original by Guillevic, *"L'Homme qui se ferme,"* preceded by this note:

> Sitting in a cafeteria one afternoon in the spring of 1964, I made a first draft of the translation. About a year later, in another city, late one night, I happened to recall Guillevic's poem and, having neither the French text nor my version of it at hand to consult, began to improvise off fragments recollected from the original, almost as if I were remembering a tune, or tunes. The city was Miami, and a certain desolate stretch of the bay there and a memory of an old lighthouse on Key Biscayne entered into this new poem, which was finished in an hour or two, the quickest writing I have ever done. . . .

The translation, at 171 lines chopped into twenty-one irregular segments, is the most ambitious of Justice's sight readings. Like a latter-day, more laconic Prufrock, ill at ease in the purgatory of the natural world, the man closing up "holds in his hand / Something threatening. / He hopes that some day / He will know what to do with it." A generic enigma, the stick-figure of a man in a scale model, with a craving for dead leaves, a knack for calculation, and little else. *Chacun ses monstres . . .* against which he has "cooked up / His little song."

> Much like the man
> Who, naked, would put on the skin of a stag
> Still warm from the last chase.
>
> And speaks like someone
> Who'd have something to say
> From the center.
>
> It remains to be seen what to make of it,
> Of what he says.

Justice's delicately balanced equivalent—impossible to quote effectively—is a long snake of upended dominoes.

The "improvisation" had already appeared in *Night Light* (1967) (there titled "The Man Closing Up" and subtitled "Improvisations on themes from Guillevic"), severed from the translation in which it began. The man closing up is seen in close-up, coming to life, a human figure in a seascape, pinpointed in the note. Unfolding so that it can be read alongside the translation (the book is ingeniously constructed), the improvisation is more vivid, more desperate, a scenario of claustrophobic deprivation:

> There is a word for it,
> A simple word,
> And the word goes around.

It curves like a staircase,
And it goes up like a staircase,
And it *is* a staircase,

An iron staircase
On the side of a lighthouse.
All in his head.

And it makes no sound at all
In his head,
Unless he says it.

Then the keeper
Steps on the rung,
The bottom rung,

And the ascent begins.
Clangorous,
Rung after rung.

He wants to keep the light going,
If he can.

But the man closing up
Does not say the word.

"Probably more than other poets I know, I play games in my poems (as I do in life), and one of the unwritten rules of the game for me, as I like it played, is that you can risk this much personality or that much confession if the voice is promised to be that of someone else to start with. . . ."

VI ■ *Blood brought to ghosts . . .*

Transformations and re-creations abound in *Departures* (published in the same year as *The Man Closing Up*), a work of inspired ventriloquism. They multiply in *The Sunset Maker*

and the two volumes of selections, most notably in the experiments based on Baudelaire.

Miami, Florida, c. 1936

Je n'ai pas oublié, voisine de la ville,	a
Our new house on the edge of town	a
Notre blanche maison, petite mais tranquille;	a
Looks bare at first, and raw. A pink	b
Sa Pomone de plâtre et sa vieille Vénus	b
Plaster flamingo on one leg	c
Dans un bosquet chétif cachant leurs membres nus,	b
Stands preening by the lily pond.	d
Et le soleil, le soir, ruisselant et superbe,	c
And just as the sun begins to sink	b
Qui, derrière la vitre où se brisait sa gerbe,	c
Into the Everglades beyond,	d
Semblait, grand œil ouvert dans le ciel curieux,	d
It seems to shatter against the pane	e
Contempler nos dîners longs et silencieux,	d
In little asterisks of light,	f
Répandant largement ses beaux reflets de cierge	e
And on our lids half-closed in prayer	g
Sur la nappe frugale et les rideaux de serge.	e
Over the clean blue willowware.	g

In *Departures,* Lorca and Vallejo make cameo appearances,
along with four ancient Chinese, not to mention Anon,
author of a well-known Old English riddle. There is even a
departure from another man's translation: "1971" remodels
John Batki's version of Attila József, transposing it, stars and
all, from Hungary to America.

The fascination with Guillevic centers on questions of
technique: "Just to read him seemed to constitute a kind of
discovery for me. I had, for a while, the ambition to translate

that *style*, as it were, into American verse. . . . What I tried to do, once I found a style in another language which was to me of great interest, was to put it into American." And, "I suppose, now that I think of it, I was interested in the fact that his poems looked as if they should sound like Williams and they didn't. There was a sort of challenge to me to find out what the secret of that was, and I tried to invent or duplicate that kind of effect for myself."

There were other inventions, including several from the work of Rafael Alberti. "I've taken three different poems by Alberti and modeled an English poem on them. Not in what Lowell calls an imitation, and not a translation, not an adaptation. . . ." Again, the technical challenge—*la difficulté vaincue*—provides the starting point for these reworkings, some characteristic of the structure of the originals that catches his eye. And the care with which Justice distances his own enterprise from Lowell's is worth noting.

To imitate is to ape and follow suit, parrot and take after. To depart from is to vary and change, swerve and diverge. On a sliding scale of strategies for transformation, departure is a natural step beyond the notion of imitation. The original poet and the original poem slowly vanish as the Justice version comes into focus. The task of the translator becomes something new, "Something Better, 'tho it want yet a Name."

A method not without dangers and temptations. The temptation, of course, is to smash and grab, to plagiarize and purloin another man's inspiration, run off with his muse. And the danger is that one's translation may cast a shadow over the foreign poem, as Santayana's immaculate conversion of Gautier's *"L'Art"* exceeds its original. *A translator is to be like his author*—Dr. Johnson speaking—*it is not his business to excel him*. Hence the modesty of Justice, and the tact, the scrupulous tracking of origins and sources, the giving of credit where credit is due, even to the dead, especially to the dead. This eases the dangers if it does not erase them.

AN INFORMAL INVENTORY OF
DONALD JUSTICE'S TRANSLATIONS

The Summer Anniversaries, 1960. Revised edition, 1981.

Rimbaud   "The Poet at Seven" echoes *"Les Poètes de sept ans"*

Dante   "A Dream Sestina" recycles opening lines of the *Inferno.*

Baudelaire   "A Winter Ode . . ." echoes *"Les Sept Vieillards"*

Contemporary French Poetry: Fourteen Witnesses of Man's Fate, 1965.

(All the poems in this book are translations, French texts *en face*. Justice was the co-editor, with Alexander Aspel; he chose the translators and the translations and worked on eight of the poems, as follows.)

Ponge   "Rule": *"Règle"*

Michaux   "Tomorrow is Not Yet . . .": *"Demain n'est pas encore . . ."* (translated with Dori Katz)

Char   "Lightning Victory": *"Victoire éclaire"* (with Dori Katz)
           "The Library Is on Fire": *"La Bibliothèque est en feu"* (with Ralph Freedman and Paulène Aspel)

de Mandiargues   "The Color of Cold": *"La Couleur du froid"*
           "High Place": *"Haut Lieu"*

Jaccottet   "Sonnet": *"'Sois tranquille, cela viendra!'"*
           "The Crossing": *"La Traversée"*

Traversées, 1966. (Poems in French by Paulène Aspel. Two translations in the book are by Justice.)

Aspel   "Winter": *"Hiver"*
           "Diptych for Paul Klee": *"Diptyque pour Paul Klee"*

Night Light, 1967. Revised edition, 1981.

Guillevic   "The Man Closing Up": *"L'Homme qui se ferme"*
             ("Improvisations on themes from Guillevic")
             "Hands": epigraph: *"Les mains ne trouvaient plus /
De bonheur dans les poches"*

Enzensberger "For a Freshman Reader" ("After the German of
             Hans Magnus Enzensberger")

New Poetry of Mexico, 1970. Bilingual edition edited by
Mark Strand.

Villaurrutia "Nocturne of the Statue": *"Nocturno de la estatua"*
             "Rose Nocturnal": *"Nocturna rosa"*
             "Cemetery in the Snow": *"Cementerio en la nieve"*

Pellicer   "Study": *"Estudio"*
             "Memories of Iza": *"Recuerdos de Iza"*
             "Wishes": *"Deseos"*
             "Studies": *"Estudios"*
             "Prodigal Poem": *"Poema pródigo"*

Velarde   "Humbly": *"Humildemente . . ."*
             "The Dream of the Black Gloves": *"El sueño de los
guantes negros"*

L'Homme qui se ferme/The Man Closing Up, 1973.
"A Translation and an Improvisation."

Guillevic   *"L'Homme qui se ferme"*
    This fine press edition contains the original French text,
with Justice's (more or less) literal translation *en face,* and
reprints "Improvisations on themes from Guillevic"
from *Night Light* on a fold-out page in the back. The
translation was begun in 1964 and first published here.
The improvisation, first published in 1967, was begun in
1965. "I am aware that at least one other reading is as
plausible as this highly personal one."

Departures, 1973.

Guillevic	"ABC": "Some images in 'B' are adapted from a series of poems by Guillevic *(Choses)*."
Alberti	"On the Night of the Departure by Bus": "loosely modeled, in structure, on . . . *'En el día de su muerte a mano armada.'*"
	"White Notes": "The first two lines, the last line, and perhaps others . . . were also suggested by passages in Alberti's *Sobre los ángeles.*"
	"Cool Dark Ode": "loosely modeled" on the fourth part of *"Colegio (S.J.)."* In an interview, Justice refers to it as "a take-off from Alberti."
József	"1971": "O Europe," "a departure from a translation by John Batki of Attila József."
Lorca	"Lorcaesques"
Yang Wan-Li	"After the Chinese": "The remote sources . . . appear in *The Penguin Book of Chinese Verse.*"
Wang Chia Ch'in Chia Chëng-Yen	
Anonymous	"Riddle": "based on a well-known Old English riddle."
Vallejo	"Variations on a Text by Vallejo": The source text is *"Me moriré en Paris con aguacero . . ."* A further note in *A Donald Justice Reader* adds "The Greek poet, Kostas Ouránis (1890–1953), deserves some credit for this motif. Though I did not come across it until years after my own version, Ouránis has a poem apparently dating from 1915, the first line of which, in Kimon Friar's translation, reads: 'I shall die one day on a mournful autumn twilight.'"
	"Presences": Described in an interview as a "borrowing from, but a more hidden one, and therefore unacknowledged."

Selected Poems, 1979. (In the section "Uncollected Poems.")

Baudelaire	"Sonnet: An Old-Fashioned Devil": refers to *"Au Lecteur"*; epigraph: *"Tu le connais, lecteur, ce monstre délicat . . ."* (dated summer, 1948)
	"Two Songs from *Don Juan in Hell*": "*Don Juan in Hell* was to have been a puppet opera, based on the Baudelaire poem." (dated 1953)
	"Memories of the Depression Years": #3 (Miami, Florida) "is similarly related to Baudelaire's *Je n'ai pas oublié . . .*"
Wang Wei	"Memories of the Depression Years": #2 (Boston, Georgia) "is a kind of *imitation* of the Wang Wei poem which has been translated as 'A Farm House on the Wei River.'"

The Sunset Maker, 1987.

Baudelaire	"Nineteenth Century Portrait": "after Baudelaire"—"See Baudelaire's *'A une Malabaraise.'* I have shifted the scene from Malabar and Paris to the Caribbean and New York. Richard Howard's translation provided the hibiscus."
Rilke	"Seawind: A Song": "after Rilke"
	"Last Evening": "after Rilke"—"Both Rilke poems date from the poet's stay in Capri during the first part of 1907. My versions came out of an attempt to write a play based loosely on that period in Rilke's life. The famous image of the death's-head shako with which *'Letzer Abend'* ends I have dePrussianized, since in my play both poet and setting had become American. See *'Lied vom Meer (Capri, Piccola Marina)'* and *'Letzer Abend.'*"
Dante	"Purgatory" (retitled "Hell" in *Reader*): "So saying he went on / To join those who preceded him; / and there were those that followed."

Laforgue   "Nostalgia and Complaint of the Grandparents":
The epigraph, *"Les morts / C'est sous terre; / Ça
n'en sort / Guère"* from *"Complainte de l'oubli des
morts,"* is turned, three different ways, into a
refrain.

A Donald Justice Reader, 1991.

Catullus   "Little Elegy": "After Catullus" *("Lugete o Veneres
Cupidinesque")*

Baudelaire "The Metamorphoses of a Vampire": "translated
from Baudelaire"—"Line 12 of the French text I
was using reads *véloutés* rather than *rédoutés*." (First
appearance: *Reading Modern Poetry, 1955.*)

"As the Butterfly Longs for the Cocoon or the Looping Net"

Richard Howard

To account for the insistent reticence of this poet, for what he himself, in a characteristic oxymoron, calls "The major resolution of the minor," we must a little recuperate the blurred meaning of elegance—a term very promiscuously accorded these days and very precariously worn—from the original sense of the term itself: a consistent choice of words and their arrangement in the exemplification of a single taste. An American impulse, as it were: from many, one. At the age of forty, Donald Justice had not produced, or at least had not ventured to publish, so *many* poems, perhaps three dozen in his first book, *The Summer Anniversaries* (which was the Lamont Poetry Selection for 1959), and a dozen more in *A Local Storm,* three years later. To pursue the patriotic figure, about as many poems as there are States in the Union. But he has written enough—as there are States enough—for us to collect from the whole sum and tenor of his discourse, as Berkeley would say, a provisional perspective, and the winnowed singleness of that perspective, the unmistakable and unmistaken unity of an artistic identity, is proof, then, of his elegance, a reminder too that the word "glamor," a cheaper sister of elegance in misuse, is merely a Scots corruption of the word "grammar":

> How shall I speak of doom, and ours in special,
> But as of something altogether common?
> No house of Atreus ours, too humble surely,
> The family tree a simple chinaberry

Such as springs up in Georgia in a season.
(Under it sags the farmer's broken wagon.)
Nor may I laud it much for shade or beauty,
Yet praise that tree for being prompt to flourish,
Spite of the worm and weather out of heaven.

I publish of my folk how they have prospered
With something in the eyes, perhaps inherent,
Or great-winged nose, bespeaking an acquaintance
Not casual and not recent with a monster,
Citing, as an example of some courage,
That aunt, long gone, who kept one in a bird-cage
Thirty-odd years in shape of a green parrot,
Nor overcame her fears, yet missed no feeding,
Thrust in the crumbs with thimbles on her fingers.

There is a glamor, certainly, about such poetry: it is there in
the voice, shifting from courtly to country, Southern and soft
and just under the tension of song, in which it is uttered so
cunningly:

By seventeen I had guessed
That the "really great loneliness"
Of James's governess
Might account for the ghost
On the other side of the lake . . .

and even so complacently:

Heart, let us this once reason together . . .
An antique, balding spectacle such as thou art,
Affecting still that childish, engaging stammer
With all the seedy innocence of an overripe pomegranate!

a voice that has studied, has mastered the cadences of Mr.
Ransom, as in this further bit from the poem I quoted first,
"Tales from a Family Album":

There was a kinsman took up pen and paper
To write our history, whereat he perished,
Calling for water and the holy wafer,
Who had, ere that, resisted much persuasion.

But it is yet a glamor of selfhood, beyond manners, not
accountable to such indenture alone—else we should have to
course after too many masters for it, from Auden:

The danger lies, after all,
In being led to suppose—
With Lear—that the wind-dragons
Have been let loose to settle
Some private grudge of heaven's.
Still, how nice for our egos!

or from Ogden Nash, of all people:

Meanwhile the petty lord who must have paid
For the artist's trip up from Perugia, for the horse, for the
        boy, for everything here, in fact, has been delayed,
Kept too long by his steward, perhaps, discussing
Some business concerning the estate, or fussing
Over the details of his impeccable toilet
With a manservant whose opinion is that any alteration at
        all would spoil it . . .

to William Carlos Williams:

Grandeur, it seems,
Comes down to this in the end:
A street of shops
With white shutters
Open for business . . .

It derives, this glamor of Justice's, not from a red wheelbarrow
or from bells for anyone's daughter, but from a special accommodation of the poem's shape and body to its impulse or

"message" until nothing remains outside the form, left over to be said in any way *except by the poem itself:* until nothing is epactal. Experience, when judged, arrested, enacted, and committed to the language in this indivisible fashion, becomes difficult to discuss, difficult to distinguish apart from the very poems, whose weather and working enforce a finer rehearsal of their "sense" than any paraphrase or reduction. But of course this is generally true of all successful poetry, and if Plotinus is right that criticism is the progressive explication of the implicit, we must be nothing if not critical in precisely the cases where the success is most evident. Moreover, for all the glamor of language which seems to slide these poems off our minds, what must attract us even further into Donald Justice's poetry is that it is alien as well as assimilable to other poetry, that it is autonomous. The differentia are there, are even there in the poems' gist, but I prefer to suggest that they are not thereby essential just because we can detach them— merely detachable. It will be *more* interesting to trace this elegant idiosyncrasy in what are mostly regarded as the poem's means and machinery, its joints and surfaces, though I suppose it is interesting enough, even so, to remark that what we must put up with here is a poetry *about* the mind's circular movement, its apprehension of an imprisonment within itself, and *about* the impoverishment of the world as a consequence of this servitude. So much for the message, then, as a sop to Plotinus, let us say; to find the means of a poetry is a surer step toward finding its real message, we suspect, and cherish an ignorance of "subject," an ignorance that is likely to be as illuminating as any knowledge we have already or are likely to come by. To the means, then, the pulleys, cranks, and motors that keep the message running. It is no accident, indeed it is a necessity that Donald Justice writes so many sestinas, for this is a strict form that bends the poem's motion, that binds and braids into a halter the poet's impulse to run away with himself in all directions; what satisfies and even delights about Donald Justice's sestinas is that they are

invented by their "sense"; called into being by their burden,
they are inevitable and necessary emanations of entrapment.
Poems about circuit and constraint, whose forced conclusions
can be unpeeled like a great onion of foreclosures:

> There is no way to ease the burden.
> The voyage leads on from harm to harm,
> A land of others and of silence.

That is the final stanza of one, with all six terminal words;
another:

> Round me they circle on the hill.
> But what is wrong with my friends' faces?
> Why have they changed that way to wood?

But perhaps the most astonishing and original of them all is
the one called "The Metamorphosis," a decorously Southern
Gothic narrative of a man proceeding homeward through an
emblematic landscape of mortal encroachment:

> Past Mr. Raven's tavern
> Up Cemetery Hill
> Around by the Giant Oak
> And Drowning Creek gone dry
> Into the Hunting Woods
> And that was how he went . . .

and finally thrusting his key into the lock six stanzas on, only
to be held fast, confiscated by the nameless horror that he finds
in his own hall:

> Then bent he to the keyhole
> Nor might his eyes withdraw
> The while the hall unwound
> That thing which afterwards
> No man should know or its like
> Whether dead or living.

But the transformation has occurred not only in the subject, as recorded or remarked by the natural terrors of this moralized landscape: "Then owls cried out from the woods," the following hound "moaned and whined / As she some fit were having"; and not only in the grave and practiced saraband of the sestina's actual structure, the last word of the first stanza's last line becoming the last word of the second stanza's first line and so on; but in the very metamorphosis of the six words themselves on which the sestina is built, so that the first stanza's "tavern" passes through "heaven," "haven," "having," and "heaving" before it becomes "living" in the last, and the other five teleutons undergo a similar process, snared yet in the pitiless rhythm of their exchanges. Everything is the same and yet is utterly different: that is the terror of "The Metamorphosis," and it is accomplished, enacted, perpetuated by the poem's formal will as by its subject or story. The nightmare is derived, in fact, from the daylight means of existence, as the transformed words are derived from the initial set: and that is Donald Justice's whole object and outrage in the rest of his poems.

For example, the abridged villanelle "Women in Love" perfectly exemplifies the paralyzing effect of feeling it discusses—"they cannot stay or go"—by its formal necessities, the three rhyme words on two rhymes and the six recurring lines out of thirteen; so that the poem's ultimate meaning is, and is only—its actual form:

> It always comes, and when it comes they know.
> To will it is enough to bring them there.
> The knack is this, to fasten and not let go.
>
> Their limbs are charmed; they cannot stay or go.
> Desire is limbo: they're unhappy there.
> It always comes, and when it comes they know.
>
> Their choice of hells would be the one they know.
> Dante describes it, the wind circling there.
> The knack is this, to fasten and not let go.

The wind carries them where they want to go,
Yet it seems cruel to strangers passing there.
It always comes, and when it comes they know
The knack is this, to fasten and not let go.

Take a further instance, neither narrative nor analytic this time, but stating a kind of artistic credo. In the little poem called "Thus," in two stanzas, the description of a piece of music, a theme and variations, is undertaken in the first eight lines—key, character, mode, and orchestration are announced; in the second eight-line strophe, the same teleutons are employed, though the meaning of the words is altered in every particular by the statements, even by the rhythms, in which they occur. So that where the first group concluded

> As for the theme,
> There being but the one, with variations,
> Let it be spoken outright by the oboe
> Without apology of any string,
> But as a man speaks, openly, his heart
> Among old friends, let this be spoken.

the second takes up the strain metamorphically:

> It would do certain violence to our theme.
> Therefore see to it that the variations
> Keep faith with the plain statement of the oboe.
> Entering quietly, let each chastened string
> Repeat the lesson she must get by heart,
> And without overmuch adornment.

Abruptly, it is the final word, "adornment," that breaks the form, the sequence—of course, one almost adds. The adornment is the variation, and how else, *where* else might it occur? The congruence, then, the mutual mirroring of means and meaning in this poetry is precisely the glamor of Donald Justice's art, and if it makes, in its stern demands, for the relatively few poems in his canon, it must also be held responsible for their elegant necessity.

∎ ∎ ∎

In an essay on Karl Shapiro's antipoem *The Bourgeois Poet,* Donald Justice once said that he liked best those parts which were at once "wildest and most formal," "surely a winning combination," as he put it then. And even more suggestively, in the preface to his edition of the poems of Weldon Kees, Justice speaks of being original "in one of the few ways that matter" as a question of a "particular tone of voice which we have never heard before." Bearing in mind the fierce adequacy of this poet's performance to his purposes, the inextricability of formal pattern and wild theme, I should like a little more emphasis on that tone of voice in which we may hear his poems. I mentioned above the gist of these half-a-hundred poems as being, when logically arrayed, the self's apprehension of its own duress and bondage to its own instruments and the consequent despoiling of the physical world: a void at the center which causes a curling of the edges, so to speak. There would seem to be a tradition, or at least a convention, in lyric poetry for dealing with a world thus enchanted, thus held in thrall, and it is this conventional tone which releases Donald Justice's "particular" gentle and ruinous tone of voice, "humbly aspiring" as James Dickey says, but aspiring to apocalypse out of a frenzy with mortality, aspiring to extirpate everything that might stand between the naked self and the absolute—which is not humble. We may trace the articulation of such a convention for dealing with enchantment, in this century, in poems by de la Mare, by Graves, by Yeats before 1916, by Frost and Ransom in America; the decorum of this kind of poetry admits of sharp observation, but not much experiment or originality with the tools of that observation, either words or senses. The language of this poetry is one already received by poets, not invented to satisfy new needs (which is why we must except the later Yeats from this group). There is, for instance,

a direct and admirable succession—though I think no immediate influence—linking these "Bells" by de la Mare:

> I saw a ploughman with his team
> Lift to the bells and fix on them
> His distant eyes, as if he would
> Drink in the utmost sound he could;
> While near him sat his children three,
> And in the green grass placidly
> Played undistracted on, as if
> What music earthly bells might give
> Could only faintly stir their dream,
> And stillness make more lovely seem.

to these "Belles," without the period inversions, by Justice:

> They lean upon their windows. It is late.
> Already it is twilight in the house;
> Autumn is in their eyes. Twilit, autumnal—
> Thus they regard themselves. What vanities!
> As if all nature were a looking-glass
> To publish the small features of their ruin!
>
> Each evening at their windows they arrive
> As in anticipation of farewells,
> Though they would be still lingering if they could,
> Weary, yet ever restless for the dance . . .

The next two lines, with their allusions to the fairy-tale,
clinch the resemblance to the poet of *Peacock Pie:*

> Old Cinderellas, hearing midnight strike,
> The mouse-drawn coach impatient at the door.

but it is the rhetoric of the ruined self, or at least of the self
incarcerated, that is more strictly analogous to de la Mare than
even the nursery-rhyme trope. The more dramatic poems in
A Local Storm extend the range of this rhetoric:

Meanwhile they quarrel and make it up,
Only to quarrel again. A sudden storm
Pulls the last fences down. The stupid sheep
Stand out all night now coughing in the garden
And peering through the windows where they sleep.

and the final one in this pamphlet makes the tone itself into a kind of *ars poetica:*

it would be too late:
The artist will have had his revenge for being made to
wait,
A revenge not only necessary but right and clever—
Simply to leave him out of the scene forever.

But though Donald Justice has made it reach farther than the sleeping princess and the broken tower, the rhetoric of enchantment is always the same, consonant with Stendhal's remark that "one must write with equal application at all times"—when one is always in the same fix, I should add. There is a deep, committed reverence about the way Justice celebrates his defeats: madness, love, old age, death—in all, the violence, the wildness is inside, working outwards, showing up the world in a reluctant, leave-taking light, either in the mode of the times:

Jane looks down at her organdy skirt
As if *it* somehow were the thing disgraced,
For being there, on the floor, in the dirt . . .

or in the mode of the timeless:

Weary the soldiers go, and come back weary,
Up a green hill and down the withered hill,
And Jack from Joan, and they shall never marry . . .

But given such a burden altogether, and such a resonance, and such a claim on the coincidence of the will's rhetoric and

the world's wreck, the wonder is not that Donald Justice had
written, for his forty years and his book and a half, only fifty
poems, but that we have an elegant monument of fifty such
poems to testify to his doomed transactions with life:

> The aging magician retired to his island.
> It was not so green as he remembered,
> Nor did the sea caress its headlands
> With the customary nuptial music.
>
> He did not mind . . .
> . . . .
> If now it was all to do again,
> Nothing lacked to his purpose, only
>
> Some change in the wording of the charm,
> Some slight reshuffling of negative
> And verb, perhaps—that should suffice.
> So, so. Meanwhile he paced the strand,
>
> Debating, as old men will, with himself
> Or the waves, though as it was the sea
> Seemed only to go on washing and washing
> Itself, as if to be clean of something.

In 1967 a dozen poems from the pamphlet *A Local Storm*
were added to another twenty-five written since 1963; the new
book, *Night Light,* is for the most part a matter of what Justice's
Prospero discovers his future to be in the fragment just quoted:
"Some slight reshuffling of negative / And verb, perhaps" to
produce "Some change in the wording of the charm"—the
charm, one notices, remaining the same in either sense ("He
did not mind . . . If now it was all to do again"). The illumination of *Night Light,* insofar as it is not merely reflected from
an earlier achievement, is low indeed, a blue glow which if not
fitful nonetheless emits as well a kind of vexed buzz close to
the fretful; as Justice says in "The Thin Man,"

I indulge myself
In rich refusals.
Nothing suffices.

I hone myself to
This edge. Asleep, I
Am a horizon.

The little lines with their rhythm of carping speech seem to be all the poet can afford, and it is remarkable, in fact, how richly he can make them work for him, or at least how readily recall the splendors that once were in his grasp: "the dream . . . repeats, / And you must wake again to your own blood / And empty spaces in the throat." The book moves from the galled expectation of song, "Orpheus Opens His Morning Mail," to the complacencies of "Narcissus at Home": "Alone at last! But I am forgetting myself . . ." And surely that is the progress, from a myth of effective music to one of self-satisfied musing, which Justice wishes us to trace. The obsessive imagery is indeed one of mirrors: in "Men at Forty"

deep in mirrors
They rediscover
The face of the boy . . .

and in "The Missing Person"

in the mirror
He sees what is missing.

It is himself
He sees there emerging

Slowly, as from the dark
Of a furnished room . . .

and in "For the Suicides of 1962"

Even
Those mirrors, to which always

> You must have turned to confide,
> Cannot have recognized you,
> Stripped, as you were, finally . . .

and in "The Tourist from Syracuse"

> Mine is the face which blooms in
> The dark mirrors of washrooms
> As you grope for the light switch . . .

and finally, most frankly, in "Poem for a Survivor"

> Holding this poem
> Close, like a mirror,
> I breathe upon it . . .

and elsewhere the pervasive narcissism is merely adulterated, not exorcized, by occasional gestures to the outside world:

> As though the simple
> Death of a pet cat,
> Buried with flowers,
>
> Had brought to the porch
> Some rumor of storms
> Dying out over
> A dark Atlantic.

The negatives reshuffled are indeed those of a consciousness held captive in the impounding self and which, being conscious, knows that it is a captive, *captivated* in precisely the sense or the two senses that Narcissus is subject to himself. Donald Justice perpetuates his powers, however low the wattage, by taking leave of them, and in the characteristically titled "The Man Closing Up" offers at least his warrantable intentions for the enterprise:

> He wants to keep the light going,
> If he can.

After the initial statement, in all its elegant postures, of the withdrawn consciousness, of the indentured ego, writing poetry is now a continuous farewell tour of duty ("The rhymes, the meters, how they paralyze"), and as the poet himself manfully asserts, in an otherwise peevish apostrophe to his own early poems,

Now the long silence. Now the beginning again.

Tradition and an Individual Talent

Dana Gioia

Anyone who reads Donald Justice's poetry at length will eventually note how often his poems seem to originate out of other literary texts. While most poems conduct a conversation with the past—if only by employing a form or genre their audience will recognize—authors, especially Americans, often exert immense effort and ingenuity to disguise their literary antecedents. If poetry grows out of the dialectic between innovation and emulation, our literature has always prized originality over continuity. Originality is, after all, America's one strict tradition.

Donald Justice, however, appears unconcerned about revealing the extent to which his poems rely on the literary tradition. *Departures*, *Selected Poems*, *The Sunset Maker*, and *A Donald Justice Reader* all end with "Notes" in which the author identifies the sources of particular poems, including some borrowing that even a sophisticated reader would not have detected. Other poems begin with clearly labeled epigraphs that contain images or phrases used later in the text. Even Justice's titles openly advertise their genealogy: "Sestina on Six Words by Weldon Kees," "Last Days of Prospero," "After a Phrase Abandoned by Wallace Stevens," "Variations on a Text by Vallejo," "Henry James by the Pacific." Whereas most writers diligently hide their literary debts, Justice practices what accountants call "full disclosure." In this respect he writes as a historian would, carefully crediting all of his predecessors to acknowledge that scholarship—like literature itself—is a collective enterprise. Justice's meticulous notation not only attests to his integrity as a writer, but it also suggests that his borrowings are a conscious and central aspect of his poetics.

Until going through all of Justice's published poetry, however, even a careful reader may not realize the full extent and
diversity of the author's appropriations. Moreover, such an
examination also reveals the surprising fact that Justice's conscious employment of other texts for his own imaginative purposes is not part of an early imitative stage but has increased
with each collection. Whereas his first volume, *The Summer
Anniversaries* (1960), contains only five poems (out of thirty-
two total) that have overt literary sources, Justice's second collection, *Night Light* (1967), includes no less than eleven (out
of forty). In *Departures* (1973), the ratio increases with ten out
of twenty-nine poems openly drawing material from other literary works. In *Selected Poems* (1979), four of the sixteen previously uncollected poems employ borrowed literary models.
(This count does not include the Tremayne poems, which
show an oblique debt to Kees's Robinson and Berryman's
Henry poems). Finally, in *The Sunset Maker* (1987), not only
do nine of the twenty-five poems owe debts to other literary
works (three are translations), but the last half of the book con-
stitutes two internally referential sequences of poems, stories,
and a memoir that borrow and develop material from one
another.

I do not claim this census is scientific. Another critic might
arrive at a slightly different total or make a convincing argument why a particular poem does or does not belong on the
list. But by any count, it appears that at least one quarter of
Justice's published poems utilize openly borrowed material—
even if it is only something as small as a memorable phrase.
His appropriations vary from entire poems (like Attila József's
1927 "O Europe," which Justice rewrote about the American
landscape as "1971") to borrowed situations and characters
("Last Days of Prospero"). He may steal an opening line (as
he did from the beginning of John Peale Bishop's "Ode,"
which now also starts Justice's "The Grandfathers"). He may
adopt elements of a poet's style (as in his Guillevic homages)
or a particular typographical arrangement (like Hart Crane's

use of marginal commentary in *The Bridge*, which found its way into one version of Justice's "Childhood" before being revised away). He also has reshaped prose passages into verse while keeping much of the original phrasing, as in "Young Girls Growing Up (1911)," which recasts an incident from Kafka's diaries. And sometimes he simply quotes an author in a passing allusion. The sheer diversity of his textual appropriations is not only impressive but unusual, as is his habit of underscoring each debt with a conspicuous epigraph or endnote that heightens the reader's awareness of the transaction. One often reads an allusive author unconscious of his borrowings. Justice, a lifelong teacher, intends his allusions to be recognized—whether the reader is prepared for them or not.

When critics discuss the debt one poem owes to another, they usually analyze the relationship in terms of influence. In understanding the nature of Justice's textual appropriations, however, traditional concepts of influence are not especially helpful. Except for a few early poems influenced by Auden (one of which, "Sonnet," is equal to anything in its model, Auden's "In Time of War"), Justice has always had an identifiable tone and manner. His obsession with formal experimentation and his impatience with writing the same kind of poem for very long have given his work an extraordinary stylistic variety out of proportion with its relatively small size. But his poetic signature remains constant—clarity of expression, relentless economy of means, self-conscious formal design, unpretentious intelligence, and quiet but memorable musicality. Reading his work, one always senses an integrating and independent imagination.

Discussing literary influences, one also looks for the critical relationships between an author and one or two dominant predecessors. Reading Blake, one recognizes the crucial importance of Milton as a model. Studying Baudelaire, one considers his obsessive relationship with Poe. A contemporary writer like William Everson, for example, cannot be understood without constant reference to his lifelong master,

Robinson Jeffers. Harold Bloom insists that such dominant influences must be seen in Freudian terms as decisive psychic struggles. In order to become strong and mature, a younger poet must assimilate and then overpower his elder authority figures. Such theories, however, do little to clarify Justice's case. Not only does one not sense any psychic wrestling with his three dominant early masters—Stevens, Baudelaire, and Auden—one also doesn't find much evidence of them in his poems outside of a few deliberate homages. Likewise, the broad range of Justice's borrowings—from T. S. Eliot's prose and Hart Crane's marginalia to Duke Ellington's lyrics and Mother Goose's syntax—makes it impossible to discuss dominant single influences. If Justice is, to use Bloom's term, a "strong poet," one aspect of his strength is the ability to draw from the breadth of world literature.

The one critic who provides a helpful model for Justice's appropriations is T. S. Eliot. In his 1920 essay on the Elizabethan dramatist Philip Massinger, Eliot wrote that one could learn a great deal about a poet by understanding the way in which he borrows.

> Immature poets imitate; mature poets steal; bad poets deface what they take, and good poets make it into something better, or at least something different. The good poet welds his theft into a whole of feeling which is unique, utterly different from that from which it was torn; the bad poet throws it into something which has no cohesion. A good poet will usually borrow from authors remote in time, or alien in language, or diverse in interest.

Except in his conscious homages, Justice does not imitate the styles or employ the thematic of the texts from which he draws material. Instead, like Eliot's mature poet, he steals an image or idea, a phrase or pattern to use in a new imaginative context. In "Counting the Mad," for example, Justice borrowed the meter and syntax of the Mother Goose toe-

and-finger counting rhyme, "This little pig went to market."
But Justice's poem imitates neither the style nor effect of its
source:

> This one was put in a jacket,
> This one was sent home,
> This one was given bread and meat
> But would eat none,
> And this one cried No No No No
> All day long.
>
> This one looked at the window
> As though it were a wall,
> This one saw things that were not there,
> This one things that were,
> And this one cried No No No No
> All day long.
>
> This one thought himself a bird,
> This one a dog,
> And this one thought himself a man,
> An ordinary man,
> And cried and cried No No No No
> All day long.

The original nursery rhyme (or at least the most common
modern variant, which Justice uses as his model) is playful and
intimate—as befitting a verbal and tactile game a mother
shares with a small child. By keeping the syntactic pattern of
the original more or less intact but substituting shocking new
subject matter, Justice achieves the double effect of familiarity and dislocation. The harmless market-day adventures of
five childlike pigs become a nightmarish tour of an insane asy-
lum. Significantly, Justice formalizes the idiosyncratic rhythms
of the original nursery rhyme into a fixed stanza. Repeating
this pattern three times, always ending with the staccato cries

of the inmate who "thought himself a man, / An ordinary man," Justice creates a formal feeling of confinement analogous to the mad's physical incarceration. Imaginative literature about insanity often tries to re-create the disjunctive mental processes of the mad. This method tends to create complex imitations of the mad's interior monologue. In "Counting the Mad," however, Justice views the insane from a largely exterior perspective. He reproduces what a visitor would see or hear, and in doing so also reproduces the horror a visitor would feel. The only projection into the interior life of the mad is in the final stanza, where he states the central figure's self-image of normality. Although Justice's subject is potentially complex and unknowable, by using the Mother Goose paradigm he makes the finished poem simple, lucid, and accessible.

"Counting the Mad" also illustrates Eliot's point that good poets improve or transform what they take because Justice's poem is both more ambitious than and different from its model. This sort of appropriation is typical of Justice. He takes something from one context and uses it in another. Reading in a newspaper about "a hatbox of old letters" to be sold at auction, he transformed the item into the elegiac poem "To the Unknown Lady Who Wrote the Letters Found in the Hatbox." Finding a striking description in a John D. MacDonald detective novel ("One of those men who can be a car salesman or a tourist from Syracuse or a hired assassin"), Justice—who was then living in Syracuse—expands the passage into a menacing, metaphysical poem, mysterious in ways quite alien to MacDonald. Justice's poem "The Tourist from Syracuse" ends

> Shall I confess who I am?
> My name is all names, or none.
> I am the used-car salesman,
> The tourist from Syracuse,

The hired assassin, waiting.
I will stand here forever
Like one who has missed his bus—
Familiar, anonymous—

On my usual corner,
The corner at which you turn
To approach that place where now
You must not hope to arrive.

The way Justice elaborates MacDonald's brief description into an independent poem is characteristic of his creative method. "The Tourist from Syracuse," however, illustrates this intertextual procedure at its simplest. Although Justice's poem achieves a degree of linguistic and intellectual complexity beyond MacDonald's original, it nonetheless bears a paraphrasable resemblance to its prose parent. Justice rarely develops borrowed material in so linear a fashion. Usually his appropriations only provide a point of departure toward an imaginative end unforeshadowed in the original.

More typical of Justice's creative method is his "After a Phrase Abandoned by Wallace Stevens," which bears as its epigraph an eight-word fragment from Stevens's notebook ("The alp at the end of the street"). Justice has revised the poem significantly since its first appearance as a three-part sequence. Its most current version reads in full,

The alp at the end of the street
Occurs in the dreams of the town.
Over burgher and shopkeeper,
Massive, he broods,
A snowy-headed father
Upon whose knees his children
No longer climb;
Or is reflected
In the cool, unruffled lakes of

> Their minds, at evening,
> After their day in the shops,
> As shadow only, shapeless
> As a wind that has stopped blowing.
>
> Grandeur, it seems,
> Comes down to this in the end—
> A street of shops
> With white shutters
> Open for business . . .

This poem does bear a family resemblance to Stevens's work. Justice not only borrows the opening line from his Hartford master, he also employs Stevens's characteristic dialectic between the sublime and quotidian suggested by the borrowed phrase. Moreover, Justice uses some Stevensian stock characters, the burgher and the shopkeeper. But no sooner has Justice established this Stevensian scene in the three opening lines than he liberates the town from the elder poet's metaphysics. The new poem uses the contrast between the cold, primal presence of the mountain and the increasingly self-contained, man-made reality of the village to make points quite alien to Stevens. Justice observes the psychological situation of the townspeople, who have banished the paternal image of nature to the boundaries of their consciousness. He postulates no Stevensian struggle with abstractions of reality. Rather than transforming his observations into the premises of a supreme fiction, Justice accepts the loss of mystic consciousness as a condition of modern life. Justice even celebrates—despite the touch of irony in the last stanza—the functional beauty of the burghers' workaday world. Without mocking Stevens's fixation on the loss of religious faith, Justice quietly moves beyond this late romantic concern to create a poem of contemporary consciousness.

Justice's poem acknowledges Stevens as its precursor. It even initiates a subtle ontological discussion between the younger and the elder poet. But there is no Bloomian struggle for displacement. Rather than the anxiety of influence, Justice displays a characteristic confidence and respectful tolerance. "True poetic history," Bloom has asserted, "is the story of how poets as poets have suffered from other poets, just as any true biography is the story of how anyone suffered his own family—of his own displacement of family into loves and friends." Justice's example demonstrates the sheer inadequacy of such Freudian theories of poetic influence. As a means of apprehending how Justice works his intertextual appropriations, Bloomian displacement offers no more insight than does the simple theory of imitation. It is more helpful here to expand Eliot's notion of the "mature poet." No anguished rebel, Justice is a thoroughly mature writer—stylistically, intellectually, psychologically. His authorial identity meets its precursors with the self-assurance, independence, and discriminating affection found in a fully developed and healthy psyche.

"After a Phrase Abandoned by Wallace Stevens" also demonstrates the unusual manner in which Justice uses borrowed material to generate new poems. There were several distinctive ways in which quotations from other texts were commonly incorporated into Modernist poems. They were, for example, used as decorative devices, arresting local effects to add interest to the surface of the poem. Although Modernist poetics minimized the notion of decorative language, properly proportioned decoration remained one of its fundamental poetic techniques. Marianne Moore frequently employed striking quotations in this manner, as in, for example, the second stanza of "England." Quotation was also used as an emphatic device to add force or authority to a passage. Ezra Pound habitually inserted classical quotations into his poems to achieve this effect. Emphatic quotation became a central technique for his "Hugh Selwyn Mauberly." Quotation was also used as a contrapuntal device to provide an ironic contrast to other elements in a poem. Eliot borrowed lines of poems, songs, prayers, and nursery rhymes to use contrapuntally in *The*

Waste Land and "The Hollow Men." Sometimes an author even used borrowed language architecturally, as Nabokov did in several of his novels, using, for instance, Poe's "Annabel Lee" as a recurring emotional scaffold in *Lolita*.

Although one finds examples of decorative, emphatic, and contrapuntal quotation in Justice's work ("After a Phrase Abandoned by Wallace Stevens," for instance, borrows a decorative phrase from Auden's song "Fish in the unruffled lakes"), Justice's characteristic method is to use quotation as a generative device. He coaxes a new poem out of the unrealized possibilities suggested by a borrowed phrase or image. His Stevens poem proceeds directly from the images and ideas of the fragment. "The Tourist from Syracuse" likewise uncovers levels of meaning in MacDonald's phrase beyond the normal depth of the detective genre.

In the work of Pound or Eliot, borrowed quotations usually maintain their original identity despite their new context. Even when they are used ironically, one hears them as foreign words imported into the new text. Their quotation marks, as it were, remain intact. The final text often has the texture of a collage in which borrowed and original materials combine to create a novel effect. But in Justice's work, quoted material usually seems totally assimilated into the new poem. Not only does it no longer seem foreign to the text, the new poem appears to have grown organically and seamlessly out of it. One occasionally sees this generative technique in the early Modernists, as in the opening section of Eliot's "Ash-Wednesday," which incorporates a line translated from Cavalcanti ("Because I do not hope to turn again"). But even in "Ash-Wednesday," Eliot ends the passage by returning to emphatic quotation. Having stolen a line to begin his poem, Eliot makes public penance by quoting the end of the "Hail Mary" as a self-standing coda.

Although Justice has appropriated other texts with the imaginative rapacity of an Eliot or a Pound, he has never been much drawn to the techniques of collage. The surfaces of his poems reflect such high polish, his syntax unfolds with such architectural assurance, that one suspects he found the disjunctive energy of high Modernist collage unappealing. Even when he began poems out of chance fragments (as in the aleatory poems in *Departures*), he left them with a seamless finish. Generative quotation has been a technique more compatible with his tastes, and no American poet has used it more effectively. When Justice titled his third collection *Departures,* he slyly but self-consciously confessed to this obsession. Stylistically the volume was a departure from his earlier formal work, but the book was also built around a series of poems that began as imaginative departures from other texts, some drawn from literary tradition, others from chance methods. Justice's title signals the author's unabashed reliance on the intertextual play between tradition and innovation. Tradition, to tweak Professor Bloom one last time, is not a threatening father intimidating creation, but a generative matrix for new poems.

The reason why theories of influence as romantic rebellion have so little applicability to Justice is that he is essentially a postmodern classicist, a contemporary artist who understands the sustaining power of tradition without seeking to stifle innovation and experiment. "Classicist" and "tradition" have often become code words for aesthetic and political reactionism, but Justice is no traditionalist in the narrow sense. As a poet, critic, and translator, he has assimilated the achievements of international Modernism, but he has from the beginning also recognized that his historical position comes after that aesthetic revolution ended. Justice's response to the predicament of the postmodern artist is part of his originality. He fostered no illusions of perpetuating the superannuated avant-garde aesthetic (a temptation that ruined many artists of his generation, especially the composers). Instead he confronted the burden of the past by exploring and consolidating the enduring techniques of Modernism to create a style that reconciled the experiments of the previous two generations with the demands of the present.

A central means of achieving this synthesis was to borrow material and techniques from the major Modernists and determine—in practical poetic terms rather than the abstract critical concepts—what remained viable for the contemporary artist. Eliot, Pound, Stevens, James, Williams, Rilke, Crane, Vallejo, Lorca, Kafka, Rimbaud, Baudelaire, József, Alberti, and others provided the material for experiment. The imaginative mission of consolidating the heritage of Modernism also explains why, despite his voracious appropriations, Justice so rarely borrows from earlier writers. With only a handful of exceptions, his appropriations begin chronologically with Baudelaire and Rimbaud, at the start of modern poetry. (And even his use of earlier sources like Dante in "Hell" often have an Eliotic or Poundian flavor.) Contrasting the chronological range of Justice's allusions and quotations with those of a Pound or Eliot, Kees or Lowell, demonstrates how closely focused Justice has been on Modernism.

In someone less talented or self-critical, Justice's allusive method might have proven dangerous. To borrow the words of great writers for inclusion in a new poem forces the reader to compare the new text with the original. Poetry so openly intertextual also risks seeming remote or pedantic, something drawn bloodlessly from books rather than learned firsthand from life. The common complaint of "academic formalism" leveled at members of Justice's generation is inadequate to address either the early work or ultimate accomplishments of poets like Richard Wilbur, Louis Simpson, James Merrill, Donald Hall, William Jay Smith, or Adrienne Rich. Nonetheless there does remain—as often is the case with unfair but enduring criticism—an uncomfortable kernel of truth in that generational stereotype. Some of Justice's contemporaries have produced dully learned and pointlessly self-conscious work. Poets are often scholarly creatures, and much intelligence and learning goes into every genuine poem. But intelligence cannot endow a poem with life in the absence of emotion or imagination. Perhaps a poet can never know too much, but a poem can.

Despite the literary models behind many of his poems, Justice rarely seems bookish. Although subtle in language and sophisticated in technique, his work—except for the overtly experimental pieces in *Departures*—is exemplary in its clarity and accessibility. One always senses the emotional impulse driving the poem (which is frequently a painful sense of loss or, more recently, bittersweet nostalgia), and that intuition clarifies all of the other elements, even when they are complex or deliberately ambiguous. But if Justice's language is often tentative, his poems never display the densely allusive or obscure manner of his teachers, Robert Lowell and John Berryman. His learning is assimilated into the total experience of the poem. One need not know the source of his allusions to understand what they mean in their new context. Even writing about literary subjects such as Henry James or the forgotten poet Robert Boardman Vaughn, Justice remains accessible. In this respect, his work reminds one of the poems of Jorge Luis Borges. Despite their formidable learning, Borges's poems are not difficult, because their intellectual content is always integrated into their imaginative and emotional fabric. Borges might have been speaking for Justice when he said, "I am also living when I dream, when I sleep, when I write, when I read." Reading is a natural part of Justice's poetic process because it is an integral part of his life.

Justice has fulfilled Eliot's challenge in "Tradition and the Individual Talent." He has demonstrated what Eliot called a poet's indispensable "historical sense," the ability to perceive the literary past in order to develop his own contemporary identity. Tradition, Eliot maintained, "cannot be inherited, and if you want it you must obtain it by great labor." Not every poet is willing to make the effort. Most are content to work within a received (and therefore entropic) idea of tradition. Aside from the sheer excellence of his poetry, Justice's importance comes from his determination to explore and redefine the traditions available to contemporary poets. The Modernists accomplished the task for their generation largely in their prose. Justice, however, has conducted his inquiries almost entirely in verse.

Prefacing *Platonic Scripts,* his only prose collection (which includes more pages of interviews than essays), Justice regrets having written so little criticism. "I see now," he remarks, "that criticism can be of enormous value in helping to define and refine one's own thinking." But even while sharing Justice's regret, one must point out that his poems have performed an important critical function in evaluating the heritage of Modernism. Without ever becoming didactic or dully programmatic, they have clarified the possibility of contemporary poetry. They are intellectually challenging without losing their emotional force. Although his poems pursue an investigative mission, they never forget that their primary purpose is to be good poetry. They are experimental in the happiest sense—experiments that succeed. His achievement has been to synthesize the diverse strands of Modernism into a powerful, new classical style.

Justice's poetry combines the concentration and energy of Modernism with the clarity and accessibility that typify classical styles. Although the tradition out of which he writes is the Modern movement, his sensibility exhibits the chief features of classicism's unity of design and aim, simplicity of means, clarity of expression, and a governing sense of form, all grounded in an informing tradition. There is also a notable element of restraint, but not in the stereotypical sense of excluding violence and emotion, which classical styles do not do (Beethoven, after all, was the apogee of classicism). Instead, classical styles control and balance emotional energy within a total design. Classicism has never had much good press in America. Our nation prefers the technicolor claims of Romanticism. But classicism is not a single style; rather, it is a sensibility that must in each age reinvent its own means of expression. At its best—which in contemporary art is very rare—classicism can achieve a unique balance of accessibility and profundity, of energy and concentration.

To demonstrate how effectively Justice's style achieves classicism's double aims of simplicity and profundity, we will end by examining "The Grandfathers." In this short, early poem Justice had already created a style with an accessible surface and complex subtext. Characteristically, he did this by appropriating another poet's words to create a subtle intertextual argument. "The Grandfathers" begins with the opening line of "Ode" by John Peale Bishop (a largely forgotten figure who wrote half a dozen of the best American poems of the twenties and thirties). Here is Justice's poem in its most recent version (*Selected Poems*):

The Grandfathers

> *Why will they never sleep?*
> John Peale Bishop

Why will they never sleep,
The old ones, the grandfathers?
Always you find them sitting
On ruined porches, deep
In the back country, at dusk,
Hawking and spitting.
They might have sat there forever,
Tapping their sticks,
Peevish, discredited gods.
Ask the lost traveler how,
At road-end, they will fix
You maybe with the cold
Eye of a snake or a bird
And answer not a word,
Only these blank, oracular
Headshakes or headnods.

On a narrative level "The Grandfathers" is a descriptive poem about taciturn country elders, the sort of old men one might observe while traveling backwoods roads. Read as a realistic lyric examining archetypal figures of American folk-lore, "The Grandfathers"—with its quirky irregular rhyme scheme and sharp images—is a haunting poem. Aside from compliments, it does not appear to need much commentary. But if one goes back to its source, Bishop's "Ode," one finds an unexpected poem, which begins

> Why will they never sleep
> Those great women who sit
> Peering at me with parrot eyes?
> They sit with grave knees; they keep
> Perpetual stare; and their hands move
> As though hands could be aware—
> Forward and back, to begin again—
> As though on tumultuous shuttles of wind they wove
> Shrouds out of air.

Bishop's poem describes a frightening vision of the three Fates, who become symbols for a tragic pagan worldview. The three sisters serve as horrific reminders of man's mortal-ity and the transience of human accomplishment. Bishop has no protection from them because his Christian faith, with its promise of salvation and resurrection, is dead. "Ode" ends

> There was One who might have saved
> Me from the grave dissolute stones
> And parrot eyes. But He is dead,
> Christ is dead. And in a grave
> Dark as a sightless skull He lies
> And of His bones are charnels made.

Returning to "The Grandfathers" after studying Bishop's poem of existential dread, one sees a different text. What seemed like a macabre but naturalistic lyric now also reads as a densely metaphorical examination of how religious anxiety persists even after the religion itself has died. One now notices, for instance, the ambiguity of reference for "they" in the opening line. Does it refer to "the grandfathers," as one might initially have assumed, or to "The old ones," or to something else left unstated (such as the "they" in Bishop's original, quoted in the epigraph)? One also notes that the grandfathers themselves may not be as entirely literal as they at first appeared. These ancient figures consistently operate on both a realistic and metaphorical level. Continuing through the poem, the reader now finds that many of these seemingly realistic details also have sinister, religious meanings. If they are indeed divinities, Justice's "old ones," those "Peevish, discredited gods," may indeed "have sat there forever." Two carefully elaborated levels of meaning coexist in the poem, each becoming a metaphor for the other. On a realistic level, "The Grandfathers" is a study of malign but impotent back-country elders; on the intertextual and metaphorical level, it describes the silent but troubling gods who still haunt the modern psyche. Characteristically, Justice designs the poem so it can be read satisfyingly on the first level alone, but he also creates a mythic subtext that can be understood only by reference to the poem's source. Justice's headnote from Bishop, therefore, isn't only an acknowledgment of the poet's borrowing; it is also a necessary clue to the poem's tradition, which includes not only Bishop's "Ode" but other Modernist poems about the death of religion.

Poems like "The Grandfathers" demonstrate the centrality of textual appropriation to Justice's aesthetic. Without understanding the intertextual complexity of his work, one cannot fully read his poems. Placing Justice in his own self-defined Modernist tradition and appreciating the hidden complexity of his sometimes deceptively simple classical style, however, reveals a profound and challenging poet. He has shown that Modernism remains a living tradition for artists strong enough to approach it with imagination and independence.

The Midnight of Nostalgia

William Logan

And what a dreadful disease Nostalgia
must be on the banks of the Missouri!
Sydney Smith

We have heard the chimes at midnight,
Master Shallow.

Falstaff

You don't have to be religious to succumb to nostalgia, though in some people nostalgia may supplant the religious instinct. The Christian present pursues its balance between the past of grace freely bestowed, fall, redemption through blood and the future of redemption in death, rise from sin, grace everlasting. As pure philosophy it is progressive, though I don't believe the angels will wear togas or holy tunics to protect their modesty. In practice, and in its daily injunctions, it tends to be backward-looking, and in its regressiveness to resemble the common operations of nostalgia.

We think of nostalgia as the vice of maturity, a disease of age; but one doesn't have to pass forty for nostalgia to press into a life, and even the very young may show its effect. In *The Oxford Book of Literary Anecdotes*, Ronald Knox is recorded as saying, during a bout of insomnia at the age of four, "I lie awake and think about the past." As a literary theme (rather than transient concern or rhetorical figure), nostalgia required a notion of the self perhaps impossible before Rousseau. Once the trivial incidents of a life had gained the authority of the poetic lyric, nostalgia became another vehicle for certain ancient, governing anxieties: the loss of the past (especially the perfected or romanticized past, an Eden), the forfeit of opportunity and regret for actions taken or mistaken, the corrupted potential or relative poverty of the present.

There was a feeling before the feeling found a name. When Shallow boasts, in *Henry IV, Part II,* "Jesu, Jesu, the mad days that I have spent! And to see how many of my old acquaintance are dead!", he mingles regret with the consolation of reminiscence, measuring the present on the terms of the past. And Falstaff, later, detects how reminiscence overwhelms the thin particulars: "I do see the bottom of Justice Shallow. Lord, Lord, how subject we old men are to this vice of lying!" (echoing his exclamation in *Part I* when Prince Hal claims the slaughter of Hotspur: "Lord, Lord, how this world is given to lying!").

The burdens of nostalgia aren't just an old man's quarrels with truth—for seeing the past, for saying the past, as better than it was. In an unsparing and sensible book called *The Burden of the Past and the English Poet,* Walter Jackson Bate reminds us that the pressures of the past have been felt since antiquity: an Egyptian scribe of 2000 B.C. named Khakheperresenb lamented, "Would I had phrases that are not known, utterances that are strange, in new language that has not been used, free from repetition, not an utterance which has grown stale, which men of old have spoken." The burdens fell differently on Shallow and Khakheperresenb, the literary construction and the literary scribe, but were jointly derived from and jointly determined by the belief that compared to a past of vital originality, the present was a withering or falling away.

The word *nostalgia* is a learnèd neologism of the late Renaissance. According to one scholar, it can be traced to an obscure 1688 medical tract, by the Swiss physician Johannes Hofer, describing a disorder found among Swiss mercenaries serving abroad in the armies of Europe. Their symptoms included melancholy, despondency, weeping, anorexia, and attempted suicide. They were, in short, desperately homesick. The first use in English isn't recorded until almost a century later, and before the present century all *Oxford English Dictionary* citations retain the sense of the cobbled-up Greek: *nostos,* a return home, and *algos,* pain.

Even used figuratively, the word remained within the pathology of homesickness: "That pond has . . . about half-a-dozen trouts, if indeed they have not sickened and died of Nostalgia" (1842). The first citation in the *OED* for our modern sense, for the "regret or sorrowful longing *for* the conditions of a past age; regretful or wistful memory or recall of an earlier time," doesn't occur until 1920, in D. H. Lawrence's *The Lost Girl.* No doubt a deeper trawl of literature would drag up earlier examples, but the shift from pathology to *pathétique* comes remarkably late.

It is widely supposed that nostalgia in literature is immitigably bad, that it protects what ought to be examined, falsifies what should be exposed, defends what must be attacked. The nostalgic impulse is thought to derive from the complacency of denial and therefore to exist wholly within the precincts of sentimentality, of the unexamined indulgence in emotional forms. But nostalgia isn't necessarily a wish to return to the past; it is the wish to be privileged to recall it, and to the extent that nostalgia is the admission of a practice, aware of limit in the character of its longing, it is a gesture of counter-sentiment. Nostalgia is the refuge of poets for whom the current modes of reminiscence have been irremediably stained with sentiment.

The sentimentalities to which our poetry is susceptible contaminate the treatment of private life. The modern poet is an adept of the material or moral condition of his own life—even love takes a poor second to the versification of domestic anecdote. When the allocating sentiment raises the trivial to the virtues of symbol, it is not the literature but the life that seems wanting. What is commonly thought to represent "risk" in contemporary poetry, the revelation of private affairs, employs an attitude to experience smug and calculating when it isn't corrupt, shameless, and insincere. From this, nostalgia can represent an escape and the radical of a reformation. It is also, of course, peculiarly permeable to sentiment; and every example of nostalgia in its reforming character may be countered by a dozen of sentimental misuse.

I have entertained these general notes before coming to the individual case because I am interested in nostalgia only as antisentiment, as the canker within sentiment. Given the rarity of a nostalgia of this condition, the subject of this essay might more usefully have been "The Abuse of Nostalgia," but that would have eliminated consideration of the reforming instance.

The method of Donald Justice's later poetry accepts nostalgia, a nostalgia with little of the emotional consolation of submission and more of the religious desolation of confession. In his arching dark ironies, Justice has long proved an irritant to the simpler taxonomies of American poetry, which find it convenient to ignore whatever lies beyond the margin of immediate comprehension. Justice almost never uses the self as the location of drama, for the great tragedy moving through the little event. In his detachment he is a modern (his most obvious forebears Williams and Stevens) at a time when the sharper reliefs of Modernism have been eroded. Modernism's respect for history, for a culture that spans millennia and not just months, has been superseded no less than its cool outward presentation of subject. No longer is Modernism's "impersonality" recognized as a matter of tension and tone: when fully employed, tension and tone don't require the outward display of emotion (Eliot's poems, to me at least, are frighteningly emotional).

The poetry of Pound and Eliot threw out grappling hooks in all directions; the poetry of Williams and Stevens was, in the main, self-sufficient. Most of Donald Justice's poems are similarly occlusive; they are the horizon of their own reference. They have practiced various strategies of impersonality, and without a side-glancing title or guarded note the reader would scarcely be aware of a debt to Vallejo, or Rilke, or Baudelaire. Justice has often made his own what is most foreign (one might see this strategy as a way of *avoiding* the burdens of the self)—the foreign landscapes become local; the references to a wider culture turn properly private. His poetry is consequent to its limitations (which is not the same as complacent in them); this may be called its modesty. Within that modesty, however, he has discovered—increasingly in the past decade—a richness and lushness located almost entirely within the remove of the past. In his use of nostalgia, nostalgia can no longer be considered a defensive exhaustion—rather it has been a recovered plenitude.

Justice's last new collection, *The Sunset Maker* (1987), is a book of assignations with the past, and it is necessary to stand a little aside from the assignatory character to observe the special conditions the artist has made in the fabric of observation. "Nostalgia of the Lakefronts," the poem in which the method most readily implicates the verse technique as well as the verse subject, opens with what seems the destruction of Sodom and Gomorrah: "Cities burn behind us . . ." But the cities burn with lights; these are not the cities of the plain, and the hints of holocaust would be a mild, damning joke if not for certain deepening shadows—of the proper end to wicked pleasures, of the punishment for those who look back.

The poem establishes itself not as a meditation but as a movement through childhood, or through the moment when childhood is "fading to a landscape deep with distance." Neither the moment nor the loss is precise—the poem memorizes, perhaps memorializes, certain summers by a lake, perhaps one certain summer, the summer of 1942, the last before war closed the hotels. The memories have wavered past precision (Justice would have turned seventeen late in the summer of '42) until what is important isn't their specific outline but their evocative ghostliness, their "indecipherable blurred harmonies"—the loudspeaker, the distant sad piano, the horn over the water.

> At such times, wakeful, a child will dream the world,
> And this is the world we run to from the world.

But in this blurring (the second line sounds like a blurred quotation of Jarrell, whose favorite word was *world*), the world inwardly dreamed and the world outwardly experienced can't always be kept apart—it is perhaps not the proper burden of the artist to keep them apart:

> Or the two worlds come together and are one
> On dark sweet afternoons of storm and of rain. . . .

The child dreaming the world may be the artist in his earliest manifestation, but the fiction of the artist is more devouring than the child's mere dreaming. The past has an achieved coherence, though here the subversion of the present by that past lies in the very innocence of its art, the art of a now vanished moment. The lake, for instance, "is famed among painters for its blues":

> Is their wish not unique—
> To anthropomorphize the inanimate
> With a love that masquerades as pure technique?

Here the artist's impersonality is the condition or cost of his feeling—the feeling guaranteed only by the purity of technique. There are two movements from this question, one through subject and one through form. In the poem the question is not answered but overridden, perhaps overwritten:

> O art and the child are innocent together!

The remainder of the poem chronicles the loss of that innocence—not the child's but the artist's. "Soon now the war will shutter the grand hotels"—this is the loss or corruption nostalgia expects, even revels in (there would be little point in setting up a stone for something that still existed). But there is a ghostlier, more painful loss in the very concept of artistry. I wouldn't wish to press the suggestion too far, at least not past the point where it is merely suggestive; but in poetry as well as painting a certain innocence (some might prefer to call it sophistication) did not survive much longer. The realism that even the Cubists subscribed to, in their way, soon became the province of the amateur only—the line immediately after the exclamation above is, "But landscapes grow abstract . . . ," and its bearing on painting (the collapse in value of draftsmanship, the triumph of Abstract Expressionism over line, the later relegation of figure to the cartoon kitsch of Pop Art) isn't wholly compelled by an abstraction of memory. In the final stanza:

> And after a time the lakefront disappears
> Into the stubborn verses of its exiles
> Or a few gifted sketches of old piers.

The verses are stubborn because they *are* verses at a time when metrical verse has long been suspect and "amateur." And those *old piers* sound grimly with the *old peers* whose techniques are vanished issues. I have taken a liberal course with the pun because of the second movement, through form, to which I alluded earlier. The poem's stanzas vary between six and seven lines, but the rhymes are all exact, sometimes a word with itself (*harmonies / harmonies*), but never weaker than a syllable with itself (*cockatoo / 1942, unique / technique, disappears / piers*). The words and syllables rhyme not with something like themselves but with themselves; and this violation of the normal prescription of rhyme isn't just the calculated echo in language of the past's vibration into the present, but the considered deviation in technique that implies, first, that the artist who would respond *to* tradition must respond *within* tradition and, second, that the history of poetry is the violation of technique, not the abandonment of it. For the artist, "Then we remember, whether we would or no." Nostalgia is not, not necessarily, the parasitic enactment of the past for its emotion, but the enactment of a responsibility by the measurement of loss.

The past is a series of half-forgotten particulars; but in Justice's poetry, to what I think is an unusual degree, the observer stands aside from the force of the particulars, not immune to them (because continually establishing relations between them) but curiously detached from their access. It is as if a poet were permitted every intimacy with a speaker except intimacy itself; that is, all the stoic intimacies of knowledge but few of feeling. This may seem the reverse of what we expect when the speaker is the poet. (The question is, of course, more vexed, but it shouldn't be made needlessly difficult—in other than dramatic monologues, the speaking voice is usually taken for the poet's. That doesn't mean the poem tells the truth.)

The inadequacy of contemporary poetry may lie in its confidence of feeling (even its representation of feeling) and its absence of a knowledge susceptible to anything outside feeling. The determinism of contemporary poetry demands that feelings be enactments of events, perhaps better the performatives of events; that is why the past in most poems is so often on trial. One of the merits of Justice's poetry lies, not in its absence of emotion, but in its withholding of confidence from emotion. The events that suffer this withholding are permitted a range of insinuation more disturbing because less mediated. At a felt distance, the past can't be revealed or reenacted, only rendered (for this reason Justice's exclamations, his mark of exhausted plangency, seem twice lonely). Such a speaker is unreliable because he will not accede to the conventions of sentiment.

The unreliable narrator provides a convenient transition to Jamesian sentiment; that is, a sentiment established and modified by the intimacies of knowing, the intimacies of detail. I don't think it necessary to establish that Henry James was sentimental, as long as I am speaking of the letters, not the literature. It was convenient, and he acceded to it, and whether it was for the sake of his friends or of his mental detachment makes little difference. Justice's poem "American Scenes (1904–1905)" is a variant instance where the use of nostalgia is formal—that is, has formal value (in the structure or the development of structure) beyond the entablature of "meaning." I take it as an example of how a mind that finds longing a kind of failing, a mind both superbly aware and superbly devious, may counter the reactionary gestures of nostalgia even while seeming to observe them. The indulgence is the satisfaction of an urge, while the countering stakes off the grounds of refusal. This is called having it both ways.

The impersonation of James requires a fidelity to external observation, as well as to the internal tones impressed by meter and rhyme (the operations by which poetry establishes its difference from prose, and so the most difficult to set in accord with it). The four sections, the four scenes that are the emphatic form through which the poem sustains its relation to James's original journey, are mere fragments, shattered recollections of a shattered sensibility: three pairs of quatrains and a sonnet epilogue. This is enough, as a matter of formal responsibility, to create the sensibility intact, or as much of the whole as applies.

Many of the phrases in the poem fall, unencumbered or unelaborated, from James's notebooks and from one of the saddest books of American travel, *The American Scene*.

Cambridge in Winter

Immense pale houses! Sunshine just now and snow
Light up and pauperize the whole brave show—
Each fanlight, each veranda, each good address,
All a mere paint and pasteboard paltriness!

These winter sunsets are the one fine thing:
Blood on the snow, one last impassioned fling,
The wild frankness and sadness of surrender—
As if our cities ever could be tender!

(James's *Notebooks*—borrowed phrases in italics)

The snow, the sunshine, light up and pauperize all the wooden surfaces, *all the mere paint and pasteboard paltriness. The one fine thing are the winter sunsets, the blood on the snow,* the pink crystal of the west, *the wild frankness,* wild *sadness*(?)—so to speak—*of the surrender.*

Borrowing is the artificial shell around which an obligation accrues. Here the very ease with which the pilfered phrases are united in the tone guarantees, seems to guarantee, the fidelity of the poem's exhausted, translucent passion, even though in James the passages are neither as richly evocative nor as exclamatory (the three exclamations create the intimacy of Justice's tone). They are reportorial, professionally engrossed, almost dry—they have leaked into style.

It is the aversion from the original, however, that rescues the richness of feeling beneath James's phrasing. I am reminded of the dramatic placements Shakespeare found for the phrases from Holinshed or North's Plutarch, or of the Elizabeth Bishop poem "From Trollope's Journal" (another version of civil war), funded on a few spare lines from Trollope's *North America*. The reproduction is the supplement to the original, yet it comes to have original force.

James had written to W. D. Howells, before leaving for America, "I *want* to come, quite pathetically and tragically—it is a passion of nostalgia." Here the meaning balances between old and new, in the passion that once was sickly possession, almost ready to detach itself from the pathology of homesickness to become mere yearning for the past. It was the past that James came for—he hadn't visited America in twenty years. He had turned sixty. And everywhere among his old haunts were the vastations and devastations of two decades of unrelieved commerce. Some of the ancient streets behind Boston's statehouse had been cleared, but the house of his childhood still stood, rich in its recollections. He looked upon it; and a month later, when he returned to look again, it had vanished completely: "If I had often seen how fast history could be made I had doubtless never so felt that it could be unmade still faster."

I have lingered over these circumstances for their relevance, not to the minor arrangements of the poem, but to the responsibilities that such arrangements assume. Any negotiation with the past, it should be clear from James, is either a surrender or a recovery. Each loss of the richness of the past, each triumph of the tawdry or the commercial, freed James from the material aspect of his nostalgia. And yet the very terms of his analysis, of his distaste, were conditioned by a past irretrievably absent. The rage to recover, the "nostalgic rage" as he called it in another context, is thus cruelly limited in its capacities of analysis—that is its pathos. Its triumph is its refusal merely to surrender to the pleasures of recall. The closing lines of the first three sections of Justice's poem mark his wary regard for this temptation, as well as his refusal of its blandishments: "As if our cities ever could be tender!"; "Of open gates, of all but bland abysses"; "and the South meanwhile / Has only to be tragic to beguile."

In the sonnet epilogue, Justice finally overtakes James:

Epilogue: Coronado Beach, California

In a hotel room by the sea, the Master
Sits brooding on the continent he has crossed.
Not that he foresees immediate disaster,
Only a sort of freshness being lost—
Or should he go on calling it Innocence?
The sad-faced monsters of the plains are gone;
Wall Street controls the wilderness. There's an immense
Novel in all this waiting to be done,
But not, not—sadly enough—by him. His talents,
Such as they may be, want an older theme,
One rather more civilized than this, on balance.
For him now always the consoling dream
Is just the mild dear light of Lamb House falling
Beautifully down the pages of his calling.

Except for the penultimate line (*Notebooks:* "the mild still light of dear old L<amb> H<ouse>"), the phrases are now all the poet's; and yet the impersonation is complete, having shifted to a manner detached no less fondly, or fixedly, than James's own erasure or self-effacement as "this victim," "the strayed amateur," "the ancient contemplative person," and especially "the restless analyst," as he variously styled himself through *The American Scene*. These scenes, this particular book, and this particular author converge in their attractions for a poet himself drawn into the "nostalgic rage." In a poet past sixty, one may read into this epilogue, "sadly enough," a disavowal, perhaps even a farewell, like Prospero's farewell, to certain ambitions (it must be remembered that Justice's poetry has been rather liberal in such disavowals since his forties). But it is also a recognition of the subjects proper to such a talent and of the home built in the present, rather than the home surrendered to the past.*

The beauty of this epilogue is the manner of its refusal, which may be called the judgment of the observations, while the judgment of the form lies in its deviations from and attachments to tradition. The feminine rhymes, for example, are usually considered a weakness, but here they bind the poem to another modern poem of loss (Bishop's villanelle "One Art," its main rhymes "master" and "disaster") and prepare the gorgeous lambency of the final couplet. Too, it is the subtlety as

---

*The sonnet might also be read as an inversion of "On First Looking into Chapman's Homer." Justice's "strayed amateur" has crossed the continent (the long way, in relative comfort, not the short difficult thrash through an isthmus of jungle and swamp), but he does not stare at the Pacific with a wild surmise—he looks back across the land at what has been lost, and what now cannot be. The discoveries have all been made; the frontier is closed. Keats thought Homer a new realm, and literature a series of lands to be discovered (this was his first great poem—he was feeling like a conquistador); for James the novel will not be written, at least not by him, and certain possibilities have finally and forever vanished. And Justice, too, no longer a young master but an Old Master, finds foreclosure and farewell. It is amusing to think of James as a stout Cortez. This section was reprinted alone in *A Donald Justice Reader* under the title "Henry James by the Pacific."

well as the frequency of the metrical reversals and the spondaic or anapestic substitutions that establishes the emphases and delicacies of tone. In these deviations—permissible deviations though they are—the accord with prose described earlier is reached, where, for the poet as well as the novelist, the past is not succumbed to but regarded, not like a yielding but like an availing.

But there, there again, is that register of innocence being lost. James's demonic eye could not help recording the subversions of landscape and manner with the most rectifying precision, even while each notation (at least in the nostalgic landscapes—he hadn't visited the South or West before) drove him further from the fond memories inhabited during his decades in England. Further, or more deeply within them, because however much the past is minutely modified by the present, it is never sufficiently vast to sustain itself as a fiction—those who would pretend otherwise must drive themselves to ever more heroic measures of submission. (What is interesting about the past is not its vastness, but the narrow channel of episodes to which our memories reduce it. We're likely to recall, in our indulgence, only what we have recalled before; in the repetitive traffic of scene and event, we worry the same wounds and the same pleasures.)

The more Justice has made the past his subject, the more richly textured and tonal his vocabulary has become. This purging of earlier dictions is most acutely evident in the long poem "Childhood," which closes his *Selected Poems* (1979) (and is dedicated, self-protectively, "to the poets of a mythical childhood—Wordsworth, Rimbaud, Hart Crane, and Alberti").

> Winter mornings now, my grandfather,
> Head bared to the mild sunshine, likes to spread
> The Katzenjammers out around a white lawn chair
> To catch the stray curls of citrus from his knife.
> Chameleons quiver in ambush; wings
> Of monarchs beat above bronze turds, feasting. . . .

It is difficult to recapture a visual innocence, but if something can be recaptured it isn't innocent. The detachment of recollection, which is often illicit, is here explicit in the system of *en face* notes that explain some of the less and most of the more obscure references to Miami in the thirties.* The notes create the double world that is the sufficient cause of longing: the modalities of pathos lie in the detachment of the present from the past. The notes are the evidence of the present; but in their admission that a distance exists, and can't be breached, the thwarted wish becomes the pathos and not the longing itself. Here, I would argue, where nostalgia is no longer a succumbing to, it has become a recovery of. The notes are the "smell of ocean longing landward."

In a poem that reveals the logic of its longing as a structural design, there are apt to be traces or accidents of that longing in the verbal play. It is not, or not just, that the reader is more attuned to such accidents by the structure; but that the divided attention of composition prepares, elicits, such slips or tremulations of reference. "Already / I know the pleasure of certain solitudes," the poet says, and we would be more certain that those pleasures were merely *particular* pleasures if we were not made aware that they might also be *assured* pleasures. Similarly, in the "cool arcades" of the shops:

> O counters of spectacles!—where the bored child first
> Scans new perspectives squinting through strange lenses. . . .

This is "a tray of unsorted eyeglasses"—the notes tell us so. And yet the deposition of the note seems insufficient, in a poem that is one long relation of spectacles,** from the world

---

*In later books reprinting "Childhood," the *en face* notes were removed and Rilke added to the dedicatory list of poets.

**And aren't the readers, to darken and deepen the pun, apostrophized as mere *enumerators* of spectacle, like Romans at the Coliseum?

beyond the horizon, the distant world of doomed republics and the nearer one where "Westward now, / The smoky rose of oblivion blooms, hangs" (the Everglades afire), to the circumscribed world of the boy's osteomyelitis: "on my knee a small red sun-glow, setting." This world of suffusions—of the globe's "blur of colors," of the "Myriad tiny suns" that "Drown in the deep mahogany polish of the chair-arms," of the "soft glow / Of exit signs," of the horizon afire and the knee's "sun-glow"—suggests the inevitable haze, the partial blur, in which the past exists. It is hardly surprising that when the boy catches sight of himself, he is not quite himself:

> Often I blink, re-entering
> The world—or catch, surprised, in a shop window,
> My ghostly image skimming across nude mannequins.

That blink, that ghostly image shimmering in the divided attention for which the structure has prepared us, is the sign of the present as it imposes itself on the past. There has been in Justice's poetry an increasing recognition—a dawning, perhaps—that there will be no hereby, no chance of alternative, and little of change. In this recognition the character of Justice's work has grown gradually Jamesian: for James, fate was only the accrual of sensibility.

If this withholding is the necessary condition for a nostalgia that eludes sentiment, it acts on itself as a loss of innocence, the loss to which these poems have obsessively returned. Those who have been expelled from the garden of the past are doomed to recall it, and all recollections conditioned by the sin of knowledge must be fictional. What such sinners re-create in the name of the past will be tainted by their own determining circumstance. (This is the retrospective burden: you can't analyze without being afflicted by the past; you can't re-create without being afflicted by the present. The acts of reference and renewal are flawed in their very terms—here literature approaches the uncertainty principle, and criticism may be substantial but must be unscientific.)

If the wilderness can never recall the garden without some acknowledgment, some trace or fleck must betray what has come after. I am reminded of James himself, having escaped in the middle of his journey, having taken refuge from the disaster of his visit to Richmond in the drafty recesses of George Washington Vanderbilt's rural mansion, Biltmore. *The American Scene* scarcely alludes to this week of "deviation"; but, in a letter to his nephew Harry, James described the misappropriation of energy that attends the attempt to create the past within the present:

> I arrived at this place, last P.M. in a driving snow storm (the land all buried, and the dreariness and bleakness indescribable), and the first thing that has happened to me, alas, has been to have a sharp explosion of gout in my left foot. But I hope to make this a *short* business . . . ; only the conditions, of vast sequestered remoteness and "form," pompous machinery that doesn't *work,* are unfavourable to it; huge freezing spaces and fantastic immensities of *scale* (from point to point) that have been based on a fundamental ignorance of comfort and wondrous deludedness . . . as to what *can* be the application of a colossal French château to life in this irretrievable niggery wilderness.

That is what the reinvented Eden will suffer, if created without continual suspicion toward its attraction, even its possibility. The knowledge from which nostalgia must descend is that the substances of the past are always a little tawdry, "Forlorn suburbs, but with golden names!" That is the final line of "Childhood." To go further, and even perhaps too far, nostalgia requires the wish for religious grace compromised by a religious scrutiny.

memoirs

Donald Justice's Miami

Laurence Donovan

Donald Justice was born two years before me, in 1925, in Miami, and I came down from the North about twelve years later. I became acquainted with him, through mutual friends, some time in my high-school days. Although his academic career kept him from Miami except for nostalgic visits, our acquaintanceship deepened over the years. The times, the settings, and the characters in his poetry and fiction are familiar ones to me.

The Miami in which Donald Justice grew up, and which he writes about so accurately and sensitively, was not the Miami widely known today. Nor was it the Miami widely known even then. To most of its natives Miami was never the grand, booming tropical paradise of bathing beauties and sunny beaches fostered by its publicists, but more of a small, unsophisticated village, one, I suppose, of "the raw towns that we believe and die in." In fact in the suburbs' and even the inner city's little neighborhoods of middle-class striving and genteel poverty we took a skeptical or amused view of the city's glittering reputation abroad, if we thought of it at all.

Perhaps more significant in our early years were the signs of decay around us, the relics of dreams shattered in the hurricane of 1926 and the depression of 1929: the Spanish-style coral rock gateways and fountains that were all that remained of the grandiose plans of the early city developers, the abandoned skeleton of the initial classroom building at the fledgling University of Miami, the long stretches of sidewalk which led into empty spaces and which even today, those stretches filled with glassy banks and high-rises, lie lonely and mostly unwalked upon. These picturesque ruins bred a feeling of distrust in, or at least indifference to, the development and progress and change that were soon to come upon us.

Don evokes this mood often in his poems and stories. As he writes in "Childhood," his moving portrait of the Miami of his youth,

> And sometimes,
> Where the city halts, the cracked sidewalks
> Lead to a coral archway still spanning
> The entrance to some wilderness of palmetto—
>
> Forlorn suburbs, but with golden names!

Sunny Isles, Golden Glades, Buena Vista, Opa-Locka contained a magic not to be found for us in Bloomingdale's, the Palmetto Expressway, Dadeland Mall, or Barnett Bank.

"Childhood" evokes many of my memories of downtown Miami, small and intimate and untrafficked enough in those days to be an after-school playground and meeting place with one's friends. I too remember the shameful "white" and "colored" drinking fountains in Richards' Department Store (where my mother worked) and "the warm cashews in cool arcades!" It was a city a boy could encompass and grow up in. My long daily walks as a fifteen-year-old copyboy from the old *Herald* building on the river to the *News* tower on the bay took me past George's hole-in-the-wall bookstore, where I bought one book a week out of my ten-dollar salary—among them the Wordsworth, Rimbaud, and Hart Crane of Don's mythical childhood (although, I fear, not Alberti!).

What we knew of the town was different in detail, of course, as were our childhood circumstances. Don was brought up in a close-knit family, whose members are familiar to his readers; I came of divorced parents, a deserted mother. While he was being tutored by the piano teachers (whom he has elegized in those remarkable poetry-prose tandems in *The Sunset Maker*), my mother scrimped to provide me with occasional fifty-cent Saturday morning cartooning lessons at a Fleischer's Studio store on Flagler Street. While he accompanied his father putting up storm shutters on the great hotels, I sold newspapers on Flagler near Harvey's Restaurant, had the archetypical bicycle newsroute (now supplanted by Hispanics in automobiles), worked as a clean-up boy in a small solar water-heater factory, and during high school carried copy at the *Miami Herald*. But these differences do not matter: our mythical childhoods in Miami were similar in so many and such profound ways that his poems always speak for me.

In his "A Winter Ode to the Old Men of Lummus Park," for instance, where old men, "ghosts" from the North, come from their lonely rented rooms along Flagler Street to take what warmth they can get from the winter sun—"wan heliotropes" is his marvelous phrase for them—Don elegizes the little park on the Miami River across from the Del Rio apartments where I lived. It was where my brother and I often hung out, and where one summer we built "The Lummus Park Special" to enter in the annual Soapbox Derby sponsored by the *Daily News*. It was an ungainly construction of wood and tin and purloined cartwheels which in the end proved, through over-ambitious adornment, too heavy to push to the finish line—an early example of the hegemony of aesthetics over practicality that was to plague our lives. And, of course, the "wan heliotropes" were always present in the park, if only to be ignored until I was reminded of them decades later in a poem.

Today Lummus Park, populated by dealers and muggers, is no longer a fit place for children, and the communal Soapbox Derby has given way to the Miami Grand Prix, a ballyhooed commercial attraction that tears up downtown streets once a year. Such changes for the worse or the dubiously "progressive" are symbolic of the dark burgeoning of this city, which provoked Don's opening remark at his Book Fair reading here a few years back: "I miss Miami when I'm away, and"—after a pause—"I miss it when I'm here."

Don's love for the Miami of the past, whose lineaments
have virtually disappeared under the malls, boutiques, condominiums, mazed expressways, and money-laundering banks
of an international metropolis, and under the hordes of non-
natives who have recharacterized its population, has been
expressed throughout his poetic career in his devoted references to his early friends, who were by and large compounds
of undirected talent, mythic story, and worldly unsuccess.
They were brilliant talkers, impractical idealists, and generally self-destructive characters. There is only space here to
speak of two of them.

Robert Boardman Vaughn, whose gaunt, wild-eyed,
apparitional figure I encountered first in my high-school days,
and to whom among his teachers Don dedicated his book *The
Sunset Maker,* was a dreamer and poet who followed his elusive
muse through the Caribbean, producing little poetry but, as
Don writes in "Portrait with One Eye," making his life a poem.
A follower of the somewhat contradictory figures Ezra Pound
and Fidel Castro, and of "Yardbird" Parker and John Coltrane,
he haunted the fishing piers of St. Croix and St. Thomas and
the bars of Coconut Grove and New York City with the fren-
zied and compelling talk that was enlivened by the alcohol that
finally destroyed him. Younger than Vaughn, I was awed by
his wit and poetic promise, but later found him a drunken
specter, a kind of raving, tropical Max Bodenheim. Mark
Strand remarked appropriately, when Vaughn made a brief
appearance in New York, that "he scared my daughter."
Vaughn later lost an eye in a fracas in Kansas City, reportedly
in search of the roots of jazz, and after a number of rumored
demises was beaten to death in the streets of Manhattan. A slim
manuscript of his poetry, gathered posthumously from old
acquaintances and lovers, proved disappointing.

Don, who, in the face of Vaughn's frequent affronts to
him, persisted in regarding him as an old friend and perhaps
the type of his opposite, the nonacademic adventurer poet,
has returned to him often and elegiacally in his poetry, as in

"In Memory of the Unknown Poet, Robert Boardman Vaughn," which concludes

> All done now. But I remember the fiery
> Hypnotic eye and the raised voice blazing with poetry.
> It was his story and would always be his story—
> The boredom, and the horror, and the glory.

Another Miamian who took on mythical proportions in our small circle was John Lenox. He is portrayed in Don's elegy "In Memory of My Friend, the Bassoonist, John Lenox," peering out myopically from his second-story porch overlooking Biscayne Bay, in the same house that provides the scene for the story "The Artificial Moonlight." For some years I lived there in an apartment below this eccentric musician and part-time welfare worker. Glum philosopher, misogynist, lover of the arts, and despiser of the decline in values he saw around him, John never aspired to writing poetry, but his conversation was often poetry itself. He brought me much happy distraction from the monotony of paper grading in those years. Shambling massively down from his untidy eyrie, blinking through my porch screen, beer in hand, John would burst into the small apartment where I lived with my wife and turn night or day into a patchwork of brilliant metaphor, either in Swiftian castigation of the tastelessness and duplicity of man or in loving and intricate elaboration of the genius of Bach or Mozart.

A memorable figure, John occupied the upper floor of the old Coconut Grove house—long since replaced by an execrable highrise called "Sailboat Bay"—looking out with hardly contained repugnance at the threatening world, precisely as Don describes him:

> In eminence he sat,
> Like some lost island king,
> High on a second-story porch
> Overlooking the bay

(His blue front lawn, his kingdom)
And presided over the Shakespearean
Feuds and passions of the eave-pigeons.
Who, during the missile crisis,

Had stocked his boat with booze,
Charts, and the silver flute
He taught himself to play,
Casually, one evening.

And taught himself to see,
Sailing thick glasses out blindly
Over some lily-choked canal.
O autodidact supreme!

Original thinker, scorner of success, poet of paranoia. His every action seemed emblematic, an expression of an inner world superior to the absurd one he saw around him. For instance, John's desire to escape the missile crisis, to which Don alludes in his poem, was compounded when Nixon came into office. He immediately spent some weeks marking off on the front lawn a diagram of the sailing boat he intended to build in which to depart the continent for securer realms, carefully outlining its shape and lineaments with pegs and string. To anyone wishing it, John gave a tour of the boat, walking through it from stem to stern, stepping, in his lumbering way, across its deck and around its various appointments and up over the hatch as if these objects were actually there. Of course, in his mind and its whimsically phantom world, they were.

I might add that when reluctantly obliged to leave his private kingdom for work at the welfare agency or the symphony hall downtown, John drove an antique Cadillac, which I believe he prized for its vintage shabbiness, its elegant decay. One morning the owner of our building came to where I lived in the back and politely, hesitatingly asked: "Can you tell me who owns the Cadillac in the attic?" On investigation it turned out that John had purchased another wreck of a similar model for its salvageable parts and, disassembling it, had snaked it through the tiny trapdoor in the hallway, where he reassembled it intact in the attic. The relative mildness of the astonishment of our landlord at coming upon this seemingly impossible object speaks of the tolerance we all felt for John's characteristic and wonderfully quirky way of doing things.

Such incidents in the life of a man who turned his vision upside down in psychological research for a college thesis, and then couldn't see to write it, are legion, but I must stop here. John died many years ago, at a tragically early age, of disorders consequent upon alcoholism and a world that was unfit for him.

Robert Vaughn and John Lenox are only two of many figures of remarkable talent and interest who were bred in Don's older Miami, and whose romantic viewpoints predate the vast shambles of greed and faddishness it has become today, and who are now dead, all at pitifully early ages. I think of, among many others, Eugene Rosenbloom, James McDaniels, and the young poet Ronald Perry, who came among us in later days, and whose work Don selected for the National Poetry Series in 1980. Ronald was the only one of the group to receive any sort of national recognition for his talents.

Of the remainder, the characters upon whom Don based his fictional account of those old times in "The Artificial Moonlight," all, including myself (I appear as Hal), are more or less alive, and indeed grateful that they have not qualified for the poet's elegiac pen. But the old pine-and-rock house is gone, and most of the Grove as we knew it, and most of downtown Miami. Although perhaps all men, in their generations, think of their youthful past as poorly lost, I believe that Don records in his writings the passing of a time and place that were truly unique, and that bred a type of American now disappearing from the scene.

John, where you are now can you see?
Do the pigeons there bicker like ours?
Does the deep bassoon not moan
Or the flute sigh ever?

No one could think it was you,
Slumped there on the sofa, despairing,
The hideous green sofa.
No, you are off somewhere,

Off with Gauguin and Christian
Amid hibiscus'd isles,
Red-mustached, pink-bearded
Again, as in early manhood.

It is well. Shark waters
Never did faze you half so much
As the terrible radios
And booboiseries of the neighbors.

Here, if you care, the bay
Is printed with many boats now,
Thick as trash; that high porch is gone,
Gone up in the smoke of money, money;

The barbarians . . .
                            But enough.
You are missed. Across the way,
Someone is practicing sonatas,
And the sea air smells again of good gin.

A Very Few Memories
of Don Justice

Richard Stern

A pleasant red-haired man
Noticing my red hair
Predicted a great career,
But for the asking mine,
Though whether of sword or pen,
Confessed he could not tell,
So cloudy was the ball.
Now how could a person
Know that words from a stranger's mouth
Could seem the simple truth
To a boy of seven or eight?

This stanza will not be found in Donald Justice's as-yet-uncollected *Collected Works*. My somewhat unreliable head may be its only residence, though in its perfectly correct, if discarded form, it will be found in one of the hundreds of wonderful letters from Don I have saved over what is now almost a half century.★ Helped—I think—by noting that the poem "The Summer Anniversaries" is dated 1955 in the "Uncollected Poems" section of the *Selected Poems,* I'd guess that this stanza—which may once have belonged to it—came my way that year or the year before. Was it Don or I who said of it, "Too Yeatsian"? Probably Don, although over the

---

★For students, or just fanciers of fine epistolary prose, the letters are found in the collection of my papers in the Regenstein Library of the University of Chicago.

years in which we carefully criticized each other's poems and stories, no criticism, however harsh, was out of bounds.

How many other slightly damaged beauties exist only in the letters and memories of Don and his friends? Collect these discards, and they would make a decent reputation for a lesser poet. Not that I can be objective about Don's poems. They are part of my life, my sensibility, my long friendship.

It was, I think, October 1944. I was sixteen, a freshman at the University of North Carolina in Chapel Hill. In the library, I'd just, an hour before, come upon a wonderful book, the enormous anthology of *Modern British and American Poetry* edited by Louis Untermeyer. I'd become a poetry reader four years earlier, when Pocket Books issued its first book, *The Pocket Book of Verse,* edited by M. E. Speare (shorn of the magic "Shake," but sacred nonetheless to me). In Speare's marvelous zoo were the English poets up to, I'd guess, the Yeats of "The Lake Isle of Innisfree." I knew nothing of poems written after that until that hour in the library.

I felt someone looking over my shoulder at the book. "Good stuff." A soft voice, hardly Southern. A long-faced fellow with horn-rimmed eyeglasses, tall, thin. "Like it?" Surprise and pleasure, inflected with the slightest patronage. He was nineteen, worldly, from Miami, on his way to New York. In Miami, he'd studied composing with Carl Ruggles (of whom—like so much else—I hadn't heard). We must have exchanged addresses, because I think the first of the letters came from New York that fall. Months, or was it a year later, Don came back to Chapel Hill to do graduate work. I'd formed a literary group, a few students and a few instructors who met once a week to discuss a book, *Madame Bovary, Crime and Punishment, Walden.* Each meeting was led by someone. I think Don's book was *Walden.* I was starting to write poetry. Don introduced me to the rigors of composition. He was generous, too; had to be. Any half-decent turn of phrase or meter fired the generosity. When I finally wrote one fair line, "The sun makes shadows of us all," the generosity confirmed my vocation.

In 1945, or perhaps early in '46, I wrote my first real story. (I'd written a few sketches in high school.) Don was very kind about that, and my vocation sharpened. We worked for the *Carolina Review,* and wrote for it the only joint piece we ever finished, a movie review of *The Big Sleep.* By then, we were part of a group, including Don's fellow graduate student, Jean Ross, who became his wife in the summer of 1946. For a wedding present, I sent them the just-issued tome of one of our masters, Yvor Winters, *In Defense of Reason.* We also read the *Kenyon* and *Sewanee Reviews,* and occasionally the *Partisan.* I think the *Southern Review* had stopped publishing, but we knew its back issues. Jean had a foot in the door of new writing: her sister Eleanor was married to Peter Taylor, who taught at Greensboro. Peter's roommate was Robert Lowell, and when we went over to the writers' conference at Greensboro, we met him and Red Warren, whose *All the King's Men* was our favorite new novel.

In 1947, Don and Jean were in Miami, and I in New York and then in Evanston, Indiana, where I spent a miserable two months working in a department store. A girl to whom I'd given a ring lived in Orlando, Florida. I went down there, was discouraged by her mother, and took a beautiful bus ride to Miami and stayed with Don and Jean in, I think, the garage apartment adjacent to his parents' house. The two most memorable events of a lovely week were meeting our dear friend Norma Troetschel (who died in 1992) and, with Don, picking the winning round of, I think, the Walcott-Marciano fight and collecting fifteen dollars, which paid for that night's—and several other nights'—beer.

When Don and Jean went out to join our friend Edgar Bowers in Stanford the next year, I went to Harvard, and the year after that to France on a Fulbright. There were many wonderful letters from the Justices, including those that, in 1952, determined me to go to the Iowa Workshop for my doctorate.

It was brutally hot when I arrived in June 1952. I stayed

with the Justices under a bookshelf of the Baconian landlord's works on the true authorship of Shakespeare's plays. Don and I wrote couplets which began

> Two Iowan Baudelaires,
> Sweating out tetrameters . . .

After rough weeks—I'd been away from taking classes for three years; my wife was expecting our second child; Iowa City looked grim and ugly after Paris and Heidelberg; and money was very tight—I began to love Iowa. The Army-McCarthy hearings were on. We watched them, raging and cheering. Every afternoon, after classes and teaching, we had a savage croquet game on the river, Don and I against Don Petersen and Tom Rogers. Don Justice was a maniacal games-man, willing to risk fracturing his foot to get better purchase on a ball he'd club into the shrubbery.

Games, poetry, and stories dominated our lives. (There are certain Rilke poems that have a garbage aroma for me, for De Snodgrass and I discussed them while we emptied pails in the communal garbage house.)

In 1954, after graduation, I got a job at Connecticut College (then "for Women"). In April 1955, Don wrote that he'd been offered a job by Walter Blair of the English depart-ment and Norman Maclean of the Committee for General Studies in the Humanities of the University of Chicago. He wrote that Chicago, both city and university, scared him; he turned down the appointment and took a job at the University of Missouri. Oddly, the Chicago job was offered to me. (I've been there since.)

Almost every Christmas the Justices came to Chicago, from Missouri or St. Paul or, mostly, Iowa City. Christmas offered a new world for our gamesmanship, the kids' new toys. One year, we raced jack-in-the-boxes hour after hour. Another, we played tiddly winks for most of the night. Norman Maclean, who came by every Christmas morning with a bottle of wine, laughed his head off at the two maniacs keeping the kids away from their toys. (When the kids were older—say five—Don competed with them.) Our competition died with Pounce, a game of double patience. (Patience!) I retreated from competitive frenzy and saved myself an ulcer.

■ ■ ■

Don and I had our ups and downs. There'd be some dumb slight or imputation which would rupture relations for a week or a month. Once we decided to write a play together. We laid it out, scene by scene, and began writing. There was only one comfortable chair in the house. One of us had it one day, the other the next. One day we argued about whose turn it was; that finished our collaborative life.★

During the last twenty years, we have exchanged fewer letters and seen less of each other. To some degree, our tastes have diverged, and we've worked different sides of the street. But our old friendship is very strong, and for me Don's beautiful poems remain one of my life's resources and standards. I'm proud that a rather mysterious one is dedicated to me. The poem, in some ways a slight one, was written, as I recall, in a bad time, when Don was teaching out in San Francisco and was not in good shape. The poem is from the volume *Night Light*.

Poem for a Survivor

For RGS

Holding this poem
Close, like a mirror,
I breathe upon it.

I watch for some sign.
There is a faint mist
Spreading across it.

★I finished the play. It was called *The Gamesman's Island* and is included in *Teeth, Dying and Other Matters*.

It takes hold. It clings
To the lean hollows
As the sun rises,

This sun that is going
To burn the mist off.

I give you the chamois
To clear the surface.

I give you this sun.

The gift of the chamois and the sun stand in my mind for much that Don has given me of clarity and the light behind it.

Graduate School:
The Thin Young Man

Jean Ross

The graduate Chaucer class at Chapel Hill met first hour in the fall of 1946—a small class in a small classroom, so that it was not possible to come in late unnoticed. One student, a tall, thin young man in black horn-rims, came in late more than once. He was also lacking a book and, since he had taken the seat beside me on the back row, asked to look on mine. I was not eager to share it, feeling that in the mind of Professor Kaufman (learned and dour, with a wintry smile) I might become associated with this unserious person.

The thin young man, later addressed as Mr. Justice, wore his hair a trifle longer than was customary at the time, at least at the University of North Carolina. Later I learned that Don's maternal grandmother had once sent an anonymous packet of hairpins to a young man to tease him about the length of his hair and that eventually she had married him. Lacking her example, I merely disapproved, though mildly. (How conservative that length would seem now.) In general his appearance was *hip,* no doubt partly as a result of his having spent the year before in New York.

In the lobby of a movie theater one afternoon I identified him for my roommate as "the guy who's going to flunk out of graduate school." He didn't flunk out, of course, but wrote a thesis on the poets of the Fugitive Group, taking a master's the following summer.

■ ■ ■

Neither of us has a clear recollection of our first date. Soon we were eating dinner together much of the time, at one of those wonderful Chapel Hill restaurants—the University Cafe, the Porthole, Danziger's. We worked in the library (I was working on Faulkner); we listened to music in the Union's listening rooms. We went to the movies—*To Have and Have Not, The Big Sleep, The Best Years of Our Lives.* (I feel sure that Don could not only say what other movies we saw, but name the theater and the compass direction we were facing.) We saw a production of *The Rivals,* and one of *Macbeth,* in the Forest Theater.

Chapel Hill was a campus of sandy paths and old landmarks; town and campus joined comfortably. Don lived in a basement room some distance out on East Franklin Street, in Mrs. Caldwell's house. Her son Dallas, who was around his age, became a good friend, and they frequently sat up late talking or listening to music. One night, late, they ran out of cigarettes and, after what must have been some hesitation, smoked the remains of a pack of Sweet Caporals that had been in a box on the mantelpiece ever since Dallas's late father had given up smoking twenty years before.

It was the President—Senator—Frank Graham era, and there was a good deal of political activity; the SCLC rang doorbells on Saturday afternoons. One of my roommate B. A.'s friends and ping-pong partners was Al Lowenstein, later a congressman from New York.

And there was the Saucer Club, our writers' group. It may have been Edgar Bowers who christened it ("If the saucer fits, wear it"), though the name was a rather fleeting fancy. We read and discussed our work, of course—Edgar, Ken Rothwell, Dick Stern, Paul Ramsey, my roommate Betty Anne Ragland, Don and I, and several others.

In the spring we went to Greensboro to the Arts Forum at what was then the Woman's College of the university, where I had gone as an undergraduate. My sister and brother-in-law, Eleanor and Peter Taylor, were at the college, which made it all the pleasanter to go over. The Arts Forum issue of *Coraddi,* the student magazine, included poems from our crowd by Edgar, Paul, and Don, as well as work by others who would distinguish themselves later (Anthony Hecht, Roger Hecht, Flannery O'Connor). Robert Penn Warren, John Crowe Ransom, and Robie Macauley were among the visiting writers; Randall Jarrell and Peter Taylor, teachers at the college, were also panelists. I remember our enormous interest and our feeling of partaking of the future.

■ ■ ■

In the spring Don came to Norwood and met my parents. At the beginning of the summer I went home, and Don went to Miami but returned to work in the UNC library. He took his degree in August. We were married later that month and went down to Miami, where he was to teach at the University of Miami (his undergraduate college) and where I was to find a job in the university library.

■ ■ ■

We went to Miami in a 1938 Buick convertible, a classy-looking car that Don remembered fondly for years, in spite of its many failings. A year later, in the late summer of 1948, we sold it in Charlotte and were lucky to unload it. We were preparing to go to California, where Don was entering graduate school at Stanford. Edgar Bowers had gone out the year before to study with Yvor Winters and had sent back good reports.

We had spent the summer of '48 in North Carolina, partly with my parents, but chiefly with the Taylors in a house they had bought on Rocky River near Norwood, a house built by my great-great-grandfather. In late August we sold the car and got on the bus for the four-day trip to San Francisco.

In the western half of the country the bus was often almost empty, and for a long time the only other passenger was a quiet, pleasant Okie, who showed up later in a poem. I remember trying to sleep on the long rear seat of the bus— roomy but jiggly.

In Palo Alto, housing was tight; thirty people seemed to answer every apartment ad. For several weeks we lived in a room some distance out and rode a Greyhound bus in. We bought a '32 Ford coupe, a convertible, but one day it stopped in its tracks. It was diagnosed as having extremely serious problems, but Don sold it to an optimistic undergraduate and later saw it tooling around campus.

An apartment turned up in Mountain View, then a dingy little town, and we took it. But we heard about a house for rent in La Honda, up among the redwoods, and had the idea of sharing it with our friends Herb and Jody Shore. We would need transportation, of course, and Herb and Don went up to San Francisco to look at cars. All they found that we could afford was a jeep, an honest-to-God olive drab ex-Army jeep, and they came back in it. They set off for La Honda to scout out the prospective rental, but the jeep disliked the terrain; soon it was steaming. They didn't even get to look at the house in question. It may have been just as well: even from Mountain View into Palo Alto, it was a very chilly ride those mornings in an open jeep. In another few weeks we found an apartment in Palo Alto and made the Shores sole owners of the jeep. The apartment was on the third floor of a house on Forest Avenue; it had attic ceilings, and the kitchen had a small lavatory instead of a sink, but it was a find all the same. We used the owner's wringer washer on the back porch, and the family dog came up to visit when it was lonely.

Since Don was teaching two classes, he was allowed to take only one course per term. The head of the department thought that entering graduate students should begin with sterner stuff than writing courses, so Don only audited Yvor Winters' poetry class. The teaching assistantship was essential (my job in the geology library was not high-salaried), but at this rate Don would be middle-aged before he got a degree. When he pointed this out, however, Professor Jones was unyielding. Still, Don was sitting in on Winters's class, learning more about meter; and the company was agreeable.

It was our first time in California, and the very air seemed different, with its smell of eucalyptus. Remembering the campus, we often think of a terrace near the Union where people sat with coffee and snacks, the bees from the nearby shrubs occasionally exploring the cups. The graduate students' hangout was the Briggs Room, but at first I thought it was called the Bridge Room in honor of the game played there.

Edgar had a car, as well as an instinct for good living, and took us to San Francisco (Omar Khayyam's, the Top of the Mark, the Zebra Room). There were the usual graduate-student sociabilities, including a party given by the tenants of a Frank Lloyd Wright house, which we and our companions had to circle repeatedly before we could locate the door of. There was an evening at the Winters's house, when he played records of poets reading their work and poked a little mild fun at some of them. He spoke of the pleasure of living in California. ("There's Allen Tate living in some New York apartment, mushrooms growing out of the walls . . .")

In the spring Don won a prize in a short-story contest with his story "The Lady." We left at the end of the year, and the prize money got us back East by train, through the Rockies and flat, fertile-looking Iowa. Back to Miami, to teaching and library work.

■ ■ ■

In Miami, in 1950, Preston Dettman printed a chapbook of Don's work, *The Old Bachelor and Other Poems*. In the spring of '51, however, the University of Miami let some forty English instructors go, waiting unconscionably late in the year to do it. We went to North Carolina that summer, and in the fall the Taylors kindly let us use their house in Hillsborough. Toward Christmas we returned to Miami, and Don drove a cab for ten days. In the first weeks of 1952 we were again selling a car—again a convertible, though less beautiful than the Buick. (Perhaps this piece should be called "Selling the Convertible.") Again we were about to set out on a long bus trip to graduate school, this time to the University of Iowa.

From the train a few years before, in the month of June, the dark soil and green growth of the Iowa farmlands had looked pretty; in January, as the bus rattled through small towns in Illinois and Iowa, the homely houses huddled together with their porch swings drawn up to the ceilings for the winter, it all looked less promising. I was relieved to find that Iowa City wasn't flat and, though the January thaw wasn't pretty, that it wasn't bitter cold. Don phoned Paul Engle, who said, "Two days on the bus? You must be basket cases," and came down to meet us with his young daughters. He had arranged lodging for us at Mrs. Bristol's on South Johnson Street—a three-story yellow brick house that included several apartments. We were on the second floor, the bedroom across the hall from the living room; there was a fireplace and much marble-topped furniture. Out in the hall near the wall phone one sometimes came across Mrs. Bristol's note cards; she was working on a treatise meant to show that Shakespeare had not written Shakespeare. We both remember standing at the windows of that apartment and looking out at the first big snowfall, watching a couple of dogs cavort and dig in the snow.

■ ■ ■

If Iowa City lacked the style of Palo Alto and the long history of Chapel Hill, not to mention climate, it had a body of congenial people who welcomed us hospitably. The Writers' Workshop was Paul Engle's creation, and he took a thoughtful interest in a great many of the students; Mary Engle sometimes rounded up household items and baby beds for them. Often, at the beginning of the fall term, there was a Workshop picnic at the Engles' summer place, an old mansion near Stone City, and a caravan of cars would go out from Iowa City, becoming eventually a dusty caravan. There had been a quarry and later an artist's colony at Stone City; it was near Anamosa, the site of a prison camp from which inmates occasionally escaped, and at least once after an escape we scanned the countryside from the roof of the house—not expecting to locate the escapees exactly, just looking. A few years later two escapees did enter the Engle house, and the family took it with considerable aplomb.

A number of the Workshop poets lived downtown in apartments over stores, in buildings later torn down when urban renewal struck. Don and Jeanine Petersen lived over Ewer's Shoe Store, opposite the Moose Hall, from which they observed the members hobbling out after the Saturday night dances; Anne and Bill Belvin lived above a feed store, and the stairs to their place often had a pleasant, haymow kind of smell. I seem to remember going to a party up a monumental flight of wide steps over an automobile showroom, the cars gleaming down below.

We too moved downtown in early summer, to a large apartment across from the campus on Washington Street, up a flight of squeaky stairs to a door that later, as the election neared, bore a large color picture of Adlai Stevenson. The apartment had probably been a suite of offices once, for there were frosted glass panels set in the walls between some of the doors. Don began to paint the living room, possibly a pale raspberry sherbet shade, though I hope this memory is false; Somner Sorensen, a chess champion but a rather monotonous reader, came over and treated him to selections from Shelley while he painted. Jack Roth painted some Chinese characters on the glass panel that separated the living room and a small and superfluous bedroom. Rachel Chester began a picture of us while we lived there but complained that we didn't look the same for any two sittings.

We did not lack amusements; the problem was getting enough sleep. Dick and Gay Stern arrived from Germany that summer—we'd known Dick at Chapel Hill—and with them we went to see *Cosi Fan Tutte* in MacBride Auditorium, where bats sometimes circled high over the heads of the singers. In the Iowa Memorial Union there was a show of paintings by the patients of Independence State Hospital, a mental hospital; we were struck especially by the work of Patient B, which became the subject of a poem. In our apartment, at the rickety golden-oak dining table, we played penny poker with the Petersens, Tom Rogers, and sometimes the Sterns. Tom taught us a vicious multiple solitaire game called Pounce, which we played chiefly with him and Jeanine. It must have been the next spring that the croquet games began; in some open fields by the river, Tom, Dick, and the two Dons played a cutthroat game that led to quarrels and grudges. We went canoeing on the Iowa River with Tom, there being a canoe rental concession behind the Union in those days. When we reached the bank by the Barracks, the student housing, De Snodgrass strolled down and called pleasantly, "Two people almost drowned along here an hour or so ago." I couldn't swim, and sat pale and terrified till we were back on dry land.

Kenney's was the Workshop's favorite tavern and the place to which the students often adjourned after a class session. In 1952 it was on North Clinton Street, opposite the campus, next door to the Airliner, which was one of the more satisfactory restaurants at the time. Many of the others were jokes— the Princess Cafe, Reich's pseudo-Chinese, the Bamboo Inn, where one night we came upon an Indian acquaintance, Dr. Jayapathy, eating a plate of spaghetti, a scene that might have testified to the international character of Iowa City if either the restaurant or the spaghetti had been more authentic.

■ ■ ■

Sometime in the next year we exchanged apartments with the Petersens, who were going to have a baby; they took the big Washington Street apartment, and we took their place around the corner. It was tiny but even cheaper than the other (thirty dollars a month) and had a pleasant bay window looking out over the street. I think Don got a good deal of work done there. He often worked late and must have seen dawn come over Clinton Street more than once. Sometimes when

I came home for lunch, up the hill from my job in the university library, he would breakfast as I lunched.

The Workshop poets were publishing—in *Poetry, Furioso, Botteghe Oscure* in Rome, the *New Yorker,* and the *Western Review,* which had come to the university along with its editor, Ray B. West, Jr. Don and other students read for the *Western Review,* as well as for the O. Henry Prize story collection when its editorship passed for a time to Paul Engle and Hansford Martin. Paul had many projects, and the students normally assisted with them.

It was Paul's custom to bring in visiting poets to teach for a term or so—Karl Shapiro, who commuted from Chicago, where he was editing *Poetry;* Robert Lowell; John Berryman. Don considered Berryman a superior teacher. Berryman was newly single, however, and prone to desperate, foolish crushes on the wives of students. There was a night when he felt suicidal and called Don to come over and save him. The sight of the straight razor and the prospect before him made Don feel ill. He told John he had to lie down, and John busied himself looking after him.

■ ■ ■

We bought an old car in '53, to go South to see our families. Not a convertible, but an ugly brown sedan with a noisy engine. John Berryman said it sounded like a motorboat and would cry, as we cruised up to Mrs. Bristol's to let him off, "We're coming in to the landing!"

In the spring of '54 we moved yet again, to an apartment over a store on College Street. (All of our addresses had "½" at the end of the number.) When I think of the dining nook, which resembled a restaurant booth, I see John Berryman sitting there, lamenting the fact that he had turned forty.

■ ■ ■

How many interesting people there were! There were the Lowells, who had us to Thanksgiving dinner (goose) and with whom we watched television in the Petersens' living room on

Washington Street (our old living room, with the Chinese characters on the glass panel). I think of the Belvins' party for Randall Jarrell, which was perhaps where Meryl Johnson read his palm; of Berryman listening to someone singing "Matty Grove," his eyes blazing with emotion. It's tempting to try to fill in the blanks and put it all back together. When did we meet Henri and Jackie Coulette, Jacqueline Ragner (Rogers), the Burfords, the Londons? And where, exactly, was Helen and Ace Levang's apartment? Who, besides Tom Rogers, was host of the Friday afternoon cocktail parties of one era?— perhaps his roommate David Clay Jenkins, an Alabama fiction writer and our first Iowa City friend, though I don't think the parties were in their place on South Linn Street. And who lived over the auto showroom?

Don took his doctorate that August. It was not the last year we were to spend in Iowa City but was the end of graduate school, which he regretted. He used to say he would have been happy to remain a student, to go on to law school or library school. But I wonder where we could have found a place and companions as congenial as those we were leaving.

With Don and Jean Justice at Chapel Hill

Edgar Bowers

After three years in the army, I returned to Chapel Hill in the summer of 1946. I met Paul Ramsey and Ken Rothwell; in the fall, they introduced me to Don and Jean, who were graduate students in English, and to Dick Stern, like me an undergraduate. There followed six months of pleasure that seem to me now a little *annus mirabilis,* with the exclusiveness, mild intensity, and timelessness of an idyll. Our essential bond was an interest in literature and in writing poems, an interest formalized by a more or less regular meeting as a group to read and discuss our work; probably more seriously we talked and laughed much, at Danziger's as a gathering place over Viennese coffee, where we amused ourselves with the formation of the Saucer Club and a partly facetious formulation of principles (we even planned a magazine, *Factotum,* which Paul was to edit the following spring), during meals at the Porthole and the Carolina Inn, after movies, on picnics—all in the happy way of students, which I in a sense, because of the war, had not enjoyed. We were youthful, open, interested in one another, having fun, sharing our experiences and our concerns, with more future than past. Our camaraderie eventually included many friends and acquaintances, some ambitious to be writers, some not; so our bond was also that we liked one another's intelligence, high spirits, and good humor and sought each other's company for sympathy. I think also that all of us enjoyed Don and Jean's being so intelligently and nicely in love, planning to be married in the summer, which seemed an especially likable return to the normalcy of comedy after the extraordinary events of the war and its aftermath.

■ ■ ■

What was most important for me, though, in this time, was my friendship with Don, which was of great influence in my intellectual life. I had friends who read and wrote poems in high school (we even had a Writers Club and published a newspaper and a magazine), and then again in the Army Specialized Training Program at Princeton, but none so knowledgeable as Don, with as much literary acumen, talent, and informed opinion or, I should really say, convictions. I realize now that what I especially liked and admired in him was just his willingness to have and to defend his convictions and to understand their importance. In the company of such an intelligent friend so seriously committed to being a writer, the decision of my youth to make writing poems my first concern seemed natural, rational, and good. My formal studies continued to be in French and German, but because he and the others were studying English I began to realize that English might be my proper study also, and as a graduate student at Stanford. My decision to go there was discussed several times at Danziger's and seemed almost a decision by committee! All of this seemed given further credit when, during spring break, I went with Don and Jean to the writers' conference at Greensboro, where Peter Taylor was teaching. Robert Penn Warren gave a talk on Frost; there was a performance of Campion's songs by the glee club; and Warren, Robert Lowell, and William Blackburn discussed our poems that had been printed in the student magazine *Coraddi*. In the summer, I joined Don at his parents' house in Miami and made my contribution to the thesis he was writing on Tate by speculating with him about some of the more obscure passages in the poems.

Justice as Classmate

W. D. Snodgrass

Going to school with Donald Justice was enough to test anyone's ego. It wasn't that he was taking a more difficult curriculum—in fact, we were all supposedly part of the doctoral program at Iowa. The rest of us were signing up for our sixth and eighth class in Ph.D. German, Ph.D. French, Methods of Research, Early English. For myself, this was merely a ruse to keep myself in school. Don was actually getting a Ph.D. Having whizzed through the coursework (his French was already excellent when he arrived), he had taken the comprehensives, *passed* them, and was now collecting the poems for his dissertation, all in record time.

It wasn't just that Don had already studied poetry with Yvor Winters, musical composition with Carl Ruggles; that Peter Taylor was his brother-in-law; that he seemed to know most of the New Critics and Southern Agrarians. It was not just that his intellectual and aesthetic principles seemed fully formed and relatively unshakable.

It wasn't just that he handled his personal affairs with apparent dispatch and practicality. Don and his wife Jean seemed constantly affectionate, constantly thoughtful of each other. My wife and I, by this time, did not speak to each other except efficiently. Divorce was looming, and we were already struggling over my daughter. I was not alone in this: the strains of a situation where wives supported the family at some dull and often menial job while husbands went to classes, studied subjects they really loved, and were, meantime, surrounded by exhilarating classmates (some of whom were also attractive young women) were evident in more than one household.

It wasn't that he turned out poems so steadily and with so little visible effort. The rest of us were so often blocked that we sometimes inverted this into a matter of pride—whoever had been longest blocked could claim the greatest suffering and martyrdom. I remember once saying to Don that I had been wretchedly blocked for a long period. "Me too," he said. "I don't think I've written a word for two weeks!" I had meant something on the order of two years.

It wasn't just that his poems were so daunting—even when you *were* writing. You suddenly became suspicious, not only of your own poems, but of the whole philosophy and motive force behind them. Among the poems he turned in to the workshop were "Ladies by Their Windows," "In Bertram's Garden," "On a Painting by Patient B of the Independence State Hospital for the Insane," and "Counting the Mad." How could anyone take such simple, straightforward subjects, not trying to foist either any explanation of their cause or any high-flown interpretation of their meaning, but trusting simply to one's own voice and style to give them the reality, the elegance and thrust to make them whole?

It wasn't that the poems could shake even our teachers. John Berryman, during the semester he taught there, gave his workshop class formal assignments. That group included Philip Levine, Henri Coulette, William Dickey, Jane Cooper, Melvin Walker LaFollette, Robert Dana, and myself (though my own affairs were so snarled by this time that I seldom got to the class meetings). When his students turned in the sonnets he had assigned, Berryman sat at his desk idly leafing through them, then stopped, stared, and read one of the sonnets to himself. His face aghast, he turned then to the class and said, "It simply is not right that a person should get a poem like THAT as a classroom assignment!" He was holding Justice's "Sonnet: The Wall" about the angels lifting their gigantic and fearful wings above the gate through which Adam and Eve were driven out into the world.

Indeed, Don even had poems which I liked better than

he did! Surely that must suggest that not only his poems, but
also his standards, were superior to my own. I think particularly of a poem about the devil which was published in *Poetry*
but which he felt was unworthy to be collected in a book.
Even more, I think about (and believe I remember correctly
after forty years) his sonnet about the death of Hamlet's father,
which began

> As Hamlet the king was sleeping in his garden
>> His brother poured some poison in his ear.
> He felt, at once, his limbs begin to harden
>> And the red leaves were tangled in his hair.
>
> And, suddenly, he turned so pale no one
>> Could see him.

The rest of that sonnet was weaker; if I recall, Don did several versions in which this was the case. Not surprisingly; how
could you cap that? It seemed—it still seems—the best joke
in any poem I know. But even if I hadn't been able to cap
those lines, to finish a sonnet which maintained at least that
level, even if I hadn't been able to add so much as one line
to what is there, I'd have invented a new form for it, have
titled it "Fragment," have found some way to put those lines
in print. Don was such a perfectionist that by now I may be
the only one left who remembers those lines.

No, the real trouble, the real seed in your dentures, the
sand in your jockey shorts, was that he seemed to do it all
effortlessly. These things all seemed play for him—it looked
as if this was just another game, and not, perhaps, even his
favorite. When you ran into him at the student union, he
would be playing bridge, playing ping-pong, playing chess
against the Midwest champion. He was later a member of that
poker circle which included Nelson Algren and which some
sharpers expensively invaded. He became a member of a croquet circle where tempers grew so fierce that several players
did not speak for months at a time. In softball games, he (who

must have weighed about 125 pounds, wringing wet) became so truculent that fist fights became a distinct possibility.

One day, I ran into Don on the street. "I've been wanting to ask you something," he said. "Didn't you once play the violin?" I allowed that I had played; my claim to incompetence, though, probably sounded more like modesty than like the flat truth it actually was. "Well, I wonder if you'd mind looking at a string quartet I've been writing—I've got the first violin in a higher position and I'm not sure the passage is playable." My own abilities had, in ten years' playing, scarcely risen beyond the first position. My only resort was once again to claim incompetence and, this time, make it convincing.

A Reminiscence

Mark Strand

I met Don in 1961. He had just turned thirty-six, and Jean, his wife, was about to have, or perhaps she had just had, I can't remember, their son Nathaniel. I was twenty-seven and had just come with my first wife to Iowa after having spent a year in Italy. That year, I became convinced that writing poetry was what I would do for the rest of my life. I am sure that Don had everything to do with my new-found belief. It was under his tutelage that I wrote poems which were, for the first time, mine, and not pastiches of other people's poems. He urged me to follow my own lights and approved of what I was doing. I was flattered by his attention and encouragement. It wasn't that we spoke often of matters relating to poetry, but it was that whenever Don did speak about poetry he was enlightening. Our conversations were never long. It was assumed, rightly I think, that we shared similar tastes or preferences. But on those rare occasions when it was clear we had different opinions, we both thought it prudent to keep our mouths shut. Don's reticence in these instances was, it seemed to me, a form of courtesy. Instead of challenging me, he allowed me to believe I was his equal, or at least that my tastes were my own and that if I wanted to hold onto them I should be allowed to. Don, who knew much more about poetry than I did, and who could articulate his positions more eloquently and, consequently, more memorably and forcefully, could easily have changed my mind. And if it happened that he did say something, it was only that he disagreed, and he would say it with a peculiar mixture of force and calm, detachment and disappointment. There would be a little silence. Then we would continue whatever it was we were doing. But it was always more fun to agree with Don, to enjoy a tacit sense of unity. Otherwise one felt on the wrong side, the side without standards. Even in those days, and maybe especially then, poetry written at the Iowa Workshop was looked on with suspicion because it was "well-made," as if being "well-made" was a guarantee of dullness, a form of inhibition, a sign of insincerity. The criticism didn't especially trouble the students, but it may have troubled Don. He was our spiritual leader, our aesthetic guide, and, if necessary, our defender. And we were certain his rational and principled views of poetry would prevail.

The Workshop in those days was held in one of a cluster of Quonsets left over from the Second World War. There was just one workshop and it would meet once a week. Don and Paul Engle ran the meetings. Paul was frequently called out of the room to answer the telephone or to run an urgent errand, which meant that Don did most of the actual teaching. Adding enough praise to keep his criticism from being harsh, he guided us through poems with a skill that was as painstaking as it was graceful. I am not sure that these sessions came easily to Don. He exercised remarkable control, and we could sometimes sense his concealed impatience. After class, we would walk next door to the student union for some games of ping-pong. It was there, during our ferocious games, that Don would let go. He was intensely competitive, but, at the same time, jovial. The workshop would quickly become a thing of the past. I think the large number of games he played, and their intensity, helped Don to be as effective a teacher as he was. The year that I came to Iowa, one either talked about poetry or played games. Don was at the center of each activity, courtly and controlled when dealing with the one, emotional and competitive when dealing with the other. Games were an outlet for all of us, and we played whenever we could. When the bars closed, we would go to somebody's apartment and shoot craps or play cards. And the games might last all night. There were weekend poker games; there were softball games in which the poets were pitted against the fiction writers; there were pinball games played on dull or dark afternoons in Kenney's. And all the while we were writing poems. Had we not been, the games would have lost their urgency, would have proved useless or wasteful. The year that I met Don, I played more games than I ever had or have since, but it was also the year in which I became convinced that poetry was my calling. Beyond the classes, beyond all the games, it was finally the friendship with Don, begun that year, which made me feel I belonged within the world of poetry. I have many things to thank Don for, but that is the most important.

Jump Hog or Die

Charles Wright

Only critics, as Don himself once observed, should be fulsome in their praise. Still, I would like to make a few observations, modest though they may appear on the surface. There was, I felt, always a concentration, always a kind of fierce intensity in his demeanor—a seriousness that spoke to the seriousness of his calling. This was thirty years ago, in the autumn of 1961, my first encounter with Don in the workshop. As far as I know, in such matters—poetry and teaching—such a disposition persists. It was something in him I admired greatly.

The Iowa Writers' Workshop, as everyone must know by now, was run in those days out of Paul Engle's back pocket, and was housed in some leftover Quonset huts: left over from the post–World War II influx of students on the GI Bill. As is usual in such cases, the students went on and the huts remained—married student housing on one side of the Iowa River, art and writing classes on the other. Don and Paul were the only teachers in those days, joined by Mark Strand in my second year when he was brought up from the student ranks. Since Paul was often forced to be on the road looking for dough, Don became, more or less, the poetry workshop. And that was a good thing, at least for me, someone in need of much instruction and direction, someone, literally, just off the boat—a troop ship from Italy. Not all the instruction was found in the workshop, however. A good bit was after hours and interspersed with ping-pong and pinball.

Monday afternoons, workshop over, a group would walk from the Quonset hut to the student union. To the ping-pong room. Don, Mark, Marvin Bell, Bill Brady, Al Lee, William Brown, myself, and sometimes others. This was when I first got the notion that Don's fierce intensity was not limited to things ethereal. Did we play vigorous ping-pong, or what? Mark was a good player; I was all right, a journeyman; Bill Brady was all right. But Don was very good. I couldn't beat him. Mark may have a couple of times and Marvin, who was also a good player. But Don was both tough and tenacious, a trait I later saw on the softball field, at the poker table, at the game board (we're talking horse-racing games and war games here), anywhere. For myself, once I discovered poetry, nothing else *really* mattered. I'd tend to drift off if the game at hand wasn't going my way. I lost, in effect, my killer instinct if, in fact, I ever had one. Not Don. Everything mattered. It was *all* important. Perhaps not equally, but it all had to be done full bore. It was a quality of participation I envied greatly, but was unable to emulate. But I did play. We all played. But Don *played*. Such intensity. Such an unreturnable serve!

As I say, this concentration was much in evidence in his teaching as well. I shall never forget my first conference with Don to go over my poems. It was, in fact, my first conference with *anyone* about my poems, and I was anxious, to say the least. The subject matter of our conversation—Don's conversation—escapes me now. Some ineptitude I was trying to suggest was a poem. Something, no doubt, about goddesses and the Aegean Sea. But Don, as was his manner, was taking it seriously, very seriously. Certainly more seriously than I, having already seen in a couple of workshop sessions what the level of performance was, a level far above what I was doing. In any case, Don was patiently going over the poem. At the same time, a fly was going over it, too. And over us, circling our heads, circling the page, circling Don's face as he kept his concentration ardently on the poem and on what he was saying. I, of course, was mesmerized by the fly as it got closer and closer to Don's face and, abruptly, as Don inhaled to say something, flew into his mouth. His mouth! Don gulped. Bye fly. He actually swallowed the damn thing, so intent was he on the poem at hand. "Did I swallow that fly?" he asked, astonished. I allowed as to how he had. "Jesus," he said. Amazing! Then he actually went back to the poem. From that moment, he had me in the palm of his hand.

Stories. Many stories. Some repeatable, some not. Nights at Kenney's Tavern. The Famous Pig Roast at Nick Chrome's farm where Don organized a high-jumping contest over the pig still on the spit, the coals still glowing. Couples straying impassioned in the burgeoning spring leaves and long grasses of the adjoining fields. Hatchet-throwing competition. Later, knife-throwing contests in Al Lee's apartment, the knives and the distances getting larger and longer. Competition. Much competition. It had a wonderful effect on one's poems. The push to get them written. The desire to get them written right for the proper praise from the proper people.

Don was in the early stages of the *Night Light* poems then. I was in the early stages of learning *The Summer Anniversaries,* almost by heart. I learned what meter was about from his poems. The first successful poem I wrote at Iowa (it took me seven months) was an imitation of the meters and structure in "Landscape with Little Figures." He was a teacher in the best possible ways—he opened you to what was possible and was impeccable in his own work. Surely, as he might say himself, a winning combination.

That was 1961–1963. I went away for two years with my M.F.A. degree to the capitals of Europe. When I came back for a second (shorter-lived) go-round in 1965, Mark had gone to New York City and Marvin was teaching. And Don. This was a good time for his poems. He wrote many, especially in syllabics. And since he was writing in syllabics, we were writing in syllabics. The old order was starting to break apart and a new, looser order was looming.

As always in Iowa City, it was a good time to be there. I remember one night I saw him going from town back down to the Quonset huts, to his office, and asked where he was off to. "I've got an idea for a poem," he said. It turned out a few days later to be "The Missing Person." Nelson Algren was in residence that year. Marathon high-stakes poker games. Classes on Stevens and Williams. "Variations for Two Pianos," "The Man Closing Up." I still can't read *Night Light* without an almost unbearable nostalgia. For the things we did, for the poems that were written, for who we were, for our gloriously happy and unhappy selves. There was never a better teacher. There were never better poems to learn from. He is the Thin Man. Such rich refusals!

Syracuse Years: 1966–1970

Philip Booth

I met Donald Justice the September after Donald Dike, George P. Elliott, and I hired him to teach in the Syracuse Creative Writing Program, then in its third year. The English department, in 1966, still held sway on the second floor of a nineteenth-century rockpile called the Hall of Languages; and there, that fall, coming toward me down a corridor jammed with unregistered students, was a singularly lank figure—head hung slightly sideways, one shoulder lightly hunched—who could only be Donald Justice. Suddenly, as he recognized me, he whipped a Chapstick across his lips. I reciprocated in kind, and with mutual amusement we shook hands.

We'd both won Lamonts for our first books and had had the luck of first fellowships; we both had been hired as associate professors; we both took the dry off our lips with Chapsticks pulled out of our left pants pockets. For four high years we were friends and colleagues as different and similar as strong friendship allows. Don knew music in ways I knew not; he wrote late and slept late while I sagged long before midnight and woke early to write. Neither of us, in those years, wanted to fly. Whatever our various neuroses or defenses, each of us allowed the other his own, without comment. He was still smoking cigarettes then, I held to a pipe; I drank beer to his gin; he played ping-pong anywhere while I punched a speed-bag in my cellar. I skied on days when he was still deep in all-night high-stakes poker.

Given the freedom to schedule our workshops and seminars in the afternoon, we routinely saw each other in the department mailroom at noon and often walked down over the hill to Marshall Street for lunch. Once, early on, when he was opening his mail on the great HL steps, I remember Don's grin as he reared his head back and handed me an envelope from Alaska, with its poker check for seven hundred dollars enclosed. He exhaled something between a *Whew* and a *Whoo* and told me it came from a game five years before: "I thought I'd never hear from that son-of-a-bitch again." No exclamation mark, simply a wry detachment, matched with profound amusement.

We talked a lot, wandering easily between his ground floor office on the far west side, and mine in the north corner, both with heating pipes all over the place, cracked or leaky ceilings, and drafty windows at ground level. I think we each had a two-course teaching load: if a graduate workshop, some sort of undergraduate course; if a graduate seminar, quite likely an undergraduate workshop, alternating semester by semester. I taught seminars under such rubrics as "Postwar Poets" (commencing with Williams and Stevens, moving to Bishop, Roethke, et al.); his were typically focused on "Poems in Translation" or "The Lyric." I, by his courtesy, kept on teaching first-semester graduate workshops; he (or W. D. Snodgrass, who came to the program two years later) did second semesters. Don's equanimity in trading off notably "difficult" students, or equalizing thesis loads in our graduate poets' final years, was inherent; he was, literally, *devoted* to teaching, as remarkable as a colleague as he already was as a poet. Different as our workshops were in emphasis and practice, I'm told by old survivors that we weren't dissimilar in our manners of teaching, and were equally intense.

Strange. For all his aggressive gamesmanship at the ping-pong or poker table and for all the master poems that catalyzed his masterful own, Don never took teaching to be a competitive sport. All of us learned from his sense of prosody, not least because he was then newly interested in syllabics. I learned from his love of Weldon Kees; he introduced me to poets like Vallejo and Guillevic. Meticulous as his own poems were, his gently wry bearing was equally elegant. In a city that was, even in its raw winters, not without civilization, Don was a major *presence*. He got on amicably with most of the department; he was gladly familiar with students who played games as well as they wrote (most notably Larry Levis and Stephen Dunn); he was happily part of whatever doings his writing program colleagues were up to.

We were, in fact, up to fall and spring picnics, and winter night parties, in direct ratio to how close we lived to the university. Since Donald Dike (a fine teacher with a permanent writing block) lived thirty miles south in the hills, it usually fell to him, as founder of the program, to direct students and new staff to his eyrie before the first snowfall. De and Camille Snodgrass, almost equally far in blizzard country, rarely gathered students before spring; as did Margaret and I, who for some several years put on a May Day touch football (later soccer) picnic that invited the entire student-staff membership of what came to be called the Syracuse Stein, Sport, and Spondee Association. We lived only thirteen miles out; half that distance in a suburb called Dewitt, Bill and Rose Wasserstrom gave the most diverse parties: his devotion to Freudian criticism, her circle of ceramicists, surrounded the writers with all manner of doctors and fine food on great plates. Just around the corner from the Hall of Languages, George and Mary Emma Elliott (she still on the *Hudson Review* masthead) seated eight for gourmet dinners and orchestrated table talk on an elegant level. Even with a very young son in a narrow house (on Clark Street off Westcott off Euclid—a triad which still feels to me like an incipient Justice poem), Don and Jean gave Iowa-style parties, "after-the-reading" and otherwise. Maybe a board game in the kitchen near the bottle shelf and fridge, graduate students clustered around such visiting stars as Mark Strand. And Don, I remember, once clearing the piano bench, late, to illustrate on the keyboard some point of prosody to a young instructor I'd never before seen. And never saw again.

The parties, and the poets grouped in a given year's workshop, meld into each other like years. But what seems not long after Don, George, De, and I—introduced by Donald Dike—read in a downtown church to benefit Gene McCarthy's presidential campaign, I remember, in what may have been the week after the massacre at Kent State, the bomb scare in the HL dean's office that sent all five floors of humanity out onto the campus sidewalks. Most of us had heard the fire alarm; all of us save one had been evacuated from the building by monitors. Donald Justice, not unjustly, was angry beyond measure, having been left behind in his office at the far end of the building where, for some hours, only the bomb disposal squad and he were quietly at work. His frustration (to speak mildly) may also have owed to the fact that he remembered how his head felt when part of his office ceiling had fallen on it the winter before. Once out, Don refused to reenter the Hall of Languages until the semester was over. For the ten days remaining, he taught his workshop off-campus and held his conferences in the breezeway under the building next door that housed the French department. I have a deep image of him, precariously tipped back in an arm-rest classroom chair, going over the poems of a similarly seated graduate student who looked considerably older than he did—this thin-man poet with his sleeves rolled halfway up, paying no attention at all to chanting protesters massing through the breezeway to the quad, itself loud with rock music and brilliant with frisbees.

The chief distinction of Donald Justice's office (narrow, like his house) was a light tan three-cushion Naugahyde couch on which, somewhat slumped, he held conferences. When he took a year's leave from Syracuse to go to Irvine, I grandly offered to see the couch safely kept in my office until he returned, both of us realizing that he might well be going to Irvine in order to circle back to Iowa City. Indeed, that happened, and I inherited the Naugahyde couch that Don had liberated from God knows where. And for another fifteen years I held hundreds of conferences on what I thought of as the Donald Justice Memorial Couch. More than once I eased a stressed conference by introducing a young poet to its history; much more often I recalled what I continue to think of as my own final conference with Don when the couch was still in his office and his to command.

Never in our few years as colleagues was he so openly anxious as when he was writing what would soon be his Elliston Lectures at the University of Cincinnati. Before he left for that eight-week stint, I recall being in his office, saying praises and skepticisms of the first three lectures, which he had asked me to read in draft. He was leaving within a week and was now realizing that he'd have to write the remaining lectures once he was in residence. This in itself was nerve-wracking; but what cubed his tension was that John Cage would also be a distinguished visitor during Don's stay. He valued Cage's distinction, beyond question, but Cage's aleatory ways of composing filled Don with theoretical *Angst*. "You know," he said, almost confidentially, "he's the Enemy."

I had a card from Cincinnati soon after Don's first lecture, saying it had gone well, that he was well into writing the further lectures, was finding some poker players and tennis friends; and, indeed, that Cage had attended the initial lecture, and spoken to him so generously that they'd gone out afterwards for some beer.

Weeks pass, Don returns to his leaky-ceiling office, and he's telling me about Cincinnati, the cardsharps there, his prime tennis partner, and what had clearly become his working friendship with John Cage. I forget the tall tales and short stories, as such. I indelibly remember being treated to a working conference with Donald Justice on his Naugahyde couch.

He reached from his end of the couch to the top of his desk and, with hands accustomed to poker, began to riffle a set of 3" x 5" cards. These, he explained with the utmost casualness, were his syntax cards, a small pack, in which each card abstractly diagrammed a potential sentence: adjective-noun-verb, for instance, in that order, each diagram differing from all other permutations and combinations of those parts of speech. Next in the magic show were three slightly thicker packs of 3" x 5" cards: one pack of specific verbs, one of adjectives, one of nouns, each set deriving from words in poems Don loved, or simply made up. Don shuffled one and another, and another, of the packs, and reshuffled his syntax pack to let me in on his new-found pleasure in finding new ways to compose. They delighted him, they made sense to him as possibility; he, with inherent Justice, made sense of them. Let scholars look into *Departures* for whatever key, if any, need be found to Don's poem "The Assassination," a response to the murder of the man a good many of us were by June 1968 turning toward, though we had read for Gene McCarthy only some months before.

I cannot, even now, forget Vietnam years, and the terrible days of November 22, 1963, or April 4 and June 5, 1968. I cannot help but remember, counter to such national anguish in that decade, the Syracuse years when I had the luck of being Donald Justice's colleague. These twenty years later, a thousand miles from where he now lives, what I have most wholly at heart is that couch conference full of Cage-cards, of Don's glittering eyes and self-amused smile.

Justice and *The Death of Lincoln*

Edwin London

I went to Iowa City in September 1952 for no more compelling reason than to elongate the days before I would have to get and hold a job. Within the first few weeks I had decided, rather naively and somewhat self-consciously, that I was going to be a composer. Hurrah for naiveté and self-consciousness.

Those school days provided the opportunity, as it turned out, to define myself, in *Portrait of the Artist* style, as an artist. The first week there I talked with Robert Lowell by phone; he invited me to come around to the Poetry Workshop with my poems. I didn't go—I had no poems to bring around. But I had a few friends who *were* part of the Workshop, and I heard from them about a bebop poet from Miami. Laughable as it may seem now, this was Donald Justice. Don travelled in hipster music circles as a youth and was up-to-the-moment in Diz, Bud, and Bird. His poetry never did come across as beboppish.

I'm not sure whether we met each other during my two years in Iowa City, though my first wife wrote a play for a master's degree under Don's supervision. It was not until my second tour of duty there (1958–1960) that our paths really crossed. Occasionally I would accept an invitation to play poker in a long-established game with artists and towns people. Don was a regular—he played to win with passionate acumen. We were able to exchange musical pleasantries (Schoenberg versus Stravinsky and Ives). Through the good grace of Paul Engle, I spent an afternoon in New York with e e cummings. The discussion with cummings was about his *Santa Claus: A Morality,* which I was planning to set to music as a mime opera. I did so without changing a word of the original text. That wonderfully caring arts-politics journal, the

Iowa Defender, ran a two-page rave critique, by Don Justice, of my mime opera. His only quibble (a portent of things to come) was about the syrupy sentimental ending.

Time passed. Don went his way, garnering respect for his brilliant and finely wrought poems. To some degree I kept up with his work. I had come to grips, too, with career and employment, and at least thirteen years passed. The narrative resumes in 1972. After my second "opera," *Tala Obtusities* (a musical play on the words of Charles Dickens), was produced at the University of Illinois, I was offered a grant—for composer *and* librettist—to write another theater piece. As a lark, I called Don (then back in Iowa City) to discuss the project. I didn't want to set any sort of pre-existent play in word-for-word fashion, as I had with the cummings, nor did I want to write my own libretto. I read through Don's poetry again and thought that he (a bebop simpatico of mixed musical affinities, who had studied with the iconoclast composer Carl Ruggles) was the right person.

The accomplished American tenor, David Lloyd, at the time head of the University of Illinois Opera Workshop and the Lake George Opera Festival, drove with me over to Iowa City in the fall of 1973 for a lovely lunch at the Justices'. Don and I agreed to collaborate. The date? As David and I sped back to Urbana that evening, Archibald Cox was being sacked by Richard Nixon. It was the Saturday Night Massacre.

Now began a period of frequent contact, when we were in search of the right subject. The impending bicentennial turned our minds to Americana, and then quickly to Lincoln. David Lloyd worried about selling an opera with the word *death* in the title, but Don and I had agreed on the subject, and the title seemed inevitable. After Santa Claus and Charles Dickens, Lincoln would complete a trilogy of works about bearded men. Don was anxious to use historical sources (indeed, a verbatim account of Lincoln's last speech) to motivate our collaboration. His research was meticulous. We were at odds, though, about my wish to have rhyme and meter sufficient to distinguish recitative from arioso and full-blown aria. At Don's suggestion we subtitled the work "A Documentary Opera." A team player, he achieved a fine balance between Lincoln's prose and the artifice of meter and rhyme.

Don is an inveterate letter and postcard writer (his longhand sometimes demanded eyes keener than mine for correct reading). A barrage of envelopes, big and small, began flowing my way. There is a sheaf of this correspondence (oneway, since I use the phone) stashed in bulging file cabinets. Some intrepid scholar might usefully study the various shapes of the libretto as it developed.

Perhaps the most enjoyable time in making the opera was the spring month we spent at the MacDowell Colony. In the morning I'd set a problem of prosody or accentuation— perhaps I needed a more singable phrase. By afternoon Don had found an imaginative solution. Later in the evening we would repair to the library, which had a slightly out-oftune grand, where Don (an able pianist) and I would sing and play Schubert, Schumann, and Brahms songs, for no one in particular.

For reasons which are not clear to me, the premier of *The Death of Lincoln* was not going to take place in the summer of 1976, as originally planned. Postponement followed postponement. The large-scale opera was near completion, but sadly it has never been heard in the original version. We decided to make an oratorio out of the opera's epilogue for a 1976 program which juxtaposed Dudley Buck's optimistic centennial commission with our graver bicentennial mood.

For our oratorio, "Iron Hand," Don skillfully adapted Herman Melville's poetic threnody for Lincoln, "The Martyr," and mixed it in effective sequence with small bridges from the opera itself. The performance, in the winter of that year, was with one hundred fifty voices, a full symphony orchestra, and the artistry of the distinguished bass-baritone William Warfield.

In the summer of 1980, three scenes from the opera were produced—successfully, it would seem—at Lake George, but with piano instead of orchestral accompaniment. Don and I commiserated from time to time over the hard labor that had not reached fruition. Finally in 1988, in Cleveland, the opera received its first complete dramatic presentation. Don provided yet another version of the libretto, extirpating some characters, adding a narrator, and adapting the orchestral setting to chamber proportions. This version showed once again the consummate librettist's skill in making substance through accommodation. It was no surprise that an angry Don fought, as best he could, the un-Chekhovian staging of the last scene. For him there was no need to read good/bad, happy/sad, separation/reconciliation into what was best left to the analytic capabilities of the audience.

The opera has not had many performances. One, unstaged, at the Civil War Institute at Gettysburg, advertised it as an atonal opera and failed to mention librettist or composer. How elevating to feel like medieval artisans, in no particular key. So many years have passed since the beginning, I often wonder how Don feels about making *The Death of Lincoln*. In one sense there is little to show for it. I like to believe that he feels as I do, that every moment was worthwhile. His libretto is a real example of excellence in a virtually forgotten art.

Iowa City, 1976

Jorie Graham

I would know from the sound of his galoshes sluicing down the hallway that it was Don, key in hand, wet bangs like seaweed over his brow. As he went by, irritated, it always amazed me how frightened I was of him.

But there was a tradition involved in fearing him. My teachers whose teacher he'd been feared him. His colleagues feared him. The secretaries feared him. Each was a different fear. But we all shared one desire: we wanted him to be worthy of our fear. We passed stories around to keep him scary. X feared him utterly. Y would never, in this lifetime, contradict him. Z would rather die than be caught smoking dope in his presence . . .

And, indeed, there was objective ground for the fear. It was the fear surrounding the amount of *work* we knew we had to do in order even to call ourselves apprentices to the craft (he knew everything). It was the fear that yawned at us from the dizzying lengths of tradition we hardly dared peer back towards (he could recognize and quote everything—couldn't you?). It was the nauseating sense that the stuff one was handling was stolen (indeed! but can you quote your source?) and that the theft was always more visible than the invention (to his encyclopedic memory it *was*). You felt seen-through, small, inept, hopelessly unequal to the task. It felt great. It made the task hard enough. Nothing you ever brought in for his scrutiny could possibly hold up, or be surprising, or *clear* enough. He knew—because in less than ten words he could fashion a question that would blow your knot of words open like thistledown . . .

How can I make this palpable to those who were never in his clear-eyed, stubborn, cranky, breathtakingly precise, wry, elegant presence? We knew there was someone who could find us out. We realized that as long as we could be seen through, as long as we could imagine there existed eyes and ears capable of discerning *difference,* the task was thrilling enough, the victories (if those were ever to come) meaningful.

I used to think the anecdote where Berryman recounts that Frost told him that Yeats told *him,* "Don't worry, you never do get found out," simply revealed the sense of guilt many of us feel when at work in the communal field of the Imagination. It was Don who showed me how filled with regret and longing that remark is.

So, real and imagined, there is an auditorium-full of us who keep him where he belongs and where we need him: on a small stage—or, no—at the head of a lousy formica and plywood table—dishevelled, casually peering up at us as the silence grows—"Ah, you hear the echo in these lines, don't you?"—and our hearts sinking or, no, our hearts rising with the thrill of our smallness and the heroic size of the task . . .

And then, once we had grown up a bit, there was, is, the beauty of the work to contemplate. Poems built up from the unsaid at precisely the rate such transactions should take place—out of exactly the number of words needed—making the silence the necessary weight and speed by their presence— stones rippling and livening the stream, crackling it, purifying it, adding to its power, brightening, deepening, but not altering its course.

Once I sat before him with a bad attempt at description. I watched his hand hold the paper—everything I thought I knew was on it. Watched the light from the window behind him make the paper look even thinner, my own words bluing through like a tattoo on the skin of something dead. Words written backwards. The paper held up—as was his wont—from the bottom of the sheet, up into the room's surrounding openness. I heard the wheels on his chair creak as he pulled back from the desk between us. He put the paper down. He stole a look out of the large window, then looked back into the enclosed space. "Jorie," he said, "you have to learn to give in to the destructiveness of the subject." And I looked out the window, squinting. Saw something, but what? Saw the words down there on that paper, flat now, on the empty table between us. Saw that they were still mine, all mine, nothing but mine. That I was still alone. That they could take me to where I wasn't alone if I knew how to handle them. He picked up a pencil and did nothing. When I left I looked back at him to say something charming and polite, but the window behind him, very bright, blacked him out. He never did like to turn the light on. I saw the frame very clearly and something very, very white in it. I mumbled a few words. I imagined he heard them.

"It Figured":
Donald Justice at the Racetrack

Brian McCrea

Tampa Bay Downs, the racetrack Donald Justice and I visited during the late 1980s, is not in Tampa but in Oldsmar, a village northeast of Tampa, an area away from the Gulf shore that is only now and irregularly being overtaken by "development"—that word used in Florida to describe the proliferation of mobile-home parks, golf-course subdivisions, and, occasionally, large resorts as well as the strip malls, 7-11s, Publixes, and Winn-Dixies that accompany them.

The last turn for the Downs is unmarked, probably because a small street sign does announce that you are at a junction with Racetrack Road. Miss the turn, as we twice did, and you wind up in Oldsmar, a village characterized by feed stores and tack shops, a village that worried me because its smallness suggested that racing at the Downs might be contested within a tightly knit community, that insiders might have a bigger edge than usual.

The Downs was not a playground. Crowds were relatively small (3,000 on weekdays, 8,000 once on a Saturday when the Kentucky Derby was being simulcast), and handles (between $40,000 and $90,000 a race) were not leavened by the dollars of tourists just out to have a good time or by the contributions of fools. Because of its location, the Downs was not a place that you happened upon. People came to it with powerful intentions and, as the crowds and the handles lessened, with intensified desperation. The track was standard enough: a one-mile dirt oval; a small clubhouse painted white and light blue; a two-section, glass-enclosed grandstand; a large area of tarmac that served as a lawn; a paddock at the east end of the stands. The utter conventionality of the setup belied the extraordinary test of handicapping skill (or luck) that the Downs offered. Don and I agreed that it was the most difficult racecourse into which we had ventured.

Thoroughbred racing in the United States is hierarchical, both in its action (the various categories of ability that the horses possess) and in its scenes (the different tracks at which the horses perform). Major tracks in New York, Miami, Los Angeles, and Chicago offer the largest purses and draw horses of superior ability. But throughout the country are less prestigious tracks to which horses from the major tracks may "drop down" or at which horses that never make it to the major centers may spend their careers. Tampa Bay Downs, which holds races from mid-November through early May, occupies the very bottommost rung of the racing hierarchy.

A typical race card would open with two races for maiden claimers—that is, horses that had never won a race and could be purchased ("claimed") for a designated price—and follow these with races for nonwinners in, say, the past year. In racetrack parlance, the contestants at the Downs were "cheap horses." But they also were thoroughbreds, horses around which people had built dreams, horses you couldn't just go out and buy for your child to ride. Typically, they had been bred at small operations in Florida and were trained and raced by their breeders. They were the products of small joint investments that usually were denominated by initials: JJ Farms, WDW Ranch, KB Stud. While their breeding and their origin were easy enough to view critically, their owners were impossible to fathom. Such people might list a horse at a claiming price that did not reflect his ability so much as their financial need.

The problem that the Downs presented for a handicapper was form—or, rather, lack thereof. A kind of sweet terror would descend upon me as I looked at the past performances of the horses, particularly those in the first five or so races.

Quite frequently, these races would be dominated by five- or six-year-old maidens, horses that in fifteen or twenty starts had never managed to win. In the later races, horses that had been running at cheaper prices (and winning occasionally) would vie with horses that had been running in better company but doing nothing. What were the owners thinking? Growing up in New York, I had led a relatively privileged life as a handicapper; at Aqueduct and Belmont, I bet on horses whose records at least seemed to reveal a pattern of improvement or decline.

Don's background as a handicapper was much broader and more diverse than mine. He had bet on dogs and jai alai, two wagers from which I always shied away, and he had spent his youth in Miami at both the classy Hialeah and the cheaper Tropical Park. He had once picked five straight winners at the latter park, a feat that I, even in my New York salad days, never approached. Don's response to the Downs—at least, the response he shared with me—was to repeat, at fairly regular intervals, one of the oldest but also most elliptical and enigmatic of racetrack phrases, "It figured." The words, of course, were simple enough, but the tone was wonderfully rich, partaking in equal parts of bemusement and amusement, resignation and some slight anger, a feeling that, the race over, the outcome made sense and made no sense, a two-word poem, finally, as elusive and ironic and yet as true as experience—at least experience at the Downs—itself.

We planned our trips to the Downs to get there early enough to study the *Racing Form,* both of us annoyed that no store in Gainesville distributed it. Don liked the cafeteria at the Downs, so our goal was to arrive around 11:30, study the *Form,* have lunch, and be ready for post time for the first race. But we usually were late departing Gainesville, so the trip down, particularly that last off-interstate stretch, required pushing. The time we might have spent discussing the races, we usually gave to music; in the two hours and fifteen minutes, we might listen to James Levine conducting the Chicago

Symphony in the Mozart Symphonies 40 and 41, Alfred Brendel playing Beethoven concertos, and, my favorite, the Cleveland Quartet playing the late Beethoven quartets.

Our trips to the Downs, particularly our first, began in great hope. I had wandered away from the 1986 MLA Convention in New York and taken the train to Aqueduct. I had been away from the track for years, so the *Form* felt alien to my touch. I played five random daily-double combinations, hit one, put half my winnings on a maiden three-year-old out of Alydar in the third race, hit for $14.20, and then put half again on a horse named Iambic Pentameter in the fourth race. When the horse named after a meter won and paid $12.60, I did a very smart thing. Realizing I was $1,300 ahead and had yet to handicap a race, I went back to the convention. Don heard me recount my good fortune to a colleague in our department office and suggested a trip to the Downs. Having beaten the big track in New York without even trying, I felt the Downs could hold no great challenge for me. I would learn, of course, that sons of Alydar did not run there and horses were not named after verse forms. The trips back from the Downs were made in darkness and punctuated by long silences. With few exceptions, we had only our losses to analyze.

Our goal, of course, was to make money—lots of it. Don was looking to retirement; I was going through a divorce. But neither of us could ever get ahead of the Downs, get in a position from which we could make big bets with the track's money, the position I had been in after that third race in New York. Instead, we spent the last three races trying to get even, to make up for the bets we lost in all those early maiden claiming races. We were wise enough never to lose very much money; anyone with a scintilla of horse sense could see that the Downs was not a place where you put lots of your money on the table. But that finally became part of the weariness the Downs inflicted upon us. We were making small bets and still losing.

Don did better than I did because he handicapped differently. He placed considerable emphasis upon what is called the "speed rating" of the horse. This figure tells you how fast the horse can go during a race; it has nothing to say about where a horse started or finished, only, on the basis of fractional times, how fast the horse ran at his fastest. My system, if that is not too kind a term, is to figure out why the favorite in the race is favored, then look for two or three horses that have a chance to beat it. The Downs bred sweet terror in me because frequently I could not see, as I looked at all those six-year-old maidens, any reason to favor one over another. Don, looking for a horse that, at least at some point, could run fast, was both more decisive and more successful than I was.

On our first trip to the Downs, Don discovered what quickly became his favorite bet there—the box trifecta. In a standard trifecta wager, the bettor picks the first three horses to finish, in their order of finish. The odds against this are long, and payoffs tend to be high. In the trifecta box, you pay twelve dollars to get the twenty-four combinations in which four horses can finish. Should one of your combinations win, you get paid on the basis of a one-dollar, not a two-dollar bet. The beauty of the trifecta box bet at a track like the Downs is that it offers a hedge against formlessness, even as it also holds the possibility of paying a fairly high price. It was a bet I never learned to like. I clung to the notion that I could pick winners.

Don would sometimes bring a camera and take pictures of horses and jockeys in the paddock area to use as the basis for paintings. I usually spent my spare time in the bar, trying to take the edge off my sweet terror, but not to become so fearless that I bet stupidly. During the long drives home, we would occasionally talk about our wagers—if we had managed to climb at least part way out of the hole in which the early races left us. That talk always, in my view, was eminently sensible. We lost, but we made good bets.

On an early trip, Don had made an absolutely inspired

bet on a horse in the last race who had been running sprints—six and seven furlong races—and seemed ill-suited for the mile and a sixteenth distance. But Don saw that the horse had speed, that in some of his past races he had shown that he could maintain speed (as much as anyone could say that about a horse at the Downs), and that he was dropping down in class. Don saw class and speed as factors in the race while the rest of us were looking at distance. The payoff was around 16–1, and gave a bit of a warm glow to the ride home. The race perhaps best indicates why we kept going to the Downs, in spite of the relative formlessness of the racing. Sometimes "it figured," and when "it" did, the ease and inevitability of "it" gave both of us that wonderful if sometimes nearly fatal sense of opportunity for profit.

On one of our last visits, we drove in separately because I was giving a lecture in Tampa. The weather was bad, so I was late arriving. I missed the first race, had some difficulty finding Don, then shared with him information I'd received from a woman who, at that time, was giving riding lessons to my children, but who had raced several horses at the Downs: she told me that the track, a mixture of sand and clay, was naturally heavy, even when fast, and particularly heavy when sloppy. The information buoyed me, and I looked, even in the sprints, for stayers, for strong finishers.

As usual, Don and I did not talk a great deal, but we both were cashing tickets, and thus got into the ninth race ahead rather than behind. Not far ahead, I went with a trifecta; Don, I assumed, boxed one. The race was a mile and a sixteenth, and so we could follow the horses, could sense the ebb and flow of our chances. At the quarter pole my three horses had separated themselves from the field, but in the wrong order. I started to shout, not seeking foolishly to cheer anyone or anything on, but trying to free the immense anxiety building within me, the thought of hitting a trifecta, of making a score so sweet to me. As I shouted, so too briefly did Don. I yelled for the eight, he for the three. The sodden clay flying in large chunks up from his hooves, the eight began to move on the three. No Secretariat-like burst here, the lead closing in feet not in lengths, but the eight gaining, the class of the race, although having shown almost nothing at a higher price, passing the three about fifty yards from the finish, my trifecta right there before me eight-three-five, me wondering how many hundreds I had won, not wondering, as I might have, why Don had shouted, the three horses having separated themselves from the field, no reason to shout with the trifecta boxed.

Typically, a trifecta at the Downs will pay $200; some pay $400 and $500, some $100. In the mist, on the sloppy track, with a field of nine runners, my trifecta paid $88.60. Briefly stunned as the figure flashed upon the toteboard, I, although a winner, felt my sweet terror return. For if the result placed the race in the category of a mystery solved, Don's shout, as the horses hit the top of the stretch, now made powerful and instructive sense. He had not boxed the trifecta because the trifecta seemed so clear; it had been a better bet to try to order the top three than to box four. The race I had so ingeniously and triumphantly worked out made the same sense to everybody else. I, unwittingly and briefly, had found the logic of racing at the Downs, but now could not say why or how this particular trifecta was so obvious. As a winner, I was almost as lost as I was as a loser. There was no need to congratulate myself or to feel exultant, although at the head of the stretch, when the eight moved, my heart had, indeed, "leapt up." All that was called for was to say, me to Don, "It figured." My tone not as rich as his, not suspending all those hateful contraries in rich ironic tension, not approaching, as the words did when he spoke them, art.

Justice in Florida

William Logan

Donald has a reputation for being a prickly character, and I have often been called opinionated myself. I date our friendship from the moment, after one of his workshops at Iowa in the fall of 1973, when he told me something I'd said had stuck in his craw. He'd already gone gray then and was no longer a thin young man (what he lost in thinness he gained in authority). I was impressed by the proprietary way, on rainy days when his shoes were soaked, he would pad around the Writers' Workshop in his stockinged feet. Some midwestern afternoons, after we became friendly, I gave him a ride home in my battered blue station wagon; once, when I'd halted too long at a stop sign by the library, a driver behind us leaned on his horn. I drove on. Don said immediately (with a hint of challenge) that *he'd* have stayed at the sign, blocking traffic, until sundown. I was delighted to find someone else who believed that conversation should be a series of minor provocations.

After I left the Workshop we corresponded, his letters following me to Provincetown, Virginia, California, Boston, and finally England. I'd been living in England for almost two years when I was asked to direct the writing program at the University of Florida, which Donald had joined the year before. I'd have been happier staying another two. Florida was everything I disliked about the South—too hot, too provincial, too sandy, too racist. The only attractions were the alligators and the Justices.

■ ■ ■

Moving to Gainesville in 1982, the Justices had bought a house in Golfview, an old housing development bordering the university golf course. Built in various styles and at various times (the earliest in the twenties, the newest so post-postmodern it was hardly a house at all), the houses had been placed on one of the few hillsides in that flat city. Some were half-hidden by shadowy grove and underbrush: in Florida what was lawn one day might be underbrush the next.

Two tall rustic stone columns flanked the entrance to Golfview—beyond, the road descended and divided around a stone fountain, long dry. Elsewhere Gainesville was a tidy grid of urban planning; in Golfview the roads had a pastoral curve and a pastoral privacy, sometimes running into mysterious dead ends—it was easy to lose the way, or take a wrong turn. It was a quiet place to walk Buster, the Justices' excitable mutt. (Buster liked quiet—he was afraid of lightning, leaping into a bathtub at any distant rumble. In Florida the lightning came on fast and hard in midsummer, and he must have felt he'd been lured South under false pretenses.)

Donald and Jean's house had begun as two flat-roofed, cypress-boarded wings, each not much more than a room and a room and a room—modest, boxy rectangles divided by a level court of grass, perhaps connected by a breezeway. In the sixties the owner, a professor of architecture, joined them (making a squarish U) with a vast, high-ceilinged living room. Built of stone, this rough, masculine room had escaped from a hunting lodge—it was a set for *Citizen Kane*. Mortared rock shelved from the walls. Tall plate glass was set in bays facing the front yard as well as the inner court. In those bays hung heavy oak doors the owner had salvaged from the demolished Gothic courthouse downtown. The doors were brooding and judicial: shut, they made the stone room a bomb shelter of sorts (the architect's optimistic idea). The Justices placed a miniature orange tree in one bay, as if to bring the tropics inside.

Two bright minimal landscapes by their friend Daniel Lang hung precariously on the rock walls: in one, a skinny smokestack mimicked the line of a palm tree. Donald's grand piano stood solidly in a corner. Nearby perched a dainty fly-like music cabinet, bought at Liberty's during a trip to London—the piano looked ready to eat it.

It was an artist's house—odd, original, and with a deepening view. Jean once called it "a former showplace, full of eccentric interest," and though at times it seemed uncomfortable (as Frank Lloyd Wright's houses were), it had its own proprieties and small dramas. The backyard stretched along the low rise of the ninth fairway. From the double bays on the inner court, a scene of parallel fairways receded, primly divided by loblolly pines and old live oaks. The house was protected from the ninth tee by a grove and a thicket, and golfers who hit towering slices found their balls tangled in the canopies of two immense live oaks guarding the rear of the Justice yard. Only a nasty low slice—a weed cutter—might skid across the St. Augustine grass toward Donald's study. Nevertheless, a basket of golf balls sat on a table in the entryway, like mints for departing guests.

The north wing contained Donald's studios—a larger and smaller room knocked together—and a guest bedroom their son, Nat, used on visits. The other wing had kitchen, dining room, a master bedroom with a marble floor, Jean's study, and a narrow television room (more a television closet). From the dining room, French doors opened onto a dark screened porch surrounding a small shimmer of swimming pool, just long enough to turn around in. The pool was troublesome to keep up, and eventually everyone seemed to forget it was there—it was a lost lake.

In later years Don wrote in one study and painted in the other. In the smaller back room he built a maze of desks and tables: two walls were filled with books, and a green light penetrated through the trees outside. The tables seethed in permanent, inventive disarray. The painting studio was in even greater disarray, watercolors tacked everywhere, and photos and postcards that might be rendered into watercolor. A small bookshelf was spared for volumes Donald had "rescued" from the university library, books he thought too valuable to be left on the open shelves. A sleek chrome-and-Naugahyde reading chair, bought out of a catalogue, had taken over one corner—it had proved difficult to assemble, and once assembled had acquired squatter's rights. Donald was always buying (or occasionally being given) something recalcitrant—a computer, a stereo, a chair, a revolving bookcase—and then morosely lamenting its complexity.

■ ■ ■

As a graduate student I had taken notes in Donald's workshop not only on what he said, but also on what might be called his character of mind. His comments on my poems were brief—a line checked favorably, a passage marked for deletion, a phrase that caught his attention eliciting a few scribbles of argument. He had a finicky sensitivity to language, and in workshop focused on a particular word or phrase, elaborating on its resonance, its possible contribution of effect. Beginning discussion with a detailed reading of a few lines or a stanza, he would explain the poet's probable intention and the passage's fulfillment of intention. Then he would pause and say, "On the other hand . . . ," and completely reverse himself, offering another reading equally plausible but entirely destroying the structure of meaning he had delicately built. And then, on occasion, he might stop and say, "But on the other hand . . . ," and produce an altogether different reading, as if the other architectures had never existed. The complexity he railed against in the mechanisms of the world were exactly what delighted him in the mechanisms of art—and it was a complexity that underlay a simplicity of surface, as in his own poems.

One of the pleasures of coming to Florida was the chance to attend Donald's seminar on meter, which provided the groundwork for his short essay "The Invention of Free Verse." He had devoted months of reading to preparation; but the heart of those seminar evenings was his interpretation of particular lines, slowly isolating and defining the artifices of art as they became the sincerities of expression, until what seemed a calm enough line of meter was charged with dangers and dissensions. Those readings would strike like a bolt of lightning. I felt like Buster.

■ ■ ■

Donald had a mild heart attack in the winter of 1990, followed by a bypass operation. He had begun to think seriously about retirement the year before, and his teaching had been arranged so that in his final three years, with the help of a sabbatical, he taught only two semesters. He had grown a little disaffected with Florida (his Miami was gone) and with the university. Perhaps the course of his teaching can be read in his dissatisfactions of place, but he took hard at Florida the general uninterest in poetry or fiction as a living art. Though there was pleasure in the writing program and applause for its success, few scholarly colleagues attended readings, any readings.

As the date of Donald's retirement approached, in the spring of 1992, he refused all usual commemoration (pressed to accept the handsome black captain's-chair the university presented its retiring professors, he directed it into my office, which it never left). Even a plan for a surprise party was vetoed by Jean. Don did agree to a farewell reading, and mischance dictated that the only room available was an oddly shaped lecture-room for chemistry, with a huge slate demonstration table instead of a podium. Campus police had failed to open the room, so on that very cool evening a crowd gathered impatiently outside. Finally a small older man—he might have been a leprechaun—pushed his way to the front clutching a ringful of keys. He turned out to be a retired university vice-president, his skeleton keys saved for just such an occasion; and he let us in through a crammed storage closet—a secret passage.

The lecture room was broad, shallow, and soon packed with undergraduates (leading Donald to believe we had papered the hall). His readings were always modestly proposed —he made the poems work out their terms with the audience.

He stood behind the expanse of slate and read from his work with a sweet and practiced confidence, but also with something like mournful or nostalgic recollection. Toward the end, he mentioned that in his rush to leave home he had forgotten two poems he'd just been working on. He was determined to recite them from memory, and asked the audience's indulgence—though the shape and rhythms were in his mind, he thought it likely that he'd forget a word or a line here and there. At first he almost gave up. Then gradually, in a kind of half-thought, he spoke one line and then the next, here and there hesitating over a word or a phrase for a long, hard moment—in the silence one could see him searching painfully for the precise word, as Wittgenstein was said to have done. Each time memory broke through, and the phrases fell in their required order, each hesitation transformed into a little stirred rush of speech. One of the poems was an elegy for his friend, Henri Coulette. It was titled "Invitation to a Ghost," and ended

> Correct me if I remember it badly,
> But was there not a dream, sweet but also terrible,
> In which Eurydice, strangely, preceded *you*?
> And you followed, knowing exactly what to expect, and
>   of course she did turn.
>
> Come back now and help me with these verses.
> Whisper to me some beautiful secret that you remember
>   from life.

The effort of memory, of memory and attention, seemed partly to exhaust Donald, and partly to exhilarate him. The applause came like thunder. And then the reading was over.

interview

An Interview with Donald Justice

Dana Gioia

*Could you begin by just telling me where you were born
and what your family background was?*

I was born in Miami, Florida. My parents had come
down to Miami from south Georgia in the early twenties.
They came from farming families, but my father had become
a carpenter in Miami, which back then was freshly urban but
still very Southern. He remained a carpenter all his life. There
must have been many young farm boys like him who could
not hope to make a decent living in those days on farms all
through the South. Many headed off to the nearest big city
and learned other trades.

*Were you the first person in your family to go to
college?*

I would have thought yes, except that one of my great
uncles, as I recall, practiced as a doctor, and he must have had
at least a little college to qualify. And a cousin of my mother's
generation had dropped out of college to teach in grammar
school. That's about it, as far as I know.

How long had your family been in the South?

We don't know. Of course, the more aristocratic Southern
families would have known a great deal more about their
past—the class, that is, from which most Southern writers seem
to have come. But except for a tale or two, our family history
went back only as far as the mid–nineteenth century. This may
have protected me a little from one or two of the vices of the

professional Southerner, though the truth is I *would* like to know more about the family past.

How did you first become interested in music?

My mother and I were in downtown Miami one Saturday night, just before the stores were closing. I was five. We happened to pass through the basement of a large department store, where little kids were performing in something called a rhythm band. We paused to watch. I must have asked my mother if I could have some sort of instrument. And for my birthday I was given a snare drum, of all things! Not the ideal instrument, but it was a start. Soon after that I began piano lessons.

When did you first become interested in poetry, or writing?

In the eleventh grade. The poem that caught my fancy was in our textbook—William Cullen Bryant's "Inscription for the Entrance to a Wood." Why it converted me I have no idea. Wordsworthian platitudes.

What was it like for a writer to grow up in Miami during the thirties and forties?

About like it must have been in many American towns then. The desire to write made for a solitary kind of ambition. I felt lucky when, as a senior in high school, I met two or three others my age who were interested in the same things. In college there were a few more. But this secret desire had no apparent connection with the life of the place. Miami was a cultural wasteland. All the same, the life of the city—the small city Miami was then—was endlessly fascinating and rewarding in itself. The excitement of the tourist season, the difference between the winter people and the year-rounders, the natural beauty, the rawness and newness of everything, the ocean itself, the sense almost of a frontier, of life just beginning. As far as I knew there were no painters, no writers; there *were* a few musicians. That was about it. There were music recitals—I can't remember a single exhibition of paintings. There were some writers of popular fiction whom one saw mentioned occasionally in the newspapers. The Sunday *Miami News* carried a column by the poet laureate of Florida. I knew better at fifteen than to believe that what appeared in this column was wonderful stuff, but it was all there seemed to be. I read it eagerly every Sunday. Come to think of it, the literary level of the present-day *Miami Herald* isn't that much higher.

Pound's poem catches some of all that when he speaks of "the helpless few" in his country "A-stray, lost in the villages . . . / Lovers of beauty, starved."

How old were you before you left Florida?

As a child I used to visit grandparents and other relatives in south Georgia every summer—Boston, Thomasville, Tifton, in there. But that was just more of the same, more primitive perhaps, more rooted. The very first time I was ever out of the South was the summer I turned eighteen. I took a bus to New York. It was love at first sight, and I still love New York City. I was overwhelmed. I left Miami more or less for good in my twenties.

Where did you go to college?

The University of Miami for a B.A. Then the University of North Carolina at Chapel Hill, then Stanford, and eventually Iowa. In Miami I started as a music student. Those were the years of the Second World War; I was 4-F myself, but when a number of the music faculty were drafted, there was really no one left to teach what I wanted to learn. My composition teacher, Carl Ruggles, wanted me to go to Yale to study with Paul Hindemith. I was faced with a decision. Not only did my family have very little money, but I suspected that I might have more talent as a writer than as a composer, much as I would have liked to go on writing music. Anyhow

Donald Justice *(second from left)* in 1945 or 1946. New York. Taken by the tabloid photographer Weegee at an after-hours jazz session in trumpeter Frankie Newton's basement apartment. A cropped version was first printed in *Weegee's People* (Duell, Sloan & Pearce, 1946), captioned "Feeling no pain." *(Weegee [Arthur Fellig] © 1994 International Center of Photography, New York. Bequest of Wilma Wilcox.)*

there came a time when I sort of gave up on music, not without regret.

You were studying with the composer Carl Ruggles?

Yes. He wintered in Miami then, and through arrangement with the University of Miami he taught a little. Not classes as such. He would choose a small number of pupils and give them private lessons in composition. Usually there were about three of us; I think one year there may have been as many as four, including one from the faculty. His teaching was a revelation for me, as much perhaps for the attitude toward art that came across as for anything more strictly musical.

The first *artists* I ever knew were Ruggles and George Marion O'Donnell, a now forgotten poet who was a second-generation Fugitive-Agrarian, a contemporary of Jarrell's.

O'Donnell was the first person ever to read my poems who knew what he was reading and what was lacking and what perhaps wasn't. Encouragement meant a great deal to me. He also got me to read Hardy in a new way—not as a rural versifier but as an experimenter. Also, for the first time, Dante. O'Donnell and Ruggles made a powerful impression on me, one that has lasted all my life.

Around this time you also met Robert Frost in Miami?

Robert Frost also wintered in Miami. I became acquainted with him through my friendship with his grandson, Prescott. Frost I now see as a very great poet, but the impression he left on me then was regrettably small compared with the others. Probably he was just too big—*too* big, for one thing, ever to stop playing his role. When he learned that I was an admirer of Eliot, that was enough to keep us at a distance—properly enough. In general he liked to give the impression of being rather anti-intellectual, unacademic, a bit folksy, more mindful of the popular view of things, of popular success, than I— a romantic-minded sophomore—would have considered fitting for a great poet. Not that he wasn't always very decent to me—it was just, I suppose, that he didn't fit my image of the poet. Still doesn't, come to think of it.

How long did you study with Ruggles?

I took lessons regularly for two years. And then I decided not to go back for more. However, I ran into Ruggles one afternoon on the street, and he asked me to come around. Who could refuse? And I continued with lessons pretty regularly until graduation, though since I had more or less given up hope, it was no longer so close to my heart.

What was Carl Ruggles like?

In appearance? He looked the way he does in the portrait by Thomas Hart Benton in the Nelson-Atkins Museum in

Kansas City. Bald, round-faced, smoking a cigar, seated at the piano. That's exactly how I remember him. He was one of those eccentric self-taught artists—homemade geniuses—of which America has had its share. Marsden Hartley, one of my favorite painters, was one; Sherwood Anderson another. Charles Ives—who was Ruggles's friend and benefactor—is a similar case, despite his musical training. Ruggles had his own love for American things—like Ives. He liked the Transcendentalists, and he admired Whitman. The musical scene he was part of was akin to other movements in the American arts in the twenties and thirties. He belonged to an international group of modern composers who put on avant-garde concerts featuring Varèse, Cowell, and the rest.

Ruggles was very kind to me. I liked him very much. Usually one part of the lesson would consist of his showing you something he was working on himself. He wrote on large pieces of butcher paper, pasted together and staff-lined by hand. Such a piece of homemade score paper would be spread across the top of the piano, too big for it, really, and he would attempt to cover great ranges of the keyboard with his stubby fingers, filling in with voice the parts he could not otherwise get in—and all the while the cigar smoldering in a corner of his mouth or burning away on the school's piano. He could sound like an orchestra!

Did studying music have any effect on your poetry?

I can't think of any effect at all. None.

How then did you come to write two poems in the form of sonatinas? Or so many poems that read like themes and variations?

Well, very little effect, then. Notions of form, really, nothing more. I don't happen to think that poetry is—or can be—very "musical." It's a figure of speech, basically. My God, how I've heard the term misused and abused! That may be how the study of music affected me—to make me less toler-

ant of the kind of nonsense uttered on this score. Some even
go so far as to speak of the melody of poetry. But the fact is
that poetry has no melody, which involves pitch. It doesn't
even have *Sprechstimme*, thank goodness. "Musical" when
applied to poetry seems to mean approximately what "poetic"
means when applied to music. And, by the way, why is it that
"poetic" or "poetical" can be used to praise almost anything
but poetry itself?

You went to graduate school at Stanford?

A master's in English at Chapel Hill. I met my wife in
Chaucer class there. Then Stanford.

Did you study with Yvor Winters there?

Yes and no. Winters allowed me to sit in on his classes. I
would have taken the classes officially—it's why I'd gone to
Stanford—except that, because of the rules of procedure as
interpreted by the then chairman of the department, I was
teaching too much as a graduate assistant to be allowed the
Winters classes, which, frustratingly, were not part of the Ph.D.
plan. Instead I had to take Old English, et cetera. The Winters
classes may not have been an unalloyed pleasure for everyone,
but for me they were—except that he didn't like what I wrote
as well as I thought and still think he should have liked it. A
great relief from Old English, nevertheless.

What was Yvor Winters like?

Stocky, a bit bearish in appearance, given to frowning
and a dogmatic manner. If I think of him as wearing a leather
jacket, that probably comes from a photo in an old Oscar
Williams anthology. I'm not sure I've got him right. But I do
remember that he always seemed dead certain of his own
positions. He knew very clearly what they were, and he had
put them down with authority and with no doubts at all in
In Defense of Reason, the collection of his first three critical

books, which had just come out at the time I was a student there. He taught from that book, and I cannot remember that he ever departed from the opinions expressed therein, not ever. Though he might add to them a bit in class. Interesting asides, further information, elaboration. Basically, what was covered in his classes could have been found in *In Defense of Reason*, which I already knew well. A friend had given me a copy as a wedding present. Winters and I got along pretty well, though I was never a member of what was clearly a sort of "inner circle." There were sides to him I never got a glimpse of. But I thought highly of him and still do.

Winters was the best reader of poetry I ever heard— aloud, I mean. Not that I heard him anywhere but in class. His way of reading imparted great dignity to the poem and made the rhythm a significant, indeed, a fundamental, part of it. His voice would drop about a fifth—a whole fifth—in pitch when he read. It sounds stagey but it didn't seem so at the time. It announced that this was not a lecture, not con-versation, but a poem—a different form of speech, let us say. Kinnell's voice I have heard drop a third, a major third, but I think that means something a little different. On record unfortunately the Winters effect does not come across. (The best reader on record is Pound, and next to him Frost.)

Did either Yvor Winters or his theories have any impact on your own poetry?

Oh, yes. I wanted to write the sort of thing he would have approved of. I don't suppose I ever managed to do that. I learned a good deal about the meters from him, for which I'm grateful. I remember writing a little poem in careful and exact rhyme and meter and showing it to him. In it was a pun on the word *rest*, which he did not take to. "Nor love the rest / Denied us here" is how it went. To defend myself, I men-tioned that I had borrowed this pun from George Herbert's "The Pulley." Winters seemed rather upset by this. He marched down the hall to his office to get his Herbert and then read the Herbert poem through aloud to the class. "Yes, it's the same pun," he said, "but in Herbert it's good." Something like that. And he was perhaps right. Funny how these little things stick in the mind all these years.

*Did you meet any fellow students at Stanford who might
have had an influence on you?*

Edgar Bowers, if anyone. But my wife and I had known him in Chapel Hill. He had preceded me to Stanford and in fact encouraged me to come out, not that I needed much encouragement. Once out there we met some of the poets in the Winters circle, Helen Pinkerton and Wesley Trimpi among them. But there seemed to be writers—a lot of them fiction writers, most of whom I never did get to know—everywhere you turned that year at Stanford, quite unlike Chapel Hill. Among writers who were just beginning to gather at universities in those early days there was a great idealism, a sort of purity—doubtless naive enough—but far more to my taste than the kind of embarrassingly naked and highly practical networking you find now.

*Was that the first time you had been in a milieu of
writers?*

I guess so. We had made—had had to make—our own little circles in Miami and Chapel Hill, such as they were. The Stanford program seemed only loosely organized in those years, and that was probably for the best. One of the good things about it was that, through a gift, there was money for annual prizes—prizes in the story, in poetry, in the novel, in drama, and who knows what else. I won second prize in the story contest that year—$150—a hefty sum back then, enough for train fare for my wife and me to escape back to Florida.

Why did you leave Stanford?

It was too expensive. Just living there cost a lot, and the tuition was high. Then the chairman was forcing me to go for the degree much too slowly. I might still be there, working on my Ph.D., if I hadn't won that second prize.

So, after Stanford, you began teaching?

I had already taught one year at the University of Miami as an instructor, and I went back there and taught a couple more years, before being let go. Lots of sunny afternoons at the races, many lazy hours at the chessboard—that's what I remember now. I wasn't getting anywhere at all.

How did you first come to Iowa?

I had been out of work for a while, trying to write, and my wife's brother-in-law, Peter Taylor, and a friend of his, Robie Macauley, suggested Iowa to me. Robie had taken a degree there. I wrote a letter to Paul Engle, who ran the program—who had practically invented it, they said—and got a very welcoming letter back, offering me the best teaching assistantship I could have possibly hoped for. And we were very happy about going. I had to take a job driving a taxi cab in Miami to get together a little stake. Driving a cab wasn't nearly as exciting as I'd thought it would be. Iowa proved far more exciting. I arrived in the dead of winter 1952, straight from Florida, wearing my uncle's old army overcoat. I was twenty-six.

How long had the Iowa Writers' Workshop been going in 1952?

Since the mid-thirties. I think the first person to take a degree in writing there was Paul Engle himself. It wasn't really until after the Second World War that it began to grow into the place so many people would later be drawn magically to, while others saw in it a symbol of what was wrong with American writing, poetry especially. Most of what anyone knew about Iowa, pro or con, was all along made up of legend and propaganda. All this was just beginning to take shape when I arrived. We weren't yet defined. There was, you might say, a ferment. Rexroth was to call us "cornbelt metaphysicals." As I recall, he was a journalist employed by the Hearst press at the time. The poetry wars were just about to get underway. It was perhaps a sort of mirror of the Cold War. The weapons were words—otherwise, who knows? Iowa was taken to represent a sort of academic "establishment." What? Out there in the middle of nowhere? Some of the people calling us that themselves wrote for highly paid publications, had excellent teaching posts, got the prizes, the fellowships, the reviews—all that. It's an old political trick, calling the others what you don't want to be known as yourself, to deflect attention. Well, it may not be over even yet, but I'd rather pretend it was.

Who were your fellow students at Iowa?

There were some fine writers. Bill Stafford was there. W. D. Snodgrass, Henri Coulette, Phil Levine were all there —and a man of infinite promise then, who has not published as much since as he should have, Don Petersen. And Jane Cooper, Bob Dana, Bill Dickey—others I surely wrong by forgetting for the moment.

During your early Iowa days, you studied with John Berryman, did you not?

He was my last teacher there. Engle's idea was to bring in prominent young poets—poets then young—for a semester. The result was that I had a term with Karl Shapiro, who was then editing *Poetry*, then a term with Robert Lowell, and finally one with John Berryman.

Did any of those teachers influence you as a writer?

To tell the truth, I don't think so—for better or for worse. But Lowell had influenced me early. *Lord Weary's Castle* influenced practically everybody I knew who was trying to write poetry in 1947. Those heavy thudding meters, the prophet's voice, the doom and gloom, the cultural overload, the psychological melodrama of it all. For a while he must have influenced all of us—all but the scruffy little bands of Poundians, who were the precursors, in a funny way, of so much that was to come. Pre-Beats. You'd come across them on every campus. They've slipped from public memory now. There was already perhaps just a hint of the poetry wars to come. Against all that stood the early Lowell manner—which represented the latest thing on the other side of the battle-lines. I had tried to write poems of that Lowell type. But by the time I was actually Lowell's student I had given up on it.

Did you ultimately take a degree from Iowa?

A Ph.D. It seemed the best way to get a university job, which is what I wanted. University life was much more humane then than it has now become. Less doctrinaire, less "correct," more open-minded. Fewer intellectual fascists about.

How did you first come to teach at Iowa?

Paul Engle asked me to replace him temporarily while he was away on a Guggenheim. I was already familiar with the way things worked, and after I came in, it seems I just sort of stayed around.

How did Iowa become America's preeminent creative writing program?

Not by deliberate plan, and certainly not by my choice. But this is for me a difficult and tricky subject. My feelings about it are mixed. Let me just say this much. My happiest memories of the writing program are of the poets and fiction writers who gathered there or who drifted through, the good writers I got to know. (Some good writers passed through I never did get to know.) I tend to remember a few scattered vintage years rather than whatever it was growing into, this thing that is now called a program. It grew by accident more than by design. It was simply one of the first, and Paul Engle —in those early years especially—was astonishingly energetic in raising money to give, in the form of small personal fellowships, to young writers he thought promising. The understanding was that they'd hang around for a year or so and try to write. This much seemed useful on the face of it, unarguably so. Better than an NEA, you might well say, being more personal, less programmatic really. For there was no deliberate plan, no mad scheme to seize world power or to influence the course of literature one way instead of another. Of course we had ideas—some of us did—of what made for good writing. Who does not? Is one not entitled? And what an appealing idea this was, to provide an oasis in the midst of what Paul liked to call the "heartland," but which might otherwise have seemed just one more cultural wasteland. The question used to come up if we should have more students. I would plead for fewer. No such luck. In the end too many people learned of this splendid half-secret thing, and that changed everything.

When you came to Iowa in the early fifties, how many creative writing programs—or graduate creative writing programs—were there in the United States?

I can think of only two: Stanford and Iowa. There may have been others, but I hadn't heard of them, still haven't. Very soon after, they began to increase in number, usually started, I believe, by writers who'd passed through Iowa. So you might say we were responsible, knowingly or not, for what was to happen.

You helped make creative writing programs part of the academic mainstream. Do you have any thoughts on that?

Fairly gloomy ones. I remember that innocent time when all we wanted was to be separate from the academic side, separate but equal. We were not equal; we were condescended to; we had reason to feel beleaguered. Beyond that there was no particular goal. Some of the students I had went out and did at their schools what we were doing at Iowa. There was a snowball—or pyramid—effect. In this I may well be guilty. I did not know what I was doing, did not see what was coming.

How do you feel about the current state of creative writing programs?

The very term itself is an unfortunate one. *Creative* has been badly used. I know that Paul Engle himself always insisted on *imaginative* instead of *creative*, and I think he was right. That aside, there are simply too many writing programs now, far too many. We don't need them. For that matter, we don't need as many *writers* as we have. Though, mind you, I have nothing against amateurs in writing who write for the sheer love of it. It's different when they set themselves and their friends up as experts. An obvious problem with writing programs today is that many of those who profess to teach poetry write very badly themselves.

Does someone need to be a good poet to teach poetry writing?

I think so. Which is not quite the same as saying that if you can write you can also teach.

You have spent your adult life as a teacher (except for that brief stint as a cab driver). Has that affected you as a writer?

Probably, but I'm not sure how. The writer in academic life probably becomes more self-conscious than one with a different job or a tidy inheritance. Is that bad? I'm a self-conscious writer, but then I would have been exactly that no matter what job I had. The relation between writing and teaching remains obscure, at least to me; perhaps nonexistent. If I had been instead, say, the master of a ship, I would no doubt have found plenty of subject matter in my work, just as Conrad did. But being on faculties, I found very little subject matter in my job itself. As subject matter the academic world is pretty much bust, a hive of clichés. But then if I had been an insurance salesman, I probably wouldn't have found much in that to write about either—or an insurance lawyer, like Stevens. The question's complicated, and it comes out differently for different people. There happen to be a lot of teaching writers who don't write in what would be thought an academic manner at all, but on the contrary seem to make a profession of hating ideas, hating to take thought. Sociologically speaking, it's a kind of self-hate —very familiar. The automatic assumption underlying the received view is much too easy—the idea that if you're in the academy, you are tamed and will write in a repressed way. Not so, really not so. In fact, academics themselves tend to love the wild-man type of writer, and not just as visitor, gone in a day or two, but as colleague, a permanent scapegoat for their own frustrated wishes and ambitions, I suspect.

What effect do you think teaching at a university has on a poet? I don't mean you particularly, but in general terms?

A poet in a university has rare privileges and benefits. First of all, more time, free from the job—time which can be spent writing. And I've always counted it a privilege (I know there are those who feel otherwise) to deal in one's job with things of value—artistic value—with things you can love and respect. I cannot for the life of me see why it is more intel-lectually stimulating to dig ditches, or to go down into the mines, as I have heard recommended, than it is to talk about *Hamlet* or *Anna Karenina* or "Sunday Morning" to people interested in talking about them with you. One lives a tamer life, I think—though, God knows, I've known some wild men in academic life. And there are many who seem altogether convinced that the tame life does not lead to good writing. It may not; then again it just may.

What writers have influenced you as a poet?

Forty years ago Karl Shapiro asked the young poets in the workshop that question, and I have the same answer now. I remember jotting down, rather proudly: Baudelaire and Stevens. I may have added other names, but I remember none. Those two I do remember. And I think that's true— Baudelaire and Stevens have influenced me. Auden also. Another answer to that question would be everybody I've read. But that is perhaps a little less true.

What did you find so attractive in Baudelaire and Stevens?

I'm not sure. In Baudelaire probably the combination of high style with decadent subject matter. In Stevens I must have been dazzled by the vocabulary, the sheer nerve of it, almost Shakespearean, but unfortunately, in Stevens, without the human drama. While dazzled, though, one hardly remembers to miss that.

Did Weldon Kees influence you?

Yes, I'd forgotten him. I came across his *The Fall of the Magicians* in the Miami Public Library one evening when browsing. I checked the book out, read it with increasing excitement, and, within a week or two, was writing a sestina based on one of his. In fact, very soon after reading Kees I *dreamed* the first eleven lines of still another sestina. (Not the one based on Kees, actually, but another one called, for obvious reasons, "A Dream Sestina.") I soon finished the poem called "Sestina on Six Words by Weldon Kees." A few months after it came out in a magazine, I had a letter from

John Kees, the poet's father. During the brief interval between my writing and publishing the poem, Kees had disappeared, had become a missing person. His father wrote me to ask what the six words were. He was hoping to find traces of his missing son and thought knowing what the words were might somehow help. I had to write back explaining that the six words were simply a part of the form of a poem his son had written, and I had borrowed them; that I had never met his son. But we began exchanging letters. About that time Kim Merker, a young printer in Iowa City, and his partner Raeburn Miller were looking for something to print. They both happened to like Kees as a poet, and I suggested that we do a *Selected Poems*. I'd do the selecting; I thought Kees's work was uneven, and I wanted to use only the very best poems so that there would be a better chance of making a strong impression. Harry Duncan, another printer-friend, talked us into doing a *Collected Poems* instead. I wrote the father and asked for permission, which he was very pleased to give. His hope that publication of the book might lead to information about the whereabouts of his son turned out, unhappily, to be a vain hope.

What is Kees's place in American poetry?

He was one of the best poets of his generation. It was a fascinating generation—that half-generation just before mine—Berryman, Lowell, Shapiro, Roethke, Jarrell, and Elizabeth Bishop. Poets that close to you in time can exert a special personal power over you—something beyond the more general influence poets possibly better but more remote in time can have on you. They become like big brothers and sisters. The poets of that generation—some of them—I knew as friends. I could read their new books as they came out with a special personal curiosity and pleasure. I'm not sure they influenced my poetry, except perhaps for Kees, but they did influence my thinking *about* poetry.

You didn't mention Delmore Schwartz in your list of the mid-century generation. Why not?

I should have put him in. Schwartz's first book was spectacular. It is almost as exciting now as when I first came across it as a freshman. Not only poems but plays and the wonderful title story. Thereafter nothing quite lived up to that blazing start.

How does a poem begin for you? How does the process of inspiration work?

Just in the usual way—with a word or a phrase, perhaps even a sort of rhythm. Forgive me—I almost said *musical* rhythm. Sometimes with a quite traditional subject, such as the death of a friend.

When you begin writing a poem do you usually draft the entire poem out, or do you work in fragments?

I work in fragments—I wish I could work some other way. I *draft* perhaps an entire *line*.

How long does it take you to finish a poem?

I've written some poems in a day—not very often. Other times I've worked over the notes for a poem for years. The poem isn't necessarily any better for that, of course. If I could write poems the way I dream of writing poems, I would dash off a poem in an afternoon. Then probably take the rest of the week off. There simply shouldn't be too many poems.

How do you know if a poem is finished?

You get a sense of things fitting together, almost locking together. Yet even after that I can't deny that I have doubts, that often I want to go on tampering, changing mostly little things by now, changing back and forth. It's as if there were

an ideal form of the poem you're trying not so much to construct as to reconstruct. Like bringing out the secret writing—
done in lemon juice, say—by holding a flame beneath the
sheet of paper. What a pleasure to watch the little brown letters taking shape!

I like to think that all true poems exist before their authors
write them down. You can picture them floating about, say,
in a sort of Platonic realm; and they are perfect there. It is our
job to see that even as they enter the dimensional world they
come close to their original form.

*You've written about the process of revision quite articu-
lately. What role does revision have in your writing?*

The best kind of revision is almost always to cut out. My
students used to hear that repeatedly. Not that they ever
believed it. Another terribly useful kind of revision is the absolutely wholesale revision—a virtual reconceiving. I hear novelists talk about doing that more than poets. It strikes me as
quite incredible that you could actually reconceive *War and
Peace* and then write it all out again. But apparently something
like that *is* done. Whereas most of the revisions I see, from
studies of manuscripts, say, or in the work of students—most
revisions in poems—are small and inconsequential. Changes
of single words perhaps, or maybe a little phrase, or the shifting of one part of a line to another. Changing what they like
to call line breaks, which, after all, can hardly matter very
much unless the piece is well conceived and the words are
right. And I must confess, that's the way I myself ordinarily
revise, but it's not what I believe in. I believe in wholesale
revision—and large swooping cuts. I do make large cuts. On
the principle, you see, of leaving out the parts that aren't very
good, simple enough—what one might call the Pound principle (not in his own work so much as in the editing of Eliot).

*You have sometimes revised old published poems, even to
the point where, when your second book,* Night Light,
was reissued, it was subtitled "Revised Version."

There were very few significant changes. I should just have
let them go. In any case I've changed some of them around
again, given another chance just now with a new volume of
selected poems. It's this impossible desire for perfection I'm at
the mercy of—as if perfection were just around the corner, a
matter of just retying this knot or that. I should have learned
by now that it doesn't work that way.

*Were the revisions merely to make them aesthetically
more perfect then? Or were there ideological revisions, the
way that Auden might have done?*

There were no ideological revisions. One of the two
poems I changed most was "Incident in a Rose Garden."
Contrary to my principle that the best form of revision is cut-
ting, it ended up longer rather than shorter. That came from
trying to work old notes left over from the first try back into
the new version. I got them in rather crudely perhaps. But
I'd been eager to get them in for years. Now I'd be willing
to go back to the original version. Both versions now seem
good to me in somewhat different ways. The awful truth is
that the revisions just don't matter as much as I wish they did.

Do you write every day?

Oh, no! I know some writers say they do, but it's almost
inconceivable to me, except for novelists on a hot streak. I
can conceive of writing every *week*. What I do is to *think* every
week about writing.

*You have produced one slender volume of critical prose.
What role has writing criticism played for you?*

A very small role. It was all done on invitation. I wish I
had written more. I liked to sidestep it because I could not

turn it out quickly. If I could have written good critical journalism rapidly, I would have. But I was too slow.

Why did poets of your generation write so little criticism?

Perhaps because they became teachers, if that's not too paradoxical—teachers of writing, that is. Teaching what used to be the traditional literary subjects—the great literature of the past—develops a critical mind; teaching writing evidently does not. Or it may just be that the old certainties tumbled and we did not know where we were or what we were doing. Writing good criticism demands a certain confidence; even bad criticism does. Look at Bly. Or Pound, after the mid-twenties.

Do you work with a word processor?

Yes, but only in the last couple of years. I was slow to come around. It must be understood that I'm not at all mechanical minded.

Did you ever compose on a typewriter?

Ordinarily not. A lecture perhaps. I prefer to make things up in my head. Then pencil, et cetera. A computer is more playful, more relaxed, more like thinking itself, like improvising.

You are also a painter.

Not really. There was a time when I might have become a musician, but never a painter. I took up painting only very recently, and it may be just for that reason that I like it so well now.

Today there is an increasing specialization in the arts. Have your own multiple interests—in poetry and, to a lesser degree, in music and painting—benefited you as an artist?

They all give a special deep pleasure, let us say. They really do make life seem more splendid. They start all from the same inner source, but beyond that I can't think that one helps you with another at all. Each has too much its own essence: one art doesn't really translate into another.

Are you a Southern writer?

At times, for better or worse. But, not the way some are. I write as I speak, without much accent. If you were born and brought up in the South—at least in my time—there's no way you could escape being a Southern writer. It's not a matter of choice—it's a fate. And that was my fate—that was the world and the life I knew, what I had to work with when I began to write. Southern not because I was the descendant of Confederate generals (I wasn't)—but just inescapably and not always too happily. You are given a subject and you do what you can with it.

What is a Southern writer?

In the past? Someone who had ancestors and a tendency to brood over the lost war. Now? One who writes about crackers and rednecks living in trailers, drinking a lot and leading lives of noisy desperation—usually in the present tense.

Do you feel in any way that you belong to a Southern poetic tradition?

In some ways I came out of the Fugitive-Agrarian line— the only one that counted really. Was there another? Poe's descendants were all French.

You have published several poems from abandoned longer poems or plays. Why have you never finished a long poem?

Katherine Anne Porter used to say that some fiction writers were born to be short-story writers; some, novelists.

Before she finished *Ship of Fools* that would have been. Well, I was born to write short poems; so it appears. Everybody tries long poems. There's this mad superstition that you have to do it to count, an idea that goes back at least to Milton. Look at all the years Pound half-wasted pursuing this notion. For American poets it comes down to those who have failed to finish a long poem and those who have finished their long poems and, in doing so, failed. Obviously I belong to the first class. It's clear I have no staying power. For one thing, I'm too finicky, have too many second thoughts, too many doubts. Nor am I such an egoist as to believe that my experience has epic importance. My senior year in high school, however formative—and it was—could never justify hundreds of lines, much less hundreds of pages. The very question of the form in which to cast a long poem—which I consider crucial—has been unanswered—in a state of crisis, really—since Pound edited Eliot. I certainly haven't been able to answer this absolutely basic question.

Plays? I've never been able to manage second acts.

Do you have any favorite poems among your own work?

I do, but they keep changing. My favorites are usually very recent.

Tell me about that early pamphlet of yours, The Old Bachelor. *This is something not even your bibliographer knew about. How did* The Old Bachelor *come to be published by Pandanus Press in 1951?*

Preston Dettman, a young man in Miami—we were all young then—had a letterpress. I'm not sure what the connection was, but I think he knew a man named Clark Emery, who taught at the university and knew the young writers. Anyway, Preston—whom I did not know very well—was looking for things to print. Emery brought us together. I gave Preston a handful of poems and he turned them into a little pamphlet. He published two or three other pamphlets of the same sort back then. Where he is now I don't know. But that was about it for small press publishing in Miami in the early fifties.

> *You were thirty-four when your first book,* The Summer Anniversaries, *was published—older than some others in your generation when they began to publish. Did you regret the late start?*

Yes, but of course it was my own doing. I hadn't written enough before then to justify a book.

> *Were you surprised when the book won the Lamont Award?*

No, it didn't greatly surprise me. I am one of those writers who always think something good will and in fact should happen. I am disappointed when it does not. The Lamont was for first books back then, and if there was a prize going for a good first book, mine deserved serious consideration and luckily got it.

> *Your first book displays a mastery of what one might call "the traditional modernist lyric." But in your third book,* Departures, *you began writing overtly experimental poems. How did you become interested in experimental writing? And why did you move away from it in your most recent work?*

I'd always been interested in what we will agree to call "experimental writing." It's just that I found it hard to do. At the same time I had always been interested in writing in traditional forms, especially when given a Modernist twist. *Night Light*, my second book, has a mixture of kinds in it. It's a transitional work. But even the "experimental" pieces in *Departures* are experimental within a traditional framework. That is, they resemble other Modernist works; they coexist with them. They show themselves aware of the poems of Williams, say, and

Stevens; of the French perhaps. They hardly chart new paths, nor did I intend that they should. I was writing what I could, when I could.

At the same time, there came a certain choosing up of sides in postwar American poetry, and some poets of my generation did move, more or less, in that direction—some very dramatically, even theatrically so. I don't think I went one way or the other for ideological reasons, as some must have done. I like doing things the hard way—a little against the grain. And what had once seemed hard for me, that is, writing more freely—began some years later to seem easy. Too easy, perhaps. As it certainly seems to be for many. I wanted more resistance. So I returned to a more traditional kind of verse. Now I want in most cases to write very strictly. This position is not, I insist, ideological. There are polemicists who say, and very shrilly, too—as you know—that if you write in the old verse forms, you're fascist, that you can only be truly hip if you do things in certain prescribed and dictated ways. Well, I don't want the world to work like that. I don't write *in* meter and rhyme for any political reason, and I don't write *without* meter and rhyme for any political reason. I write as I want to, and I want to be left alone to do just that. It becomes *political* if you try to dictate to me what I must do. Don't; don't try that. Even Robert Hass, who must know better, speaks— really he does—of the "terrorism" of a metrical orthodoxy. (He is thinking of the traditional meters, of course, not free verse, though if it applies at all, it should apply either way.) But this is overkill, another example of the application—or, rather, the misapplication—of political terms to writing. Not needed if we mean to be serious.

Several poems in Departures *were written using the element of chance. Can you describe how you started composing them?*

As I recall, I got started not long after playing poker one night in Cincinnati with John Cage. Only *I* wanted to control chance, not submit to it. Chance has no taste. What I did was to make a card game out of the process of writing. I'd always loved card games anyhow, gambling in general. As well as I can recall now what I did, I made up three large decks of "vocabulary" cards—one deck each for nouns, verbs, and adjectives—and a smaller fourth deck of "syntax" cards, sentence forms with part-of-speech blanks to be filled in. I would then shuffle and deal out a sequence of "syntax" cards, then shuffle the "vocabulary" cards in their turn and fill the syntactical blanks in. I would go through all this three times, allowing myself to go back and forth as I wished across the table of results, mixing them up to taste. It sounds silly enough, I suppose, and of course anyone could do it. But it seemed at the time to simulate, at least a little, the way the mind worked in writing. And there was enough choice left for the writer's sensibility to enter. I thought that was important.

Why did you stop writing poems according to this method?

The third set of chance cards I made up produced nothing at all interesting. Well, I knew you couldn't win every hand.

You don't see any contradiction then in writing in both "fixed" and "open" forms?

None. The early Modernist masters in English—American masters, anyway—managed to bring it off, and why not? If Eliot and Pound could do it, why couldn't we latecomers give it a try? Stevens was another who managed it—beautifully.

Does the subject matter of a poem determine its ultimate form?

How? Oh, yes, the old nineteenth-century notion—organic form. I like to think subject and form work together. They determine—if that's the word—each other.

Donald Justice in 1969. New York. Taken by Rollie McKenna in the sculpture garden of the Museum of Modern Art for *The Modern Poets* (McGraw Hill, 1970). © *Rollie McKenna*

You have published short stories, but except for "Incident in a Rose Garden" you have never written any narrative poems. Why?

Again, it was a question of form, I think. For a long while blank verse seemed used-up to me—and all the great narratives I admired in English had been written in blank verse. Now I think blank verse may have lain fallow long enough—

and I have started a narrative in blank verse. Of course, it's a *short* narrative, and at the moment it's stalled.

> *You came to maturity as a writer during the age of "con-*
> *fessional" poetry. Yet your own poems—at least until*
> *recently—almost never spoke directly about your life.*
> *Did you have a self-imposed ban on autobiography?*

No. But I happen to be somewhat reticent by nature, if not exactly shy. Nor have I cultivated the kind of life that lends itself to the drama of the confessional.

> *Did you once believe a poet should be invisible in his own*
> *work?*

Yes.

> *Some of your most powerful poems have titles like "After*
> *a Phrase Abandoned by Wallace Stevens" or "Variations*
> *on a Text by Vallejo." Why do so many of your poems*
> *begin as responses to other works of literature?*

They come naturally enough out of my life. It would be quite fair to say that I've lived a literary life. Nor do I have any wish to defend the case. I remember years ago Karl Shapiro saying, quite dogmatically, that poems should not be written about literature—I think he may have said they should not be written about art of any kind. That struck me even then as quite absurd and authoritarian. I gather that quite a few people—usually those with an anti-intellectual bias— feel that way. Well, they're wrong. There's some comfort anyhow in thinking of beautiful things being handed down from generation to generation, from friend to friend.

> *In a fairly recent volume,* The Sunset Maker, *there are*
> *a couple of new "departures" for you. The first is that*
> *you seem to be writing, for the first time, openly auto-*
> *biographical poetry. How did that come about?*

I can't really say. Do writers really think of things that way? There must be very few writers who rub their hands together and announce, "Now let me turn to autobiography." Actually, I think that did happen in Lowell's case, but it was on the advice of his doctor and the case must be pretty rare. For me it was a brief interlude at best, and hardly confessional at that. Lately I've turned to the Great Depression as a subject. I find I can get quite sentimental about the Depression. Not autobiographical at all.

What is it that fascinates you about the Depression?

It's history—and with feeling. An epic—without heroes. And then there are all the great photographs recording it. You can still see it; it is still vividly there.

Could moving back to Florida have brought out this autobiographical impulse?

Probably. Moving back to Florida—especially the first couple of years—did awaken old memories. That may be what you're getting at, but growing older had something to do with it too.

The Sunset Maker *also contained two short stories. Early in your career you wrote short stories quite successfully. Do you see yourself returning to fiction?*

I wish I could; I really do. When I wrote the pair of short stories in *The Sunset Maker*, I thought I would be writing more. I did write another story, which wasn't any good; then I started another and saw that it was hopeless. I still hope to write a good story or two one day, but who knows? I have great admiration for the art of prose, great envy of those who master it.

In The Sunset Maker *you mixed two short stories and a memoir with your poems. Had you originally planned a book of mixed genres?*

Donald Justice in 1987. Gainesville. Taken by Brandon Kershner.
© *Brandon Kershner*

No, I've never been able to plan a book anyhow.

Do you have any regrets about your writing career?

I would like to have lived in a time when the style and idiom of the period were givens. The high Renaissance, say, or the early eighteenth century. Composers and painters have faced similar problems in our time, of course. The challenges are exciting enough but in the end exhausting, defeating to some of us. And they lead to these little internecine struggles that waste good energy—they've been going on since I started writing—the poetry wars. I regret the poetry wars.

Who is your audience?

Other poets, probably. For that matter, where could you find a better audience? Nor can I see any realistic ground to expect poetry to win back a general audience—except perhaps by ways that would have nothing at all to do with poetry, such as, say, taking one's clothes off in public. That was tried, and it seemed to work. Look at the way millions of dollars were thrown away producing *Voices and Visions* for TV, apparently in a misguided attempt to win a larger audience for poetry. Rumors of some golden age when poetry actually had a large general audience are, in any case, much exaggerated.

But if your question implies do I think about an audience at any point when writing a poem, the answer is no, except that I do try to make myself clear. I assume there is an audience, if not today, then tomorrow.

reviews

Introduction to the Critical Heritage

The public record of a poet's critical reception is inevitably distinct from the private history of his or her artistic development. At least in retrospect, the reputation always seems a little—and sometimes vastly—different from the reality. There is, however, more than merely documentary value in surveying a writer's reception by his or her contemporaries. To note what they praise, fault, ponder, or debate often helps clarify our own response.

The reviews that follow provide a representative selection of the critical reactions to Donald Justice's seven full-length volumes of verse and prose from *The Summer Anniversaries* in 1960 through *The Donald Justice Reader* in 1992. (We have excluded his smaller, fine press publications since they were rarely reviewed and their contents were customarily collected in later trade volumes.) The primary purpose of this gathering is neither to vindicate nor celebrate the poet's accomplishment. Justice's literary stature is now sufficiently secure to require no critical roll call. Instead, our aim is to chronicle the public discussion of his work in order to provide a detailed and specific account of the poet and his critical milieu. Although most of the reviews are positive, we have taken special pains to reprint both mixed and negative reviews since the difficulties these critics found in assessing Justice's work illuminate the complex relationship between the author and his age. The faults that contemporaries initially find in the work of strong poets are often a clear measure of their originality.

Surveying these reviews, a student of recent literary history can hardly refrain from noticing that it has consistently been Justice's sensibility that occasioned the central arguments about his work. His craft has never been an issue. From the beginning, critics, especially his fellow poets, have recognized his verbal mastery. The feature that has elicited persistent commentary has been variously described as his "reticence," "detachment," and lack of "self-absorption"—Justice's determination, that is, to present himself in personal but carefully balanced terms. In an age of self-dramatizing and often deliberately shocking confessional poetry, such classical restraint was a sufficiently unusual quality to seem refreshing to many reviewers, though troubling to a few. There has also been much debate over Justice's bold use of other literary texts in his poems. Some critics have objected to his characteristic employment of allusion, imitation, and adaptation, finding it too literary. His admirers view the same procedures not only as proof of Justice's deep engagement with surprisingly various poetic traditions, but also as a sign of a distinctly modern (or even postmodern) kind of originality. He rarely uses a source without transforming it.

The critical heritage also reflects the growing split in contemporary letters between the ways in which poets perceive their art and the manner in which critics evaluate it. Not only have poets consistently praised Justice's work, but his admirers include members of every poetic camp and persuasion. In contrast, virtually none of his detractors have been poets. Perhaps the most surprising aspect of Justice's critical reception has been the nearly universal acceptance of the often radical stylistic shifts that have characterized his development. Neither his general abandonment of formal meters in mid-career nor his later return to rhyme and meter occasioned censure or even much puzzlement among his admirers. Nor did his experiments with aleatory technique and surrealism worry many, even among more traditional reviewers. He never met with accusations of stylistic opportunism that followed several of his contemporaries. Readers have consistently trusted Justice's artistic integrity.

In preparing this critical heritage we had to omit some interesting reviews for reasons of space, but we have been for-

tunate in obtaining permission to reprint nearly every review
we wanted to include. (Only one author withheld permission
—for personal reasons.) Several writers graciously allowed us
to reprint pieces about which they now have serious reservations, most conspicuously David Galler, who no longer agrees
with the criticisms leveled in his early review. We thank him
and all the others for their generosity in letting us create this
comprehensive historical record.

The Summer Anniversaries (1960)

Untitled Review
Howard Nemerov

The chief subject of Mr. Justice's poems is the journey from innocence to experience, the Fall, domestically reflected most often in reminiscences of childhood, that strange, lost land about which there is nevertheless "something familiar." The first seven poems, for instance, vary this subject, while the eighth makes explicit what has been happening by being about the expulsion from Eden. A couple more relate the same movement to unhappy love affairs; others extend the idea of the Fall across the generations, speaking of the decay of families, houses, life styles; while the last poem in the book sums up and generalizes these journeys in another famous fall, being a prayer "To Satan in Heaven."

Mr. Justice is an accomplished writer, whose skill is consistently subordinated to an attitude at once serious and unpretentious. Although his manner is not yet fully disengaged from that of certain modern masters, whom he occasionally echoes, his own way of doing things does in general come through, a voice distinct although very quiet, in poems that are delicate and brave among their nostalgias. Of several whose melancholy lucidity moved me and will remain in memory, I mention especially "Beyond the Hunting Woods."

Howard Nemerov. Untitled Review. *The American Scholar* 29, no. 4 (autumn 1960): 578.

A Note on Donald Justice

Witter Bynner

Donald Justice is a discovery of welcome importance in his *The Summer Anniversaries*, a 1959 Lamont Poetry Selection, and the judges who found him should be happy.

What matter that he is two persons, one assuredly a poet, the other—at least for me—not. From page 3 through page 10 ("Anniversaries," "Song," "[To a Ten-Months' Child] for M.M.," "The Poet at Seven," "The Snowfall," "Landscape with Little Figures," and "On the Death of Friends in Childhood"), he is a beautifully telling new person, alive with poetry. Then from page 11 through page 19 ("Sonnet," "A Dream Sestina," "Sestina on Six Words by Weldon Kees," "Here in Katmandu," and "The Metamorphosis"), he is a totally different person—one with no telling voice. Timidly he comes back on page 20 ("Southern Gothic"), surely page 21 through page 25 ("Sonnet to My Father," "Beyond the Hunting Woods," and "Tales from a Family Album"). But the other person takes over again through page 31 ("Thus" and "Variations on a Theme from James"). The real one returns on page 32 ("Ladies by Their Windows"), leaves on page 35 ("Women in Love," "Love's Stratagems," and "Love's Map"), returns on page 38 ("Speaking of Islands" and "Sonnet about P."), runs off on page 40 ("Another Song" and "In Bertram's Garden"), jumps back on page 42 ("The Stray Dog by the Summerhouse"), off again at page 44 ("Anthony St. Blues" and "A Winter Ode to the Old Men of Lummus Park, Miami, Florida"), on again at page 46 ("Counting the Mad"), then stays firmly present to the end

Witter Bynner. "A Note on Donald Justice." *Poetry* 97, no. 1 (October 1960): 50.

("On a Painting by Patient B of the Independence State Hospital for the Insane," and "To Satan in Heaven").

What a strange, fine book—"the different and the indifferent." I know of only two American poets in his region: Henry Goddard Tuckerman of a hundred years ago and Horatio Colony of now. Obscured they both are in fine shadow. This fellow—and I hope in more of light—will remain an honor to the Academy of American Poets.

From Four Poets
David Galler

Poets deriving from Ransom, Empson, or Stevens have obviously had a hard time of it. The best of them in a generation now in its thirties have managed to narrow their devotion, concentrating on this or that aspect of the master in question. An essay in itself . . . but suffice it to say that Donald Justice is among those at the mercy of the masters. He has much company; but it is with his book that I am concerned. Page after page of surprisingly unassimilated rhetoric owing to others prevents these poems from having at least the virtues of imitations. For lack of space, here is a partial and arbitrary list: p. 18, st. 4; p. 20, l. 3; pp. 24–25; p. 30, l. 4; p. 35, refrain lines; pp. 30–31; p. 39, l. 3; etc.

An arbitrary list of other problems might include: the proper names in st. 1 of "The Metamorphosis" and whether they contribute to the poem; the four instances of the word "father" in "Sonnet to My Father" and whether they distract from the poem, perhaps pointing ultimately to a thinly conceived vision; the perhaps overworked quaint conception (from Mann to Frank O'Hara) of "In Bertram's Garden"; a meditative discourse-pattern, perhaps also overworked, exemplified in part 2 of "On a Painting by Patient B. . . ." As the problems increased, I asked myself why Mr. Justice published "The Stray Dog by the Summerhouse" after poems by Eberhart, Kunitz, and others on the same theme with similar metaphors, similar reflections. Nor did "Counting the Mad" stack up so well against Elizabeth Bishop's poem on Pound in St. Elizabeths. Of course, Mr. Justice may not have known these poems.

David Galler. "Four Poets." *Sewanee Review* 69, no. 1 (winter 1961): 169–70.

Therefore, other problems seem more to the point. Should not a poem contain more complication than "Song"? A more imaginative metaphor than that which closes "To a Ten-Months' Child"? A more personal version of experience and more reason for calling the protagonist a poet than appear in "The Poet at Seven"? (Shades of Rimbaud!) More justification (and resulting conviction) in the use of a last line than that in "Landscape with Little Figures"? A more pointed elaboration on what is meant by "death" and why the names of games have been forgotten in "On the Death of Friends in Childhood"? A reason (perhaps in a footnote) why sentence 2 of "Sonnet" struck the poet as appropriate? A reason why postured naivete must risk the facetious as in the tornada of "A Dream Sestina"? A reason why the final stanza of "The Metamorphosis" should be expected to evoke terror (as I trust it is)? A reason why the little dictum such as opens "Thus" seems to be so comfy to live with to so many poets?

Now it has occurred to me that I fail to react to Mr. Justice's wit on the one hand and reconstructed adult-as-child simplified (sophisticated) vision of things on the other. In which event, my belaborings have been beside the point and doubtlessly this is an adequate book. . . .

Donald Justice
George P. Elliott

> *"Let us honor while we can*
> *The vertical man."*

Donald Justice's *The Summer Anniversaries* did not fare well with some reviewers; their praise for the poems ranged from the vapid to the tepidly respectful and their condemnation from the inaccurate to the malicious. The general opinion seemed to be that though he is a good craftsman he is formalistic and derivative. I wish to oppose this view on two main counts. The first is that though much of his poetry sounds like other poetry this is in itself no reason to condemn him; the second is that at his best he has a fine voice of his own.

I

First off, Mr. Justice is indeed a good craftsman. He fulfills the formal requirements of the sonnet, the villanelle, and the sestina with aplomb, and varies the forms suitably whenever his needs are stronger than the forms. He moves easily from one meter to another. He understands what a line can do and his lines do it. He employs rhyme, off-rhyme, stanza, alliteration, refrain, prayer, suppressed narrative, irony, wordplay with grace and an almost flawless control. Why is such skill an occasion for anything less than admiration?

Of itself, to be sure, verse craftsmanship—formalism—is like cabinetmaking. So? Should we not honor a good cabinet-

George P. Elliott. "Donald Justice." *Perspective* 12, no. 4 (spring 1962): 173–79.

maker? There is something churlish about the attitude: "Yes, yes, but why didn't you carve me a statue instead? We need a big statue, even though botched in the execution, more than a handsome, perfect chest of drawers." It is one of the nuisances of the age that pretension succeeds with none more than with reviewers, the one-eyed ones. Very well: Mr. Justice is no Milton nor claims to be. His reach rarely exceeds his grasp. But he aspires to more than carpentry too. He is formal to the point of elegance, and for poetic elegance nothing but respect is in order.

Well, but these days there are many other craftsmen fine in a similar way; he isn't unique. True. But is particularity a virtue in itself? One usually can spot a page of e e cummings at a glance, and plenty of his pages are very bad. Take a comprehensive volume of eighteenth century poetry and read through a page of satiric couplets; unless you happen to know the passage, can you readily identify the author? The Augustans wrote in a style stronger than any one of them individually, except for a few at their very best. The point is that the style was itself strong. It is surely better to sound like one of several good poets than like no one but yourself if you yawp. In Elizabethan days no one cared who wrote an air so long as it sang well, and some are beautiful. Go to the top: in *Henry VIII* can you tell where Shakespeare's voice stops and Fletcher's picks up? The scholars have legitimately been arguing the matter for several generations. Yet the verse of the play is quite good in the fashion of the age, far better than that of Anthony Copley, whose *A Fig for Fortune* was like nothing else for 82 years in either direction.

The New Poets of England and America edited by Hall-Pack-Simpson is a worthy collection of poets born between 1917–1935 (D. Justice b. 1925). I think it is about as good as my collection *Fifteen Modern American Poets* (born between 1904–1921). Theirs includes fewer poems by more poets, mine more poetry by each of those represented; we both include about the same proportion who are disgracefully inferior to

some others omitted. Reading through the two collections I
am struck with the greater diversity of voices of the older generation and the greater elegance of the younger, and observe
that Mr. Justice shares with other poets in *The New Poets* a
considerable accomplishment in and concern for craftsmanship. This observation does not imply that he is a lesser poet
for this but that several are excellently competent. (The editors' self-evaluation cannot be said to err on the side of modesty; they apportioned themselves seven pages apiece and Mr.
Justice three.) W. D. Snodgrass has disparaged some of his own
earlier verse by calling it "committee poetry"—it could have
been put together by some clever teacher-critic-poets. All
right. Maybe Mr. Snodgrass didn't get the best possible committee to write his earlier poetry, but one shouldn't be too
hard on committees as such. Who was it that put together the
Authorized Version of the Bible? My own view is that the
level of competence as well as the quantity of good poetry
nowadays is marvelously high. Why not rejoice in the plenty
at hand rather than bemoan our lack of a Yeats? (It's worth
pointing out by the way that the overwhelming bulk of the
poetry Yeats published before he was forty was put together
by a committee of *fin de siècle* Irish esthetes beside whom Mr.
Snodgrass's midcentury American English-teachers don't look
so bad.)

The charge that Mr. Justice is derivative can be supported
only by a reader with a tin ear. To be sure, one can find Yeats,
Auden, Eliot, and Ransom in his poetry—also "This Little
Pig Went to Market." Most of the craft of poetry is taking in
techniques, rhythms, tones of other poets and making them
one's own. To hear Mr. Justice's poetry as artful pastiche of
others is not to catch his voice. That he has a voice of his own
seems to me clear, but that one can easily not catch it is unfortunate but true. I would like to help you listen to him.

II

On the Death of Friends in Childhood

We shall not ever meet them bearded in heaven,
Nor sunning themselves among the bald of hell;
If anywhere, in the deserted schoolyard at twilight,
Forming a ring, perhaps, or joining hands
In games whose very names we have forgotten.
Come, memory, let us seek them there in the shadows.

To have come upon that poem for the first time on page 153 of Yeats's *Collected Poems,* on the page following "A Deep-Sworn Vow" (instead of "To a Squirrel at Kyle-na-no"), would have been in no way surprising and in every way pleasing. It says something worth saying and is readily comprehensible, and it is formally impeccable. It would stand up to a brooksandwarren analysis but does not need or invite one. Now the tone, not peculiar to Mr. Justice, is quiet, elegiac, and intelligent. When one isolates the poem like this or puts it in an anthology of fellow poems, one discovers that, like most good poetry in English though not like the very best, the voice in which the verse is spoken is less the poet's than one of the voices of his age. But when one reads it along with others in *The Summer Anniversaries,* one discovers that its voice is also Mr. Justice's. The tone is so unobtrusive and so traditional that a reviewer who hankers after verses that will rattle his back teeth at a first reading could dismiss it as formalistic, academic.

Such a dismissal is made the easier since some of the poems in the book are fairly insubstantial. Maybe the reviewer tried digging into "Speaking of Islands" and found it not too rewarding. Though I quite enjoy the poem I do not think the poet really meant what he says in it, and I have little inclination to go back to it. In such a one as "Sonnet About P.," however, he is free from meaning anything too troublesome

so that he achieves with it an elegance as great as the cold
beauty of the woman he writes about.

> A woman I knew had seemed most beautiful
> For being cold and difficult of access.
> My friend I saw, the cleverest man of us,
> But for a word from her to make him whole,
> Himself fall speechless, like a boy at school,
> And others also, followers of the chase,
> Look up or down but not into that face,
> Owing to the perfection of the skull.
> I knew this lady a dozen years ago.
> Since, that she has to two or three been kind,
> After long siege, and these not of her sort,
> And that she has both given and taken hurt,
> Hearing all this, and more, I call to mind
> That high, improbable bosom, which was snow.

Another reason why Mr. Justice's voice is not readily
heard is that his attitude towards such personal subjects as
family trouble is most unfashionable at the moment. Secret
misery is the nightsoil of literature without which its plants
are not so likely to bring forth splendid fruit. Six or seven years
ago Mr. Snodgrass began writing poems in which he nakedly
exposed his most private troubles to the reader's view; the
time was ripe for it, and his poems were so good, that a whole
style of confessional poetry has sprung into eminence. (To my
mind no one but Mr. Snodgrass has yet written true poetry
of that kind. How he avoids sensationalism or exhibitionism
and achieves universality is a mystery to me; my hunch is that
it is not so much his ruthless honesty—Anne Sexton is honest too and yet more ruthless—as his formal elegance. He too
is a superb cabinetmaker.) Now Mr. Justice is old-fashioned:
like his silver master, John Crowe Ransom, the closer he gets
to such matters the more he protects his readers—to the

resentment of many—from the unpleasant subject with irony, archaisms, formality. Here are the third and the last stanzas of "Tales from a Family Album."

> I had an uncle, long of arm and hairy,
> Who seldom spoke in any lady's hearing
> Lest that his tongue should light on aught unseemly,
> Yet he could treat most kindly with us children
> Touching that beast, wholly imaginary,
> Which, hunting once, his hounds had got the wind of.
> And even of this present generation
> There is a cousin of no great removal
> On whom the mark is printed of a forepaw.
>
> There was a kinsman took up pen and paper
> To write our history, whereat he perished,
> Calling for water and the holy wafer,
> Who had, ere that, resisted much persuasion.
> I pray your mercy on a leaf so shaken,
> And mercy likewise on these other fallen,
> Torn from the berry-tree in heaven's fashion,
> That there was somewhat in their way of going
> Put doom upon my tongue and bade me utter.

As for which of these two ways of dealing with private trouble is the better, I think the traditional, the Justice method is wiser for most but that the Snodgrass method is far far superior—for Snodgrass.

We do not like to have the terror let in on us, and the very elegance of a poem can protect a reader from allowing the terror to blow through it onto him—especially if he is reading with one eye or if the poem is glossily set. In *The New Yorker*, embedded in a Lillian Ross snicker-job, en face to a Soglow cartoon, even "anyone lived in a pretty how town" would look tidy and "Sailing to Byzantium" pretty. In those

pages "Love's Stratagems" was safe, but if you will read it two
or three times here on these rougher pages, you may feel from
it a cold puff of pure terror.

> But these maneuverings to avoid
> The touching of hands,
> These shifts to keep the eyes employed
> On objects more or less neutral
> (As honor, for the time being, commands)
> Will hardly prevent their downfall.
>
> Stronger medicines are needed.
> Already they find
> None of their stratagems have succeeded,
> Nor would have, no,
> Not had their eyes been stricken blind,
> Hands cut off at the elbow.

What is Mr. Justice's terror about? First and most, The
Terror itself is finally about nothing. Immediately, the main
pipe through which Mr. Justice's terror blows is presented in
the last lines of "Counting the Mad."

> This one thought himself a bird,
> This one a dog,
> And this one thought himself a man,
> An ordinary man,
> And cried and cried No No No No
> All day long.

"To Satan in Heaven" is about this too.

> Forgive, Satan, virtue's pedants, all such
> As have broken our habits, or had none,
> The keepers of promises, prize-winners,
> Meek as leaves in the wind's circus, evenings . . .

We whose virtue has been to break our bad habits pray to Satan to have mercy on us because "we have affirmed thee openly" and have "Reduced thee to our own scope and purpose" in a thousand familiar ways. The poem is nearly superb, but finally in the depths of its irony, it turns slippery, eludes the grasp.

"Here in Katmandu" is one of half a dozen that have everything. I beg you to read it more than once.

> We have climbed the mountain,
> There's nothing more to do.
> It is terrible to come down
> To the valley
> Where, amidst many flowers,
> One thinks of snow,
>
> As, formerly, amidst snow,
> Climbing the mountain,
> One thought of flowers,
> Tremulous, ruddy with dew,
> In the valley.
> One caught their scent coming down.
>
> It is difficult to adjust, once down,
> To the absence of snow.
> Clear days, from the valley,
> One looks up at the mountain.
> What else is there to do?
> Prayerwheels, flowers!
>
> Let the flowers
> Fade, the prayerwheels run down.
> What have these to do
> With us who have stood atop the snow
> Atop the mountain,
> Flags seen from the valley?

It might be possible to live in the valley,
To bury oneself among flowers,
If one could forget the mountain,
How, setting out before dawn,
Blinded with snow,
One knew what to do.

Meanwhile it is not easy here in Katmandu,
Especially when to the valley
That wind which means snow
Elsewhere, but here means flowers,
Comes down,
As soon it must, from the mountain.

Night Light (1967)

Untitled Review
Robert Pawlowski

Whenever Donald Justice's poetry is mentioned, many people who should know something about poetry say, "Justice? Oh yes; a good technician but terribly limited." The tone of their comments more often than not suggests that technical skill is something to be avoided by poets or, at best, hardly necessary to the writing of good poetry. Just as peculiar is the kind of answer they give if pressed for explanations of "limited." It turns out that they don't mean range of subject, for they agree Justice has a wide range of subject; they don't mean acuity— "extremely perceptive and intelligent," they say of Justice. Do they mean then he is sensitive to a fault? Perhaps too delicate or too quiet? No, they do not mean that because such judgments are often only a matter of taste. Do they mean he lacks the huffings and puffings of James Dickey, the pitying self-indulgence of Anne Sexton, the rhetorical *weltschmerz* of Robert Lowell, the density of John Berryman, or . . . , and the conversation usually breaks off.

Possibly the above situation reflects the problem of an evaluative age wherein we demand categorical greatness for our own conveniences, or perhaps of an age which has simply forgotten how to read poetry and respond to it in terms of the art it is. Which ever the instance, it is necessary only to remember that poetry is art. As art it must concern itself with the precisions of its forms and instruments and with the feelings and

Robert Pawlowski. Untitled Review. *Denver Quarterly* 2, no. 2 (summer 1967): 175–77.

insights of its writers. These concerns demand ultimately that the artist exercise a ruthlessly responsible and self-conscious command of them. Thus it is in these terms that one must speak of poetry, rather than in terms of themes, visions, stances, etc. And it is not that the latter are unimportant but that such things can be assumed in any good poet's work.

Donald Justice is, I think, a good poet who is as interested in life, death, hate, love, fun, and sorrow as anyone; however, I think he is more interested in how these matters receive their expression than many other poets are. For instance his "For the Suicides of 1962" is a difficult enough poem under any circumstances. Such a poem invites sentimental and hysterical gore, but Justice is able to construct a terrifying statement of possibilities within the framework of an ironically graceful seven syllable line. Note its beginning, for instance.

> If we recall your voices
> As softer now, it's only
> That they must have drifted back

Counterpointing the conditional "if" with "it's only" goes a long way toward establishing the tensions that are the shaping force of the poem. Another example of this tension comes with the use of the intentionally flat statement.

> What you meant to prove you have
> Proved: we did not care for you
> Nearly enough. . . .

Breaking the lines and then picking them up with "Proved" and "Nearly enough" surprise and jar the flatness into a highly dramatic and urgent statement. It is unfortunate that space is limited here because the poem deserves a full reading, but the closing section and its metaphor must be seen.

> When the last door had been closed,
> You watched, inwardly raging,
> For the first glimpse of your selves
> Approaching, jangling their keys.

> Musicians of the black keys,
> At last you compose yourselves.
> We hear the music raging
> Under the lids we have closed.

And so the book goes, excellence after excellence. "Last Days of Prospero," "The Man Closing Up," and "Anonymous Drawing" are especially fine—for instance the latter's incise and precise "A delicate young Negro stands / With the reins of a horse clutched loosely in his hands;" until his Lord comes ". . . mopping his brow/ Clear of the sweat of the fine Renaissance morning, . . ." Justice here, incidentally, takes the risk of using the couplet in a serious poem and succeeds admirably.

Also in this volume are two of the funniest poems of recent years—"Orpheus Opens His Morning Mail" and "Narcissus at Home." The latter begins

> Alone at last! But I am forgetting myself . . .
>
> To that other—to him I imagine crouched on the far side
>   of the glass . . . to him, indeed, it might appear that
>   I was alone.
>
> But you and I, my dear, know better.

Included as well is "To the Hawks," a moving anti-war poem which, thank heavens, does not depend on napalm imagery and venomous invective for its effects. Some parts of it follow.

> Farewell is the bell
> Beginning to ring.
>
> The children singing
> Do not yet hear it.
>
> The sun is shining
> In their song. . . .

■ ■ ■

Their eyes seem caught in
The act of shutting.

The young schoolteacher,
Waving one arm in

Time to the music,
Is waving farewell.

This is a book to be grateful for.

From Poetry Chronicle
William H. Pritchard

By contrast, Donald Justice's second volume is almost wholly about literature, often not very exciting literature. "How fashionably sad my early poems are" begins one, supposedly later, poem. But the epithet would do just as well for the present collection. Even "To the Hawks," dedicated to McNamara, Rusk and Bundy, ends up sounding sad and beautiful: "The young schoolteacher, / Waving one arm in / Time to the music, / Is waving farewell. / Her mouth is open / To sound the alarm. / The mouth of the world / Grows round with the sound." Or there is the wondering regret, or archly-wondering regret, or mock-arch-regret (what is it anyway?) on which so many of the poems turn: in "Party" "the little band of initiates / Stand about in their circle / Attempting the ancient modes / Lord Bacchus himself must have invented. / If so far they have failed / To summon up any but the / Familiar demons of a banal whimsy. . . ." What I want to know is, was Donald Justice there? Did he help out? Or was he busy writing a poem? The best line in the book is an epigraph from John D. MacDonald, "One of those men who can be a car salesman or a tourist from Syracuse or a hired assassin." Mr. Justice takes the good edge off the remark and weaves it into a fashionably sad poem: "My name is all names and none. / I am the used-car salesman, / The tourist from Syracuse, / The hired assassin, waiting." No, that was not what MacDonald meant at all.

William H. Pritchard. "Poetry Chronicle." *Hudson Review* 20, no. 2 (summer 1967): 309–10.

From Five Poets
Joel O. Conarroe

Donald Justice is also a keen self-critic. In "Early Poems" he comments on the fashionable sadness of his early work, and on its technical tediousness: "The rhymes, the meters, how they paralyze." (It is characteristic of Justice's self-irony that in this poem, lamenting the absence of daring, he employs an almost computer-like regularity.) The poems in *Night Light* still give evidence of some technical timidity, but on the whole they are not so tame, not so manicured, as those in *The Summer Anniversaries*. There is still a good deal of sadness in this collection, but it is not merely a la mode.

Justice brings a controlled, urbane intensity to his Chekhovian descriptions of loss and of the unlived life, of the solitary, empty, "sad" world of those who receive no mail, have no urgent hungers—who, in short, lead their lives but do not own them. Both the title of the book and the cover photograph (a garishly neoned *Diner*, with an empty phone booth outside, probably in some drab little town where everyone is dreamlessly asleep) signal the boredom and emptiness that permeate the work. It comes as no surprise that one of the poems, toward the end, is called "At a Rehearsal of 'Uncle Vanya.'" Its final lines summarize the book's main theme: "We sit here, doctor / In the crows' shadow."

In "American Sketches: For WCW" Justice invokes another M.D. laureate of the daily spectacle. Both his lean free verse and his elevation of the commonplace suggest Williams's marvelous domestic portraits. But as important as Williams has obviously been in shaping Justice's craft, the

Joel O. Conarroe. "Five Poets." *Shenandoah* 18, no. 4 (summer 1967): 87–88.

images that most often seem to lurk at the edge of his poems are those of lonely men in shirt sleeves, smoking in empty windows, or of hands raising dingy shades in furnished rooms. It is to Justice's credit that he has learned from both Williams and Eliot without being dominated by either. His unique voice is evident in a poem like "The Thin Man" which, among other things, reveals just how crafty he is:

> I indulge myself
> In rich refusals.
> Nothing suffices.
>
> I hone myself to
> This edge. Asleep, I
> Am a horizon.

Other poems in the book that particularly strike me—because of their technical excellence and unpretentious insights—include "The Missing Person," "The Tourist from Syracuse," "Bus Stop," and "To Waken a Small Person." The latter, apparently the cousin of Williams's "To Waken an Old Lady," is particularly eloquent, i.e., "Wake up please open yourself / Like a little umbrella." (In "Bus Stop" the umbrella becomes the tenor of the metaphor: "Umbrellas out: / Black flowers, black flowers.")

The book, which contains virtually no love poetry, opens with lines spoken by Orpheus and ends with a soliloquy by Narcissus. This is as it should be, since, among other things, *Night Light* reveals a man searching in a mirror for some clue to the song of himself. Given such a gifted guide, it is a search the reader is glad to share.

While Justice's lucid poems are all fairly accessible on one or two careful readings (though additional readings do reveal further riches) the more unconventional work in George Oppen's *This in Which.* . . .

Justice

James McMichael

Donald Justice's *Night Light* is a book of few mistakes. The same might be said of less ambitious books, for the technical control exhibited in each of its poems is not all the product of a sensibility that is clinically detached from the subject matter. Justice is tightly in charge of everything that goes on within his poems, so much so that very few of them are not almost totally accessible after careful reading. Their accessibility is a corollary of Justice's seemingly unperturbed command of his materials. But the poems are clearly not those of a man who, in order to insure such command, has separated himself from subjects that might elicit intense personal involvement. They are not calm poems. Their control and quality are the more remarkable for that fact.

The book consists of a prologue and epilogue, and three internal sections of poems. Those of the first section are generally definitions of one or another kind of personal isolation. That this isolation is never specifically the poet's own suggests that his response to his subjects may have something of the clinical in it.

> Why will they never speak,
> The old ones, the grandfathers?
> Always you find them sitting
> On ruined porches, deep
> In the back country, at dusk,
> Hawking and spitting.
>
> (from "The Grandfathers")

James [misprinted "Jane"] McMichael. "Justice." *North American Review* 252, no. 6 [n.s. 4, no. 6] (November 1967): 39–40.

The universal and impersonal "you" implies that the grandfathers are collectively isolated as much from the concerns of the poet as from those of everyone else. He is enough concerned with them to be able to define their condition with precision, and with some thoroughness, and not unmovingly. And yet we may be prompted to ask how much of him is with them there on the ruined porches.

But it is only when "The Grandfathers" and several other poems in the first section are considered separately from the rest of the poems in the book that they can be read more as descriptive exercises than as what they more energetically are: analogies for the poet's own terrors. For example, the last stanza of "To the Authoress of a Hatbox of Old Letters Recently Sold at Auction" describes the aging of the authoress in terms of the irreversible changes that she sees in the neighborhood of the house within which she has become something of a self-exile.

> The many-storied houses went
> Or in deep, cataracted eyes
> Displayed their signs of want: FOR RENT
> And MADAM ROXIE WILL ADVISE.

There is about the title, other details in the poem, and the quietly ironic incongruity of the last line a suggestion that the poet is interested less in the plight of the woman as she moved toward and into death than in the people and objects surrounding her in her last years. But were the latter his exclusive interest, his control would be no sharper and we would know less about the central subject toward which all the poems in *Night Light* contribute: the imminence of insanity. Outside the self, outside the interior security that is represented throughout the book by the house and its porches, there are perpetual threats. And Justice defines them as being threats no less for an authoress, a "Girl Sitting Alone at Party," grandfathers, and "Men at Forty" than for himself.

Once we have read "The Man Closing Up," which appears in the central section of the book, we are able to recognize more clearly that there is indeed much of the poet himself there on the porch with the grandfathers whom he has described so precisely. Isolate, like them, he struggles against the forces, things, and people that threaten in unspecified ways to annihilate his identity.

> There was no storm coming
> That he could see.
>
> There was no one out walking
> At that hour.
>
> Still,
> He closes the windows
> And tries the doors.
>
> He knows about storms
> And about people
>
> And about hours
> Like that one.

And so the threat is not wholly from without. The man closing up does not want to close up, but what he knows insists on intruding between his will and his fear.

> He would make his bed with white sheets
> And disappear into the white,
>
> Like a man diving,
> If he could be certain
>
> That the light
> Would not keep him awake,
>
> The light that reaches
> To the bottom.

The rhetoric of the diction and syntax is a special kind of understatement, special in that it is even simpler than what is usually described as understatement. Its simplicity is perfectly appropriate to the terror it is designed to elicit: for nothing is simpler than closing up—whether it be this side of death, or exactly on the other.

The Poems of Donald Justice

William Hunt

The poems in Donald Justice's new book dwell on the exhaustion that follows various passions. To use words at all a writer must exert force and this exertion precludes the representation of exhaustion directly. And indeed Mr. Justice's poems approach their centers circuitously.

The strength of the poems lies in the variegated passageways that Mr. Justice invents to reach his impasse. He does not repeat himself in his approach and the individual poems have an anecdotal interest, although the truncated and elliptic manner in which they are related embodies the exhaustion.

Night Light is a book of sad poems. But there is also present a mystery which accepts an existence beyond exhaustion. I have not the exact word available, but what I wish to indicate is that an experience has been judged and found unencompassing. Failed illumination brings ghosts. The ghosts presented here, however, are not remarked as a failure to spot every inevitability. They are utilized as restraints and boundaries. A threat exists. The poet takes the ghosts for granted as a point beyond which no one steps wisely.

But ghosts are ambiguous. They are both familiar and alien. Concerning the many ghosts in this collection the reader may judge whether they are bogey-men or the real fleshless and bloodless thing.

There is no summation of our life we can pin down. At best we are like the storm-hollowed tree the T'ang poet Han Yü describes. It is a tree that "does not care yet to be only the void at its heart." The poems in *Night Light* labor under the apprehension that once upon a time there was a possibility to

---

William Hunt. "The Poems of Donald Justice." *Poetry* 112, no. 4 (July 1968): 272–73.

get it all down on paper, for all time in one poem, but no longer.

The fault seems to lie in an academic dichotomy. Mr. Justice's poems are eloquent replies in a classical mode to the all-or-nothing element in romanticism. The best poems in the book are closest to this anachronistic struggle. They are those where the poet merges at the borders of perception with the ghosts, as in the third section of "The Man Closing Up"

> He would make his bed,
> If he could sleep on it.
>
> He would make his bed with white sheets
> And disappear into the white,
>
> Like a man diving,
> If he could be certain
>
> That the light
> Would not keep him awake,
>
> The light that reaches
> To the bottom.

This poem has two more sections and at its end a lighthouse keeper is introduced who ascends in the head of the protagonist. The keeper

> . . . wants to keep the light going,
> If he can.
>
> But the man closing up
> Does not say the word.

Night Light's last poem "Narcissus at Home" begins "Alone at last! But I am forgetting myself. . . ." It succeeds in carrying off this absurdity of self-revelation, but the initial line suggests that much of a poet's ability to please lies in the present moment unencumbered by previous decisions. Finally, a poem is also about a new experience, that of the poem itself.

Departures (1974)

From Poetry by the Yard?

Anonymous
[Irvin Ehrenpreis]

The giant race of American poets between the two world wars agreed that the great, the permanent, subject of poetry is the ennobling transformation of common existence by the imagination. Their axiom was old enough, in a sense, for they believed also that wherever art rises beyond the motives of religion, politics and vanity, it accomplishes the great purpose. So when Virgil described one more woman succumbing to irresistible passion, he wrote, "Haeret lateri letalis harundo," in a concord of liquids and a modulation of vowels that pathetically sweetened the pain of the victim while revealing the poet's compassion.

Poems draw our attention to minute effects of language. In them we discover connexions of syntax to meaning that invite a second and third review. Truth, wisdom, drama become deeper, stronger, more genuine than ordinary speech can make them. They come to seem embedded in our expression and not contrived by another mind. The poems we like best, we learn by heart. Among recent books Donald Justice's reflects a familiarity with such standards and an acceptance of them.

But few American poets now agree with him. One reads most new poems for the sake of a documentary value that hardly depends on the way the words fit together. Mr. Justice writes:

Anonymous [Irvin Ehrenpreis]. "Poetry by the Yard?" *TLS* no. 3760 (March 29, 1974): 339–40.

> Though, as G. says,
> We American poets
> No longer love words,
> It is hard not to remember
> What we felt for
> Those that betrayed us,
> Those we betrayed.

Few recent poems call one back for a re-hearing, except as one looks twice at a painful street scene, or as one's ears strain to identify a half-audible voice. One would not think of memorizing them. Few of the poems even give one a signal when their end arrives. Most could equally well be cut in half or doubled in length, like some Abstract Expressionist paintings.

Often, the fundamental wish of the young (and middle-aged) poet is to rescue the irrational, to suggest that the worst things in life are reasoned, that any craziness is better than no craziness. As documents, then, the poems bear witness to the importance of certain raw feelings, or psychological processes, or indemonstrable moral principles. Often they document the author's claim to be a poet by charting the inner course of his creative tendency. Through introspection or through his response to emotional shocks, the poet serves as martyr in the old sense of giving testimony to the powers that can save us. One remembers the fury of the Psalmist inviting his audience to seize Babylonian babies and brain them against a rock. Experiences too ugly, too deep, too private for language must be the substance of this poetry. [. . .]

With less modulation of feeling, less melody and concentration than Mr. Justice, they [Kenneth Hanson and John Logan] accept similar responsibilities. They play agreeable hit-or-miss games with the rhythm and sound of their words. Their light repetitions outline their forms, convey small mockeries or evoke a modest pathos. [. . .]

Mr. Logan moves one most when he uses an organizing principle less openly employed by Mr. Justice: after assembling a variety of related objects and sensations, he gives them a significant order by suddenly turning our attention on himself as the examiner, and suggesting it is not just the common world he shows us but his own. [. . .]

Mr. Justice writes only about what he can ennoble through language. People who fascinate him are elegiacally evoked by a handful of quiet images, and made fascinating to us. The poet conveys these remarkably suggestive images through a select troupe of words varied and repeated in a sustained, low-keyed music. While sounding casual, the repetitions mark rhythmic patterns and bring out ambiguities that secretly reflect a central idea. In a still subtler motion the poet shifts from third person to second, or from apostrophizing an absent hearer to addressing himself. These shifts give one a sense of suddenly coming close to a beauty that had seemed far off.

To move us, images must be sharp, fresh, precise. To move us permanently, to be worth memorizing, they must not be narrowly bound in time or place. Listeners of many ages, many cities, must recognize them. Only a gifted poet can invent such images; if the large themes of love, heroism, and death are to be handled, only a profoundly gifted poet will discover images that are not second-hand. Mr. Justice has this power. In "An Elegy Is Preparing Itself," he tells us about a death in terms of the coffin, shroud, gravestone, and lament:

> There are pines that are tall enough
> Already. In the distance,
> The whining of saws; and needles,
> Silently slipping through the chosen cloth.
> The stone, then as now, unfelt,
> Perfectly weightless. And certain words,
> That will come together to mourn,
> Waiting, in their dark clothes, apart.

The ending supplies a welcome if unexpected peripety for this lyric, because it modestly produces the imagination of the speaker inventing these lines as a center of their design. Such heightenings by self-enclosure are characteristic of Mr. Justice;

but he varies them so quietly that one feels their effect without noticing them at work.

So in "A Letter" a patient dreams of the car accident that sent her to the hospital. Images and meanings pick up one another's burdens: trees seen through tears from a hospital window become wet trees in a park where the patient was hit by a car. The invalid, a beautiful, highly-strung, over-sexed woman, dreams of cars; and they become a motorcade for the funeral of the sort of celebrity she has had affairs with. (Will she have any more?) Word anticipates and matches word, image softens into image, until the whole poem seems an unalterable pattern of hidden processes, mysterious but not opaque, sad yet celebratory:

> You would expose your wounds, pull down your blouse,
> Unbosom yourself wholly to the young doctor
> Who has the power to sign prescriptions, passes,
> Who seems to like you . . . And so to pass
> Into the city once again, one of us,
>
> Hurrying by the damp trees of a park
> Towards the familiar intersection where
> A traffic signal warns you not to cross,
> To wait, just as before, alone—but suddenly
> Ten years older, tamed now, less mad, less beautiful.

As one reads back and forth through a poem by Mr. Justice, hidden cross-references emerge from the echoing phrases, variant images, sober puns. The poem closes gently but audibly; and as it does, one wishes to repeat it. Among those that keep calling one back are "Portrait with Flashlight," "Self-Portrait as Still Life," "Lethargy," "Luxury," "The Telephone Number of the Muse," "The Assassination," "Sonatina in Green," and "Sonatina in Yellow."

From New Work from Three Poets
Richard Howard

We live in the past because there is nothing else to live in; our relation to the present is asymptotical—we are forever approaching a point, a moment, a limit which we recognize as what gives us life, yet we can make nothing of it, do nothing with it, until it is out of our hands, literally out of our senses. Asymptotes are what fail to fall together (as *symptoms* do), and it is interesting, in considering Donald Justice's later poetry, to notice that the Greek verb for falling is akin to the Greek verb for flying: here is a poet who perpetuates his powers by taking leave of them, "patient," as he says, "And, if anything, somewhat reluctant to continue." Even the epigraph of the wonderfully titled *Departures* sounds the tonality—calculated, wounded, gorgeous in that it is full of gorges, lapses, holes—which we will hear in the last line of the book, consistent from the "still slowly diminishing echo" to "Everything going away in the night again and again."

If everything goes away *again and again*, there must be a time when it comes back—and that is the present, the difficult Now to which Justice keeps making an asymptote, a reconnaissance. His preoccupation is, in every sense, with *tense*, as when he so characteristically observes: "The typewriter will be glad to have become the poem"—the future and the past conjugated in order to reach the Present, Justice's Muse, a goddess to be worshipped in absentia, "the more beautiful, and especially when suppressed." As we remember from *Night Light*, suppression is a significant way of making room for possibility in this poet's work, though of course it

Richard Howard. "New Work from Three Poets." *North American Review* 259, no. 1 [n.s. 11, no. 1] (spring 1974): 79.

is the possibility of farewells that is thus lodged in the language. "You have begun to vanish . . . ," and again, "our cries / Diminish behind us"—all of these stabs at what Justice calls "the promised absence" are so many "Furtive illuminations" of his theme, which is given in one of his most striking titles, "An Elegy Is Preparing Itself," *i.e.*, I am alive.

Life's best means of articulating an advance upon the present is that peculiarly native construction, the gerundive phrase, the ultimate asymptote: "my place in line *is evaporating*," Justice observes drily, or again, apostrophizing a star, "That fade and *are fading*, / But never entirely fading . . ." In these poems, for all their exactitude and their exactions (Justice is not easy— he is determined about his asymptote: "the address if not the destination"), nothing is either here and now, or everything is there and then. The utterance is suffused, is soaked with process, unable to initiate being, and unable to call a halt ("Is that a scar, or a birthmark?", the 19th question suggests Justice's uncertainty about beginnings and ends). These poems—odes, by title, elegies, fragments, questions, white notes, notebooks, riddles, variations, homages—are "shaken with premonitions / Of a time when they will have begun to stop," and indeed such shaking affords them their rhythm, their breath, their aspiration to movement. Death is "still to be escaped from," even as one of Justice's heroines feels life "closing about her now": here is a delicate dialectic between calligraphy ("most beautiful in its erasures") and cancellation ("eventual flame, / Some final smoke"), where the usual signs attached to remembering and forgetting are reversed: in Justice's poetry now, the positive value is not attached to what is "already falling away, / Already in memory," but rather to what is not yet experience, "A poem in hiding / . . . the unfolding page": it is the "absent flowers abounding" he cultivates, for the actual ones are erased by words, by recall . . . The last two poems in the book, "Absences" and "Presences" trade places with each other over and over again, and we never know, in these "bleached mirrors," where we stand. It is not indeed a matter of standing, of *instances,* that Donald Justice affords us, but a manner of *ecstasy,* the lunge for the present, the ablation of ontology, the denial of likeness, for as the master whom he so lovingly chides and so challengingly lionizes—as the greatest actuary of them all remarked, "identity is the vanishing-point of resemblance." There are many deprecations in this little book, many withdrawals and tergiversations, but what matters is material: some of the most assured, elegant and heartbreaking—not broken, but breaking—verse in our literature so far.

From The Importance of Being Ordinary

Jerome J. McGann

Donald Justice, on the other hand, is an aesthete in the mould of Rossetti. *Departures*, like his earlier books, is filled with Rossettian apparatus: mirrors, hypnagogic landscapes, poems about poetry and a life in art. The very opening poem seems almost to echo Rossetti's sonnet on the sonnet.

> Be the unfolding page,
>> white page, memorial to the absolute,
>> atlas of heights and depths, . . .

But different as Justice is from [Turner] Cassity, the two men share an ability to speak, and see, clearly. Justice by now knows his poetic self so well that he seems incapable of self-deception. Many of his best poems emerge as nostalgic interior landscapes—empty, silent, and moving to a slow-motion clock. But, again like Rossetti, Justice recognizes that this is not an analytic but an erotic and performative personality. His interior poems are not confessions, or acts of questing and discovery; they are abstract maps offered to the reader, who is placed, momentarily, in a landscape of such purity and stillness that he is forcibly returned to an awareness of the importance of primitive resources.

We see this clearly in a poem like "The Confession," whose subject is "intimate crime."

> You have escaped into smoke,
> Into the dark mouths of tunnels.

Jerome J. McGann. "The Importance of Being Ordinary." *Poetry* 125, no. 1 (October 1974): 45–46.

> Once in the streets you were safe,
>
> You were one among many.

Like Cassity, Justice is too busy attending to the needs of his audience and his subjects ever to get preoccupied with himself. So many times he could have fallen out of his abstraction into self-consciousness; but he almost never does, and the result is a series of splendid labyrinths.

In this place one is continually "shaken with premonitions." As Justice says in his wonderful "Poem": "You neither can nor should understand what it means . . . And there is nothing in it to comfort you." The poem speaks like the voice of conscience. It has the clarity and crypticness of death.

> This poem is not addressed to you.
>
> You may come into it briefly,
>
> But no one will find you here, no one.
>
> You will have changed before the poem will.
>
> Even while you sit there, unmovable,
>
> You have begun to vanish. And it does not matter.
>
> The poem will go on without you.
>
> It has the spurious glamor of certain voids.

"They torture you for secrets. / And you give them poems": this is the silence of the Sphinx, the analyst's reticence, the priest's reserve. Indifference is the appearance of a poetry that is both practical and morally unnerving.

Donald Justice has a symbolist's awareness of his audience. Shirley Kaufman, on the other hand, has a Romantic's awareness of her self. [. . .] Where Justice's landscape would be abstract and vaguely disturbing, Kaufman's is personal, concrete, and a pledge of some final good-will despite all the tales of loss. [. . .]

From Boysenberry Sherbet

Irvin Ehrenpreis

Donald Justice has some kinship with [John] Ashbery. The master to whom both seem deeply related is Wallace Stevens. But there is a difference between the author of "Peter Quince at the Clavier" and the one whom Jarrell named "G. E. Moore at the spinet." Justice recalls the music, elegance, and passion of Stevens, not his devotion to aesthetics. In Justice's latest book, certainly his best, the poet keeps his old attachment to the community of vulnerable creatures—lovers, children, the old, the weak. And he bestows on them the richness of sound and cadence, the depth of feeling and subtlety of language that he displayed in his earlier collections.

What draws him to such people is not their dependence but their openness to affection and fantasy, to strong emotions and wild thoughts. For Justice, the receptivity of the artist feeds both his creative imagination and his human sympathy, two aspects of one impulse. Conversely, what seems to matter most to him, in the labors of art, is the chance the imagination offers us to keep in touch with those who share our world but not our neighborhood: the dead, the remote, those imprisoned by their frailty or foolishness.

Justice has marvelous poems about the way the creative process goes: the need to be tough, violent, and fearful at the same time ("ABC"); the difficulty of the effort and the littleness of the reward ("Sonatina in Green"). One that exemplifies his power to charm us is "The Telephone Number of the Muse." Here the poet feels his talent is dwindling; his muse has turned to other, younger lovers:

Irvin Ehrenpreis. "Boysenberry Sherbet." *New York Review of Books* 22, no. 16 (October 16, 1975): 3–4.

> I call her up sometimes, long distance now.
> And she still knows my voice, but I can hear,
> Always beyond the music of her phonograph,
> The laughter of the young men with their keys.

The unfashionable refinement of the syntax, like the unfashionable purity of the language, is typical of Justice. Both these features are touching contrasts to his pathos when Justice gives in to the elegiac mood and turns to his central concern. This is with the class of people who sink in the trajectory of their wayward natures, who leave the tribe sooner than alter their own essence. I suppose that for him the poets belong to this class.

The circular patterns that Justice loves sound appropriate to the solitary character of such people, turned back on themselves, shut in willingly or unwillingly, caught in irreversible cycles. No wonder he finds so much occupation for mirrors, guitars, pianos, repetitions of words and syllables. Such images and devices, such iterative and musical designs, suit the meditations and recapitulations of the solitary life.

The dead belong here, because our relation with them must be circular. They have prepared us for their place, and we have taken it. The hushed tone that marks Justice's voice mounts to reverence as he evokes his relation to his father in "Sonatina in Yellow." Here, the ambiguities, continuities, and repetitions move parallel to memory and forgetfulness, in a sequence impressively like a musical modulation. Love for the dead suggests love for the past, the poet's desire to keep with him the beauty and awfulness of the filiation that he will hand on in his turn; and the imagination then seems our one genuine weapon against mortality:

> The pages of the album,
> As they are turned, turn yellow; a word,
> Once spoken, obsolete,
> No longer what was meant. Say it.

> The meanings come, or come back later,
> Unobtrusive, taking their places.

Solitude falls into loneliness, isolation decays to imprisonment, repression gives way to murder, as Justice travels across
his land of self-enclosures. And we meet the neurotic in the
sanitarium, longing to get back to the way of life that sent her
there ("A Letter"), or the love-hungry poet (not Justice), reliv-
ing in his poems his love-hungry youth ("Portrait with
Flashlight"). Because he has the habit of understatement and
terseness in an era when overexpression is normal, Justice may
sound too reserved. But the intensity of vision that directs his
work will be evident to those who care to observe it, as when
the poet admits his complicity in the terrors he conveys:

> You have no name, intimate crime,
> Into which I might plunge my hand.
> Your knives have entered many pillows,
> But you leave nothing behind.
>   ("The Confession")

In making these new poems, Justice discarded some of
his old traits. He has given up regular meters for free verse.
He has enlarged his allotment of dreamlike images and veiled
meanings. But his ear and his sense of design are so reliable
that the poems remain seductive in sound and shape.

He has not reduced his most engaging feature, the mixture of gentleness with power. The confidence Justice has in
his own selfhood enables him to reach out to lives that would
unsettle a thinner character; and he can obey his admonition
in "ABC":

> Be the statue leaning out from the stone,
>   the stone also, torn between past and future,
>   and the hammer, whose strength we share.

"My Still to Be Escaped From": The Intentions of Invisible Forms

Greg Simon

His first book, *The Summer Anniversaries*, follows the steady progress of a moral sensibility from adolescence to full maturity. Friends, intellect, sex and death play before a decidedly Southern and familial landscape. The memorable poems are those with the most obvious and visible forms: blank verse, sonnet, sestina and villanelle. They are effective because even their forms are biographical, and the tyranny of their classical motion left Justice free to achieve the distances his emotional intentions required; free to explicate his immediate personal horizon gracefully and with dignity. *Summer Anniversaries* consists of perfectly flawless poems, moving as inexorably as glaciers toward beautiful comprehension and immersion in reality.

In *Departures*, his third book, Justice presents an entirely new kind of villanelle in which the emotion is so closely tied to the movement of the poem, that its formal intentions are invisible. This is "Pale Tepid Ode":

> Not with the vague smoke
> In the curtains,
> Not with the pigeons or doves
> Under the eaves,
> Nevertheless you are there, hidden,
> And again you wake me,
> Scentless, noiseless,
> Someone or something,

Greg Simon. "'My Still to Be Escaped From': The Intentions of Invisible Forms." *American Poetry Review* 5, no. 2 (March/April 1976): 30–31.

> Something or someone faithless,
> And that will not return.
>
> Undiscovered star,
> That fade and are fading,
> But never entirely fading,
> Fixed,
> And that will not return.
>
> Someone, someone or something,
> Colorless, formless,
> And that will not return.

"Pale Tepid Ode" is one of the most hypnotic and sustained chords that Justice has struck. Its intrinsic mystery and elegance, the allure it has far beyond that of his earlier poems, seems to let the material of this poem fill its form in its own way, however incomplete or wayward that may be. The new Justice poem is no longer a set piece or still life, forced into shape, but vigorous and rhythmical composition, prosody at the limit of its kinetic potential.

This remarkable new intention in Justice's work accounts for the fact that the forms of the best poems in *Departures* are invisible architecture. Many of the elements of this new style come together in "Cool Dark Ode," a poem that is, as Justice notes, "loosely modeled" on a section from a longer poem by Rafael Alberti. It will not be necessary to make any line by line comparison of the two poems. A brief glance at a few lines of both is enough to see that Justice has heightened the elements in Alberti's poem into a different order of resonance, and fitted them within a theme that reverberates with the other poems in a book dedicated to the failures of its victims, to the unexpected arrivals of the unknown, its refusal to satisfy us or identify itself, and the control it maintains without seeming to be in control:

> Night, night, O blackness of winter,
> I tell you this, you

> That used to come up as far as the frosted panes, the door,
>
> As far as the edges of our skin,
>
> Without any thought, I know now,
>
> Of entering those borrowed rooms,
>
> Or even our mouths, our eyes,
>
> Which all too often were carelessly left open for you.

Justice is trying to fit himself into the life of his poems without our knowing that he has been there; trying to receive them, but not tyrannize them, or fall helplessly under their spells. In "Cool Dark Ode," Justice addresses his nemesis and adversary with the cool indifference of a gambler who is sure of what he wants, but beautifully unsure of what he may get.

The poems in *Night Light*, Justice's second book, generally abandon the looping eloquence of *Summer Anniversaries* in favor of the instinctive and defensive reactions of a more cosmopolitan consciousness. These poems are strictly arranged into syllabic stanzas that serve as road maps for a country where every object is menacing. They were meant to strike deep into enemy territory and they were made as lean and as militant as guerrilla fighters.

The poems in *Departures* sprawl across the page as the carefully chiselled forms of his previous work were never permitted to do. As if to assure his reader that some order of composition prevails, however tenuous it might seem, Justice has appended a series of notes to *Departures* that reveal his newly acquired dedication to "chance methods" and to the writing of a few very fashionable French and Spanish poets. In these notes, Justice gives credit to these other writers for lines and images in almost half his poems. Such an admission by a poet lacking the formal credentials and previous accomplishments of Justice would be the only criticism the book would require.

Only "The Evening of the Mind," of all the poems in *Night Light*, prefigures the new line of investigation Justice was to adopt for *Departures*. From this point on we are to see "shadows moving down the page," "the aura, the coming on"; poems that delve into unmapped interiors where the demands of intimacy turn the poems in tighter and tighter circles, over the contours of the mind, and have nothing to do with limits posed by classical or syllabic concerns. Such a poem turned loose on itself, but dating in origin from the same years as *Night Light*, is "Fragment: To a Mirror":

> Behind that bland facade of yours,
>
> What drafts are moving down what intricate maze
>
> Of halls? What solitude of attics waits,
>
> Bleak, at the top of the still hidden stair?
>
> And are these windows yours that open out
>
> On such spectacular views?
>
> Those still bays yours, where small boats lie
>
> At anchor, abandoned by their crews?
>
> The parks nearby,
>
> Whose statues doze forever in the sun?
>
> Those stricken avenues,
>
> Along which great palms wither and droop down
>
> Their royal fronds,
>
> And the parade is drummed
>
> To a sudden, inexplicable halt?
>
> > Tell me,
>
> Is this the promised absence I foresee
>
> In you, when no breath any more shall stir
>
> The milky surface of the sleeping pond,
>
> And you shall have back your rest at last,
>
> Your half of nothingness?
>
> 1963–1972

For the first time, we find unanswered questions in a Justice poem, we find lines that stop and start in a faithful imitation of the temporal consciousness they mirror. The poem makes no promises. Its subject matter is nothingness and darkness; and we are led, when we think about this poem, to what the poem neither names nor commands. We confront the reticence of Justice, the obvious scarcity of lies in this book, the fact that Justice has produced fewer lines and fewer poems in twenty years than others, the Kuzmas, Tates and Bells, are able to publish in two. But reticence is an attitude toward writing that Justice has assumed with malice of forethought. We *have* every word that Nixon ever said . . . And Justice, the mystery writer, cables his new works from places that scent them with unfamiliar musk, with longing and invitation, and the desires of unrequited lives.

My own attitude toward *Departures*, based on what I understand of the new directions in Justice's work, is that this book contains too many poems. The core of the book is still the absolutely indispensable *Sixteen Poems* that Justice published in a limited edition in 1970. Few of the newer poems (the exceptions are "Fragment: To a Mirror," "A Letter," and the exquisite and sequential "Absences" and "Presences" which close the book) are equal or superior to his three odes, the five portraits, the poems based on chance, and the sequences that appeared in the little book. New poems suggesting the ironical aggressive positions of *Night Light* look unnatural among their affluent and exotic successors; the tragically fascinating women who wander in and out of "A Letter," "Portrait with Tequila," "Luxury," and the poem that perhaps serves as a measure of the depth of the entire collection, "On the Night of the Departure by Bus":

> Tell me if you were not happy in those days.
> You were not yet twenty-five,
> And you had not yet abandoned the guitar.
>
> I swore to you by your nakedness that you were a guitar,
> You swore to me by your nakedness that you were
>   a guitar,
> The moon swore to us both by your nakedness that you
>   had abandoned yourself completely.

Who would not go on living?

The typewriter will be glad to have become the poem,
The guitar to have been your body,
I to have had the luck to envy the sole of your shoe in the
dead of winter.

A passenger has lost his claim-check
The brunette her barrette,
And I—I think that there are moths eating holes in my
pockets,
That my place in line is evaporating,
That the moon is not the moon and the bus is not the bus.

What is the word for goodbye?

These women and their lovers are the captives of change ("my place in line is evaporating"), and that is the one condition that Justice explores and condones and follows through its asymmetrical maze in *Departures*. ("Some day you'll wake up / Back on that Christmas morning / In Mexico, still a virgin.") These are poems of lament, realized through the lives of those who have been tamed and addicted, whose defenses have already been pierced by the insidious devices of memory and time. ("Night is a giant cactus / Blooming at your window. / Potent, aromatic, / The liquors you press from it.") And that is why the clues to the movements of these poems reveal themselves in retrospect, in their unhurried but insistent return to the calm that precedes sadness and joy.

When poets have grown complete in whatever apprenticeship they may have chosen, and are ready to say what they must say: there are no visible forms that can hold them. This holds true all the way back to Milton, who wrote the first "free verse," and it is intoxicating to see Justice now unfettered by the forms that circumscribed and dictated the action in his early poems; and to see him working with sources that are not only energetic and new, but demanding in conception and daring in stance. Justice writes in "Warm Flesh-Colored Ode":

> . . . it is still possible to imagine
> That there are one or two hands
> Which do not know, or which do not yet know,
> Anything of either that face or the shadow
> Which does, after all, follow . . .

The epigraph† to *Sixteen Poems* (not reprinted in *Departures*) is from Lorca's "Llanto por Ignacio Sánchez Mejías":

> No one knows you. No. But you are the one I sing of.
> (No te conoce nadie. No. Pero yo te canto.)

---

† *text:* epigram

Departures:
The Poetry of Donald Justice

Joseph Di Prisco

For the last twenty years or so, while several other poets have acquired the major prizes and been honored (or broken) by national attention, Donald Justice, in comparative obscurity, has written the finest poems recently published in this country. His book, *Departures*, is an altogether brilliantly achieved book deserving of much wider critical interest and acclaim than so far has come its way.

Perhaps his obscurity is a function of the nature of his vision. The poems refuse to advertise themselves or their maker, and perhaps Justice's meticulous care, his absolute refusal to strike the fashionable pose, his unwillingness to work for the easy effect, his strong and quiet confidence— are ultimately accountable for his obscurity, but at the same time accountable for that alluring and suggestive quality which radiates within his work.

Over the course of Justice's three small and beautifully accomplished books (*The Summer Anniversaries* and *Night Light* before *Departures*) the gradual unfolding of his imagination has been taking place. And after the uncanny "Furtive illuminations" of his *Night Light* these newer poems constitute, in several senses, departures. His poems trace the echoes of remote stations of the dead; they are endlessly, painfully, elegiac. They form an exquisite, elegant, perfect, and moving farewell to everything and everyone—as it all fades away from consciousness.

Joseph Di Prisco. "Departures: The Poetry of Donald Justice." *San Francisco Review of Books* 2, nos. 3–4 (July/August 1976): 27–28.

And all that I saw was someone's hand, I think,

Thrown up out there like the hand of someone drowning,

But far away, too far to be sure what it was or meant.

["Presences"]

These are poems about departure in and from the world. Though sometimes humorous (see, for example, "The Telephone Number of the Muse," and "Portrait with Short Hair"), Justice is never vulgar, meretricious, or morbid. Mainly, he is obsessed by death and death's imaginings.

Donald Justice is dead. One Sunday the sun came out,

It shone on the bay, it shone on the white buildings,

The cars moved down the street slowly as always, so many,

Some with their headlights on in spite of the sun,

And after awhile the diggers with their shovels

Walked back to the graveside through the sunlight,

And one of them put his blade into the earth

To lift a few clods of dirt, the black marl of Miami,

And scattered the dirt, and spat,

Turning away abruptly, out of respect.

["Variations on a Text by Vallejo"]

The world, and all that can be said about it, calls up in Justice an elegy, as in "An Elegy Is Preparing Itself":

There are pines that are tall enough

Already. In the distance,

The whining of saws; and needles,

Silently slipping through the chosen cloth.

The stone, then as now, unfelt,

Perfectly weightless. And certain words,

That will come together to mourn,

Waiting, in their dark clothes, apart.

The poems are departures, too, from the earlier work, from the occasional Frenchified fastidiousness which slightly

mars his first book. This book significantly departs, also, from
the Williams line which extends in *Night Light*, and it offers a
serious, definitive criticism of Wallace Stevens in "Homage to
[the Memory of] Wallace Stevens." In this poem Justice passes
through a wonderful and exact imitation of the Stevensian
mode in Part I—"Hartford is cold today but no colder for your
absence"—to a final accommodation of that poet and his relationship to him:

> And there are heroes who falter but do not fall,
> Or fall without faltering and without fault,
> But you were not one of them. Nevertheless,
>
> The poet practicing his scales
> Thinks of you as his thumbs slip clumsily under and under,
> Avoiding the darker notes.

And, recalling Stevens's "Man on the Dump" Justice writes
with playful conviction:

> The *the* has become an *a*. The dictionary
> Closed at dusk, along with the zoo in the park.
> And the wings of the swans are folded now like the sheets
>   of a long letter.
> Who borrows your French words and postures now?

Justice does, but with a difference. What is finally left for him
is the *putting away* of instruments like the blue guitar. The poet
sums up with dignity, with serene and contemplative courage,
a world which is simply not surging with Romantic connec-
tions. "This poem is not addressed to you," he writes in
"Poem." "Not" is astonishingly prominent in his vocabulary.

Despite the frequent allusion to film and the stage (see "A
Dancer's Life"), Justice is a non-dramatic poet. His theatrical-
ity is private and self-performative, and his imagination is primarily verbal ("Is there some word for calyx in your tongue?"
he asks). One might be tempted to say that this is a poetry of

pure voice, of song, of voice which is transparent and song which is translucent—like the chandelier in motion in "ABC":

> "C"
> See how the fearful chandelier
>   trembles above you
>   each time you open your mouth
>   to sing. Sing.

All we know about the poem's voice is its capability of speech and song:

> The poem will go on without you.
> It has the spurious glamour of certain voids.
>
> It is not sad, really, only empty.
> Once perhaps it was sad, no one knows why.
>
>   ["Poem"]

This is the extreme of reticence, but it does not imply a withdrawal or a denial of responsibility. It's simply a matter of the right observation, which is only *apparently* minimal, because, really, Justice always permits himself the luxury of the rich and exact perception (as in "Luxury"). The seeming tonelessness and voicelessness, however, can narrate—almost beneath its breath—the complex history of a troubled woman, for example, in "A Letter." The surface is furiously calm, and the serenity of his approach allows the woman to come to life, in all of her suffering, as, growing older, she looks on the trees "wet with tears each morning when they wake you / Out of the sleep you never quite fall into." Without the slightest pull of the organ stops, and stopping just short of manipulating and indulging our feelings, Justice gives us a terribly moving understanding of her life:

>   And so to pass
> Into the city once again, one of us,

> Hurrying by the damp trees of a park
> Towards the familiar intersection where
> A traffic signal warns you not to cross,
> To wait, just as before, alone—but suddenly
> Ten years older, tamed now, less mad, less beautiful.

As he asks in another poem, "Behind that bland facade of yours, / What drafts are moving down what intricate maze / Of halls?" There is always *more* in Justice, always some *thing* at stake even as he speaks of his loss and his emptiness. Always there is the unfolding and deepening of confusion, the flickering of comprehension.

Perhaps the way to understand the problem of tone and voice in *Departures* is to recall the appeal of music throughout. It is a strange music of absolute tonality:

> Repeat it now, no one was listening.
> Repeat it, the air, the variations.
> So your hand moves, moving across the keys,
> And slowly the keys grow darker to the touch.
>
> ["Sonatina in Yellow"]

Donald Justice has perfect pitch: he can hear everything that is and everything that is not, and his poetry is the record of his listenings and yearnings to hear what is no longer singing and speaking and making the *white notes* of music. And here I have come to the end of this review without mentioning perhaps the greatest poem in the book, "The Assassination." Somehow it seems fitting to acknowledge my inability to say anything about it. These poems *are* departures, and the book takes one to a place one has long since forgotten leaving, and a place, upon re-entering, one cannot imagine staying in without the poetry of Donald Justice.

Selected Poems (1979)

From Two Hedgehogs and a Fox
Vernon Young

For the sake of the literary figure, Donald Justice is more hedgehog than fox but the image is actually ludicrous when applied to his poems; they don't bristle and they are hermetic in quite another way from [Richard] Hugo's, for instance, or I might say from Richard Wilbur's. I doubt if there are six poems in this selection which could be claimed for the public sensibility. But Justice has written a dozen lyrics I'd call virtually incomparable—of a kind rivaled only by W. S. Merwin or the early Merrill. And it's my sad duty to acknowledge that most were written fifteen or twenty years ago. Justice has lacked the gift for renewing himself poetically; however, the initial gift remains sufficiently impressive to inhibit critical reproaches.★

The first poem in this selection, from *The Summer Anniversaries* (1960), has long been a favorite of mine; with some incredulity and a degree of pique I have wondered why innumerable anthologists have passed it up. "Ladies by Their Windows" has three divisions, composed of nine six-line stanzas, all but one of which are unrhymed, and it's among the loveliest musical and purely evocative things I know in contemporary verse: it never descends to the explicit and is one of the last poems I should ever want to overhear an

---

★And to procure him the Pulitzer Prize for Poetry.

Vernon Young. "Two Hedgehogs and a Fox." *Parnassus* 8, no. 1 (fall/winter 1979): 234–37.

"explanation" of in a Creative Writing Class. Listen to the two opening stanzas:

> They lean upon their windows. It is late.
> Already it is twilight in the house;
> Autumn is in their eyes. Twilit, autumnal—
> Thus they regard themselves. What vanities!
> As if all nature were a looking glass
> To publish the small features of their ruin!
>
> Each evening at their windows they arrive
> As if in anticipation of farewells,
> Though they would be still lingering if they could,
> Weary, yet ever restless for the dance,
> Old Cinderellas, hearing midnight strike,
> The mouse-drawn coach impatient at the door.

Sustained at the same level of elegiac fancy, the beautiful cadences move on, in measured stanzaic waves, to their radiant and funereal climax.

> So ladies by their windows live and die.
> It is a question if they live or die,
> As in a stone-wrought frieze of beasts and birds
> The question is, whether they go or stay.
> It seems they stay, but rest is motion too,
> As these old mimicries of stone imply.

Keats, of course: the animating theme of the Grecian Urn sounds clearly in that chiming stanza and in the lines that immediately follow:

> Say, then, they go by staying, bird and beast,
> Still gathering momentum out of calm,
> Till even stillness seems too much of haste
> And haste too still. . . .

I offer the usual reviewer's apologies for not quoting the whole of a lengthy poem, at the same time hoping that readers will be moved by my fervor to rediscover this magnificent lyric.

After that, anything further is shadowed by anticlimax. There is not, for me, another poem by Justice that equals this one, although "Tales from a Family Album" is as deftly modulated (in nine-line stanzas with eleven-count lines) and as fraught with skilled echoes. Both in this volume and in *Night Light* of 1967 there are several poems that bear remarking for their pristine melancholy elegantly controlled, sometimes in sonnet or sestina form (the sestinas do not have conventional line lengths). Almost always, the conditions mirrored are those of loss, of the irrecoverable, of the transitive and the doomed. A short, formal but unrhymed poem, "On the Death of Friends in Childhood" is a succinct example of the tonal center to which many of these verses are keyed.

> We shall not ever meet them bearded in heaven,
> Nor sunning themselves among the bald of hell;
> If anywhere, in the deserted schoolyard at twilight,
> Forming a ring, perhaps, or joining hands
> In games whose very names we have forgotten.
> Come, memory, let us seek them there in the shadows.

"Ode to a Dressmaker's Dummy," "Last Days of Prospero," two exiguous poems suggested by Chekhov plays and one suggested by Guillevic, "Hands"—"And all that they grasp is air"—reveal the poet as inexorably, if wittily, dedicated to a kind of shadow-play experience in which he notes absence more sharply than presence, senses the pain of things but is more readily disposed to translate it into études than commit the vulgarity of expostulation.

With the *Departures* collection of 1973 there is a definitive thinning out, I would say, something akin to exhaustion (but *not* to imprecision of the word). The embracing title was a nod of recognition: *departure* is certainly the most prominent activity recorded, as in the poet's sardonic farewell to his Muse or, as it is centrally announced in a poem called "Presences":

> And all that I saw was someone's hand, I think,
> Thrown up out there like the hand of someone drowning,
> But far away, too far to be sure what it was or meant.

And Justice moves forward, at a stroll: announces themes for variations which are only half-executed or quickly fade; writes a poem that pertly excludes the reader; predicts his own death in the manner of Vallejo (I suspect this is a tongue-in-cheek adaptation); plays with visual motifs from Ingmar Bergman. Then, having failed to find a new source of integrated lyricism, he returns in quiet desperation to scenes from his childhood.

I call it desperation because Justice had already distilled the subject in earlier poems and had seemingly turned his attention, if obliquely, to the more complex world of culture and the faintly absurd. The predicament is fairly common among American poets when they begin to dry up. A European, at this stage, is never without history at his back to inspire or torment him. Few American poets can make much of history and they are seldom attached with any affection to the ongoing public life of the nation. Whereupon they start writing or rewriting odes to their grandfathers and their wives or their cousins and their sisters and their aunts—above all, to themselves, way back there in that swimming hole of innocence or terror. If I were to try deducing a cultural ethos from the practise of American poets I would conclude that for most Americans the only memorable thing that ever happened to them was being a child!

Since poetry is where you find it, one accepts the source. Among the Uncollected Poems at the end of this volume, undated, is at least one, "In the Attic" (p. 130), which is drily

reminiscent of the early, inventive Justice: the scrupulous
music, the Proustian consolation.

> There's a half hour towards dusk when flies,
> Trapped by the summer screens, expire
> Musically in the dust of sills;
> And ceilings slope toward remembrance.
>
> The same crimson afternoons expire
> Over the same few rooftops repeatedly;
> Only, being stored up for remembrance,
> They somehow escape the ordinary.
>
> Childhood is like that, repeatedly
> Lost in the very longueurs it redeems.
> One forgets how small and ordinary
> The world looked once by dusklight from above . . .
>
> But not the moment which redeems
> The drowsy arias of the flies—
> And the chin settles onto palms above
> Numbed elbows propped on rotting sills.*

---

*Pedantic note: each end-word of a line appears twice in the poem but
none is repeated within the same stanza.

From Anniversary Portraits

Charles Molesworth

In a rather grim comparison, Basil Bunting once said that a person working on his *Collected Poems* was like someone selecting planks for his coffin. A *Selected Poems* is, perhaps thankfully, less final—more like a 25th-anniversary portrait. Still, the occasion—and the object—can be daunting, and even perplexing. What some might see as proper formality might strike others as unnecessary stiffness. This difficulty is compounded in the case of Donald Justice, for his poetic sensibility can be seen as centered either in virtuous modesty or inescapable limitation. How you see Mr. Justice at this formal turning of his career depends a great deal on how urgently you feel about scale and subject in poetry.

Mr. Justice's first book, *The Summer Anniversaries* (1960), deals mostly with a poetry of small scale dooms and dim light. The opening poems present a group of frail women ("Autumn is in their eyes"), old men ("Unseeing and almost unseen, / Halting before the shops for breath,"), and the insane ("their / Impassivity masks an essentially lovable foolishness,"). His second book, *Night Light* (1967), continues the exploration of a dim or twilight perspective verging on total darkness. The other senses are equally choked back: We hear a "thin, skeletal music" and even though the "twilight sound / Of the crickets" is "immense," it fills the woods "Behind [the] mortgaged houses."

But with this second book Mr. Justice begins to deal more openly with what becomes a central, perhaps *the* dominant, theme in his work: The lack of an ennobling subject

Charles Molesworth. "Anniversary Portraits." *New York Times Book Review* (March 9, 1980): 8, 16.

brings about a poetry that deals with the reasons for *not* writing. In a startlingly self-conscious poem from *Night Light* called "Early Poems," we hear the poet say "How fashionably sad those early poems are!" But this poem concludes: "—Now the long silence. Now the beginning again." Here those who appreciate Mr. Justice will hear the tone of beleaguered honesty, an indomitable trust that is earned both through and with a clear-eyed humility. Others will hear a doomed, almost Pavlovian tenacity that is less to be applauded than simply endured. (Note that he says "beginning again," not beginning "anew" or "differently," so that we cannot expect much in the way of radical change.) In "The Evening of the Mind" we're told:

> The ether dream of five-years-old repeats, repeats,
> And you must wake again to your own blood
> And empty spaces in the throat.

Are those empty spaces possible sites for renewal, now that the obsessive dream has been cleared away, or are they never-to-be-filled absences, words unsayable in the waking world? And "wake again to your own blood" suggests that the American notion of autonomy and self-creation may be founded on delusion.

In his third volume, and in the uncollected poems from throughout his career now gathered together in this book, Mr. Justice continues to explore the problematic nature of his vocation. His voice often has the sound of the true "native strain," and as Richard Howard rightly observed, his early master was John Crowe Ransom. (One thinks especially of that Ransom poem that ends by describing the fingers as "Ten frozen parsnips hanging in the weather.") Sestinas and rondeaus appear less often than they did in the earlier volumes, but there remains a chaste quality to the prosody that sometime recalls W. S. Merwin. Here is a complete poem, "The Thin Man," from the second book:

> I indulge myself
> In rich refusals.
> Nothing suffices.
>
> I hone myself to
> This edge. Asleep, I
> Am a horizon.

Again, the minimalism here can be seen as an opening out to the richness and promise of that final word. And from the third book we have two stanzas from "Poem," where we can hear echoes not only of Merwin, but of Mark Strand,

> It is not sad, really, only empty.
> Once perhaps it was sad, no one knows why.
> It prefers to remember nothing.
> Nostalgias were peeled from it long ago.
>
> Your type of beauty has no place here.
> Night is the sky over this poem.
> It is too black for stars.
> And do not look for any illumination.

Mr. Justice is capable of wit, but it is often the wit of the defeated. In "The Telephone Number of the Muse," he tells us:

> I call her up sometimes, long distance now.
> And she still knows my voice, but I can hear,
> Beyond the music of her phonograph,
> The laughter of the young men with their keys.
>
> I have the number written down somewhere.

The self-deprecation here has many American precursors, from Edwin Arlington Robinson to Frank O'Hara's "I do this, I do that" poems, and the tone will continue to attract younger imitators. It is to this poet's credit that he doesn't

shrink from his own selection of scale. I can't help but wonder if he knows how fully cynical and deadening are the
implications of those sounds coming to us from "her phono-
graph." But if you are the sort of reader who occasionally suspects too much of poetry's grandeur is "pre-recorded," then
the whisper of Donald Justice may be music to your ears.

The Present Bought on the
Terms of the Past

William Logan

Every unhappy imagination is unhappy in its own way. Beneath the elegant expressions of Donald Justice's poetry lies a despair that, however disguised, infuses any act, however heartening. His poetry triumphs over modern desperation, becoming one of our acute imaginative voices, but in the process Justice becomes a modern turned inside out: confession is silenced, revelation masked, statement disavowed.

From his first book, *The Summer Anniversaries* (published in 1960 and perversely titled after a poem uncollected until now), Justice has stood outside his poems, beyond the scope of action. When his presence intervenes, he has suppressed his individuality, rendered experience as dream or drama, or performed in personae. Given this self-exclusion, the concerns of his first book are remarkably personal: memory, childhood, and the old familial drama. It is precisely in order to discuss the most personal subjects that Justice must set them at a distance. His early poems constitute a family album, but the family includes the mad, the weak, and the lost, lives past their meridian and beyond hope. To examine that decaying world, the world whose myths are the Fall and the curse on Atreus, he is willing to explore the polar regions of thought: madness and dream. "On a Painting by Patient B of the Independence State Hospital for the Insane":

> One sees their children playing with leopards, tamed
> At great cost, or perhaps it is only other children,
> For none of these objects is anything more than a spot,

William Logan. "The Present Bought on the Terms of the Past."
Crazyhorse 20 (spring 1980): 65–70.

> And perhaps there are not any children but only leopards
> Playing with leopards, and perhaps there are only the spots.

The bitter wit derives not just from frustration at madness, but from despair at interpreting any work of art. Similarly, the transfiguring dreamscape of "Sestina: A Dream" becomes analogous to the poetic act itself; that is, to the sestina which shapes experience. In both poems form revises the inadequate assumptions of a content-ridden self.

Such self-mastering through form could not, perhaps, be long sustained, and in his second book, *Night Light* (1967), the form begins to ravel in favor of content. A new course in art appreciation, contained in "Anonymous Drawing," formulates, as Richard Howard has noted, a crucial ars poetica. A petty lord has kept an artist waiting, and

> However fast he should come hurrying now
> Over this vast greensward, mopping his brow
> Clear of the sweat of the fine Renaissance morning, it
>   would be too late.
> The artist will have had his revenge for being made to wait,
> A revenge not only necessary but right and clever—
> Simply to leave him out of the scene forever.

To abolish himself from the landscape, to observe only what lies before him, the poet must keep the self, that petty lord, off the premises of the poem or so heavily disguise him that he is not easily identified. To this practice of self-effacement Justice has become devoted. Like doorways into and out of *Night Light*, "Orpheus Opens His Morning Mail" and "Narcissus at Home" introduced just those voices through which the poet could speak, that domestic reduction by which mythic figures are shrink-wrapped around the self. In this poetic of indirection, even poems seemingly most personal may derive from foreign originals or the operations of chance. Such games played to engage the imagination provide his forms; the self-effacement practiced to protect the imagination becomes his subject, strategy begetting substance. For other poets, poetry is the soul's flattering mirror; in Justice the self turns away from the mirror, renouncing self-observation only in order to write of it obsessively, leaving the mirror empty, and hence an obsessive symbol.

Like any repression, the drama from which the self is excluded provokes a symbolic reaction—the poet's chafing at the very boundaries he has created. His vengeance on drama, like his vengeance on form, is to transgress what has been announced as limitation, and so the title of *Departures* (1973), his maturest and most troubled book, signifies not merely stylistic leave-taking—poetry fragmented, poetry called into being by chance, poetry less and less formal—but also psychological rupture and separation. The movement of these poems is not line to line, but from inside to outside, from here to there. His first seven poems, as arranged in *Selected Poems*, concern a mirror, a group of inanimate objects, two vices, a dancer, a crime, an anonymous man, and an assassination. The eighth addresses twenty questions to an unknown entity ("Is there no word for calyx in your tongue?"). The ninth shrinks from its reader. A poetic world has been constructed outside the self, which no longer has intimacy with it.

Justice's recourse to emblems of solitude—music and mirrors—is no less significant than his attraction to drama, the disguise of self. An important theatrical closure occurs in "Homage to the Memory of Wallace Stevens," in which "The *the* has become an *a*." Referring to the final line of Stevens' "The Man on the Dump" ("Where was it one first heard of the truth? The the"), the poet laments the particular becoming general, the definite growing indefinite.

> The opera of the gods is finished,
> And the applause is dying.

■ ■ ■

What has been good? What has been beautiful?
The tuning up, or the being put away?
The instruments have nothing more to say.

■ ■ ■

Now all quotations from the text apply,
Including the laughter, including the offstage thunder,
Including even this almost human cry.

The last line's self-mocking alienation is appropriate to such a symbolic closing, which betrays fears of mortality and silence. This withdrawal begets others, but only death is the encore for such absolute self-effacement. For a poet so entranced by blank mirrors, it is curious Justice is not attracted to the demonic Doppelganger of fierce poets—the vampire. Would it not be an appropriate figure for a poet who has ransacked foreign poets—Alberti, Vallejo, Guillevic—for inspiration? To suck another's blood, as only the strongest poets know, is to become original, and from his influences—Stevens, Hardy, Auden—Justice has fashioned an original, compelling voice. It is typical for this poet, this consummate gamesman, that the most frightening subject, his own death, has been—had to be!—approached through a poetic borrowing in "Variations on a Text by Vallejo":

Donald Justice is dead. One Sunday the sun came out,
It shone on the bay, it shone on the white buildings,
The cars moved down the street slowly as always, so many,
Some with their headlights on in spite of the sun,
And after a while the diggers with their shovels
Walked back to the graveside through the sunlight,
And one of them put his blade into the earth
To lift a few clods of dirt, the black marl of Miami,
And scattered the dirt, and spat,
Turning away abruptly, out of respect.

Perhaps not surprisingly, little poetry immediately followed the disavowals of *Departures*.

The tactical feints Justice employs have allowed his imagination, sufficiently armored, to disclose what it otherwise would conceal: the battle to sustain feeling, to defeat silence. What have been the costs of his reticence? First, the loss of self as a foreground subject. Second, a lack of love poems (except of the wriest sort—"Ode to a Dressmaker's Dummy"). Third, a weakness in the poems of pure observation or recollection, whose proper center—the poet affected by his past—is offstage, unavailable to the reader. Such poems do not complete dramatic actions for their meaning. Interior photographs, their privacy seals them up.

The disparity, throughout Justice's work, between those poems merely observed and those imaginatively enacted implies not that two men wrote them, but that one man wrote at very different levels of imaginative engagement. The poets to whom that higher imagination is most closely allied are Anthony Hecht and Elizabeth Bishop. Though Justice lacks Hecht's overwhelming (and sometimes overweening) angst or Bishop's electrified landscapes, he shares their lunar attention to language, their precise modulations of feeling, and the wit they have embedded in form. In addition, he has mastered an elegiac intensity, a rueful elegance that heightens the everyday while declaring its frailty. His poetry, unlike the encrusted jewelry box of so many intellective poets, is an intricate watchwork, a mechanism with purpose (*to tell time*), fine gears moving in close tolerance. What is required for such poetry is forbearance, a withholding of the self from the object of concern without losing a sympathetic excitement, a satisfaction not in tragedy but in the surrender to demands the world makes of us all.

Selected Poems has allowed Justice to sweep out over two dozen poems from his canon (though, lamentably, such housecleaning has caused the loss of "Narcissus at Home" and "To Satan in Heaven"), to refurbish a number of old ones (to considerable improvement in "Last Days of Prospero"), to rectify sins of omission with a half-dozen uncollected poems, including a fragment from an abandoned long poem, "Bad Dreams," and to add a small wing of ten new poems. In his new poems Justice has returned from his *Departures* to restrictions of form and his comforting obsessions, childhood and memory. From those obsessions emerge two of his strongest poems, "First Death" and "Childhood," the latter a poem of extravagant seeing:

> Winter mornings now, my grandfather,
> Head bared to the mild sunshine, likes to spread
> The Katzenjammers out around a white lawn chair
> To catch the stray curls of citrus from his knife.
> Chameleons quiver in ambush; wings
> Of monarchs beat above bronze turds, feasting . . .

Justice's is a poetry of loss; to thwart that loss he attempts to solidify the world of his past in his poems, a private archeology preserving what otherwise would vanish. His achievement has been to write ever more cunningly of a poet's central concerns: his loss in time, his imaginative gain—the present bought on the terms of the past. Only the spareness of his output and his characteristic self-abnegation have denied him a more general recognition.

The eighty-eight titles of *Selected Poems* (a number significant to a poet who would rather have been a pianist) now secures his *made* past, his past as a poet. The poems have been rearranged chronologically, showing, for example, the progressive remission of form in *Night Light*; new typography has considerably enhanced the warmth and vision of his first two books. That vision finds expression in the final line of "Childhood," the final poem in this fine, extraordinary collection—"Forlorn suburbs, but with golden names!" Language may redeem bleakness, even while the poet recognizes the false show such language enacts.

From Identifying Marks
Alan Young

Poetry in North America seems now to be very much its own terrain. Trepid explorers from Europe soon begin to discern, however, many familiar shapes in the landscape, comforting reminders of home. Complacency is the danger for them then. American poetry, though directed initially from European contours, twists vigorously to create a distinctive identity.

Donald Justice's *Selected Poems*, a choice made from three volumes published between 1960 and 1973 with sixteen previously uncollected poems added for good measure, enables us to see this identity-creation at work. An authentic voice found by an American poet is also new territory gained for the American language. *Summer Anniversaries* (1960) was published when Justice was thirty-five years old, yet many of these poems have the feel of apprentice pieces, a formalistic and workshop atmosphere pervading the whole volume. The somewhat awkwardly worked frames of sonnets, villanelles, sestinas, odes, and other formal poems do not entirely constrict a naturally lyrical talent. The first poem in the book, though with echoes of late Eliot, has gentle rhapsodic bursts to ruffle the generally detached posture:

> The light in going still is golden, still
> A single bird is singing in the wood,
> Now one, now two, now three, and crickets start,
> Bird-song and cricket-sigh; and all the small
> Percussion of the grass booms as it can,
> And chimes, and tinkles too, *fortissimo*.
>
> ("Ladies by Their Windows")

Alan Young. "Identifying Marks." *TLS* no. 4027 (May 30, 1980): 620.

By the time of *Night Light* (1967), Justice has moved an appreciable distance from academic and provincial formalism. "Early Poems" is an act of renunciation: "How fashionably sad those early poems are! / On their clipped lawns and hedges the snows fall." The influence of William Carlos Williams is evident in poems of the American landscape, and there is a hard-won new simplicity of diction in his improvisations on themes from Guillevic ("The Man Closing Up"). "Men at Forty" shows the gain in both freedom and control of this sparer medium: "Men at forty / Learn to close softly / The doors to rooms they will not be / Coming back to."

Departures (1973) is the harvest of Justice's search for a voice. Even when he employs chance methods (sparingly) as in "The Confession," "The Success," "The Assassination," and two "Sonatinas," the way of saying is authentic. Imitations of poems by Vallejo, Catullus, and Baudelaire have his own assured, cool and elegiac manner too. There are several very early pieces as well as new very nostalgic verses among the previously uncollected poems; it is as though he has decided to settle for the contrary yet complementary moods of his poem "Tremayne"—mild despair and contentment. It would be sad if Justice, who has struggled through to a polished and urbane yet completely American manner, should have persuaded himself that the muse favours only the new generation:

> I call her up sometimes, long distance now.
> And she still knows my voice, but I can hear,
> Beyond the music of her phonograph,
> The laughter of the young men with their keys.
>
> I have the number written down somewhere.
> ("The Telephone Number of the Muse")

From Poetry Chronicle
Emily Grosholz

Donald Justice's *Selected Poems* play variations on the themes of time's passage, mortality, afternoon and autumn. His writing never succumbs to the black despair which corroded the poetry of Weldon Kees (whom he served so well as editor), but is held by a kind of mental equipoise and illusionless wit. It is grave, measured, detached, never cold but breathtakingly formal. I would say that any young American poet must come to Donald Justice's work sooner or later to learn the state of the art, even though he characteristically protests to his students:

> No more!
> There has been traffic enough
> In the boudoir of the muse.

A few examples must suffice here to exhibit his concerns and the perfection of his severely self-selected oeuvre. Often he writes of neighborhoods, quiet with the stillness of desolation, anonymous and American: though one senses behind them Baudelaire's *Tableaux parisiens*, the same charitable attention to the old, the lost, the trapped and dying. For example, "Bus Stop":

> And the last bus
> Comes letting dark
> Umbrellas out—
> Black flowers, black flowers.
>
> And lives go on.
> And lives go on

Emily Grosholz. "Poetry Chronicle." *Hudson Review* 33, no. 2 (summer 1980): 304–6.

Like sudden lights
At street corners

Or like the lights
In quiet rooms
Left on for hours,
Burning, burning.

Here is real chastity of diction, a reproach to our tribe's ner-
vous, adulterated language. "A Winter Ode to the Old Men
of Lummus Park, Miami, Florida," recalling Baudelaire's *"Les
Petites Vieilles,"* concludes:

Poor cracked thermometers stuck now
At zero everlastingly,
Old men, bent like your walking sticks
As with the pressure of some hand,
Surely we must have thought you strong
To lean on you so hard, so long!

Dante, Milton, Baudelaire, Rilke, Alberti, Guillevic,
haunt the pages of this collection, a recurrence not at all
inconsistent with the fact that Justice's landscapes and characters are thoroughly American, and that he rarely treats
Europe itself directly. The tacit presence of European culture
is what gives substance and resonance to his reflective preoccupation with the past.

From Men at Forty
Derek Mahon

The first poem by Donald Justice I ever read was the much anthologized sestina: "Here in Katmandu":

> We have climbed the mountain.
> There's nothing more to do . . .

It seemed to me then, and seems to me now, a beautiful and mysterious object, resonant and yet resistant to paraphrase. It might be said that it is a poem of regret for the death of idealism, a poem about coming to terms with quotidian reality, and, therefore, in some sense about "the way we live now." But these thoughts, although suggested by the poem, are not contained in the poem, which has a purely plastic quality, a quality emphasised by the highly artificial sestina form. It is, in Beckett's words, an example of "light commenting bodies, and stillness motion, and silence sound, and comment comment." It enjoys a Zen-like repose, and is at the same time mildly witty, as in the two variations Justice permits himself on the word "do." One is "dew," pronounced perhaps in the American way to rhyme with "do," not "due"; the other is the "du" in "Katmandu":

> Meanwhile it is not easy here in Katmandu.

Wit of this nature, based on word-play, reminds us that Justice was born and bred in the American South, and alerts us to the possibility that he might show signs of having been influenced by the Fugitives; indeed, the shades of John Crowe Ransom and Allen Tate seem to hover around many of the

Derek Mahon. "Men at Forty." *London Review of Books* 2, no. 16 (August 21–September 3, 1980): 22.

earlier poems in this volume, poems with titles like "Ladies by Their Windows," "Landscape with Little Figures," "Beyond the Hunting Woods," "On the Death of Friends in Childhood," "The Grandfathers" and "Incident in a Rose Garden." There are the same muted tones and gentle ironies beloved of the Fugitives; but there the resemblance ceases, for Justice has moved well away from their more limiting conventions and established a lucid, forceful manner of his own. Several of these poems, including "Here in Katmandu," already have the status of minor contemporary classics of American poetry: not massive classics like Lowell's greatest work, pregnant with private turmoil and public significance, but classics in a minor key and on a single instrument—spinet or tenor sax. "Counting the Mad," apparently so simple, even naive, is to American poetry what Stevie Smith's "Not Waving but Drowning" is to English. Beneath the sing-song, nursery-rhyme surface lies an infinity of pain:

> This one was put in a jacket,
> This one was sent home,
> This one was given bread and meat
> But would eat none,
> And this one cried No No No No
> All day long.

Justice's Southernness expresses itself in a formal, even slightly quaint diction and an evident respect—more common in the South than elsewhere in America—for the traditional English modes. In Justice's case, this means that he works, as often as not, from a basic pentametric line, describes recognisable scenes, and frequently comments on some aspect of life as, say, Hardy would have done, or as Larkin generally does. "Time and the Weather," "The Grandfathers" and "Men at Forty" are, in fact, strikingly Larkinesque. Justice's "ghostly furniture," "Sunday prisons" and "miraculous escapes" are properties we often encounter in Larkin. Old men nod and spit on "ruined porches"; middle age becomes conscious of itself:

> Men at forty
> Learn to close softly
> The doors to rooms they will not be
> Coming back to.

And in "Bus Stop":

> Lights are burning
> In quiet rooms
> Where lives go on
> Resembling ours.

If there is a Hull in Georgia, this might be it. (There is even a sequence in praise of water.) But French influences are in evidence too, especially and explicitly that of Guillevic, whose mischievous obliquity and animism seem to appeal to one aspect of Justice, and some of whose elusive verse he translates or adapts. This is a varied and marvellously accomplished volume, and if it seems a little short on ambition—there is no major attempt at a comprehensive statement—at least he knows what he can and cannot do. Measuring the successes against the failures in these 130-plus pages, one is left in no doubt that here is a very fine poet indeed, and one who, on this side of the Atlantic at least, has yet to receive the attention he deserves.

From Good for Nothing?

Alan Hollinghurst

Donald Justice's poems, however, persistently haunt and are haunted by the past, to the extent that their present is characterised by a weary passivity, a lack of vitality that is supported by fastidious formal elegance. They do not need to say that what happens now is pointless as there seems no likelihood of anything happening anyway. Anthony Hecht, in a generous blurb, calls Justice "the supreme heir of Wallace Stevens," but if that is so the Stevens heritage is weaker than one hoped. The poems lack urgency from early on—typically motiveless sestinas, for example—with a habit of elegance which cushions meaning, and a lack of colour and surprise. He will over-explain his material, flattening a striking comparison of a childhood memory with a Griffith film by including: "But already the silent world is lost forever"; or in a (late?) poem, also of childhood memories, adding unnecessary glosses: "Once more beneath my thumb the globe turns— / And doomed republics pass in a blur of colours . . . (Czechoslovakia, e.g.)[.]" The poems occupy a cultured space, as aware of European poetry as of American (though in a way typical too of the British awareness of American poetry, that of a couple of generations earlier)—but with a certain lassitude and narcissism, looking in the mirror as much as out of the window. Formal but *fatigués*, they create the impression of getting great job-satisfaction without actually doing much work. It is unfair but true to say that the beautiful printing and production of the book increase this sense of artistic complacency which further reduces the emotional pressure of the work.

Alan Hollinghurst. "Good for Nothing?" *New Statesman* 100, no. 2579 (August 22, 1980): 18.

Platonic Scripts (1984)

From Poets' Prose
Richard Wertime

When we turn from the accumulated weight of [Howard] Nemerov's volume to the handful of essays in Donald Justice's *Platonic Scripts*, the comparisons which follow are bound to be unfair. They shouldn't be, ideally. Justice writes prose with a deceptively subtle and quiet sort of tact.

Justice's book begins with a brief, poignant Preface that modestly makes this admission:

> Of all the poets of my generation who did not get much into the habit of criticism—and that would include the great majority of us—I may be the only one with any regrets at having kept my thoughts more or less to myself. I see now that criticism can be of enormous value in helping to define and refine one's own thinking; and there is always the chance, if it is any good, that it might do the same for another's.

I like the honest emphasis on the poet's self-interest here: criticism as a working-through of the poet's own ideas disciplined by attention to the needs of other readers.

Justice is a passionate poetic technician, and the essays in this volume deal with one of two subjects: the evolution of certain of his own poems, and the business of metrics. The first sort of essay has generic liabilities, inasmuch as talk about one's own compositions risks a tone of self-absorption and

Richard Wertime. "Poets' Prose." *Yale Review* 74, no. 4 (summer 1985 [July 1985]): 608–9.

the charge of narcissism; and since there are so many notorious instances of essays-after-the-fact, one finds the genre very hard to trust. And in truth, the first two essays of this sort which Justice offers, "The Private History of a Poem" and "On Writing 'First Death,'" have a somewhat straight-faced quality that causes me discomfort.

But then comes an impressive pair of essays, "Meters and Memory" and "The Free-Verse Line in Stevens," which helps me understand why Justice's tone is so detached when he speaks of his own work: it's the *principles* of composition that really occupy him, not his own life; and so, when I return to the more recent personal essays at the end of the volume, I see much better what objectives he has in mind. The final essay, in fact, is really quite impersonal, and offers a quiet manifesto for change in modern poetry that is as inwardly ardent and firm as it is quiet; speaking of his aesthetic stance as "radically conservative" in a nonpolitical sense, Justice proposes that the anticlassical movement in current poetry is dead:

> The age of experiment is exhausted and moribund, temporarily at least. There is no one with the brilliance and authority of Williams, and the whole lineage that came after him seems to be wearing thin, like soil needing rotation. . . . Let us consider instead the twenties and thirties: Brecht and Alberti, perhaps. . . . Not Neruda or Vallejo any longer now, however passionate and sincere, but rather the cooler technical brilliancies, the mysterious precisions of Alberti. A tradition could be put back together starting with not much more than this. Not forgetting rhythm; not forgetting truth.

"The mysterious precisions"—it's a resonant phrase that brings together, at last, all of Justice's critical work. The essay on Stevens is a critical *tour de force*. Equally remarkable for argumentative care and vigor is "Meters and Memory," where Justice argues that "The meters seem more to resemble the hammer-work of carpenters putting together a building, say, than waves coming in to shore or the parade of seasons," and concludes in the following vein:

> Meters do accompany the sense, like a kind of percussion only, mostly noise. Over and above syntax, they bind the individual words together, and the larger structural parts as well, over and above whatever appearance of logic survives in the argument; as a result, the words and parts seem to cohere, more perhaps than in plain fact may be the case. How they assist the recollection is by fixing it in permanent, or would-be permanent, form. This, for the poet, may be the large and rather sentimental purpose which gives force to all their various combining and intersecting functions.

Would that these three authors, [John Frederick] Nims, Nemerov, and Justice, could be heard speaking *together* in one book about such matters.

The Sunset Maker (1987)

From Heroes and Villanelles
Edward Hirsch

In his fifth collection of poems, *The Sunset Maker,* Donald Justice establishes himself as an elegiac poet of the first order. He may be, concomitantly, the resident genius of nostalgia in the ever-expanding house of American poetry. Mr. Justice is a scrupulous tactician of melancholy and loss who approaches his subjects with what one of his poems calls "a love that masquerades as pure technique." His temperament is wryly romantic—as he puts it in "Villanelle at Sundown," "One can like *any*thing diminishment has sharpened"—but his style is firmly classical. His new book is a little anthology of the strictest traditional forms, including a few slyly complicated nonce forms of his own devising. If, as Ezra Pound once said, "technique is the test of a man's sincerity," Mr. Justice is surely one of the sincerest poets working today.

He has reinvented the poetic vignette and his characteristic strategy is to evoke an otherwise neglected scene with a few precise notes. We are given moments out of the past, local scenes illuminated with a grainy photographic light—"Young Girls Growing Up (1911)," or "Mule Team and Poster" (Alabama, 1936), or "Manhattan Dawn (1945)," or Henry James visiting Coronado Beach, Calif. The novelist that W. H. Auden called the "master of nuance and scruple" is a presiding formal guide to these evocations of American landscape and past, though when Mr. Justice turns to the psychological as well

Edward Hirsch. "Heroes and Villanelles." *New York Times Book Review* (August 23, 1987): 20.

as geographical space he terms "My South," his work reads a
little as if Henry James and Walker Evans had collaborated on
lyric poems.

At the heart of *The Sunset Maker* is a group of poems and
a prose memoir about the experience of taking piano lessons
in Miami in the 1930's:

> Picture me, the shy pupil at the door,
> One small, tight fist clutching the dread Czerny.
> Back then time was still harmony, not money,
> And I could spend a whole week practicing for
> That moment on the threshold.
>
> > > Then to take courage,
> And enter, and pass among mysterious scents,
> And sit quite straight, and with a frail confidence
> Assault the keyboard with a childish flourish!

Learning to play the piano was apparently one of the formative experiences of the poet's life and he writes about his
early teachers with tender irony and affection. His piano
lessons come to represent moments of intense happiness (as
well as awe and dread) from the receding world of childhood
and adolescence, and his poems about the experience become
rescue operations of the past.

Indeed, in his title poem and in his short story, "Little
Elegy for Cello and Piano," Mr. Justice suggests that a single
ghostly phrase of music is all that survives of a dead composer's
life. All that gifted labor comes down to a few hauntingly specific notes. Mr. Justice's own work will last in greater dimen-
sion. In at least two of his elegies—the memorial poem to his
mother, "Psalm and Lament," and the dark, exacting villanelle
"In Memory of the Unknown Poet, Robert Boardman
Vaughn"—he counters our inevitable human losses with an
unforgettable and permanent music.

From The Poetry in Things Past and Passing

Bruce Bawer

As its opening poem "Lines at the New Year" makes plain, *The Sunset Maker*—Donald Justice's fifth collection in 28 years, and his first book since *Selected Poems* (1979)—is pre-occupied with the remembrance of things past: "The old year slips past / unseen, the way a snake goes. / Vanishes, / and the grass closes behind it." Suffusing most of the 24 poems, two stories and one prose memoir that compose this graceful volume are the author's affectionate memories of events and people—including his own younger self—that have vanished, with the lost years, into the high grass. Solemn and stately, taut and tender, these writings are nonetheless often startling in their raw response to the fact of mortality: *"The dead,"* runs the old refrain in "Nostalgia and Complaint of the Grand-parents," *"don't get around much anymore."*

In another poem, "Nostalgia of the Lakefronts," Justice recalls a setting associated with his long-gone youth, and—as he does continually in this book—links natural phenomena to memory, to history: "Nostalgia comes with the smell of rain, you know." Time and again he contrasts the blithe naivete of the young, in regard to their own mortality, and the sad knowledge that has come to him with age: in "Children Walking Home from School through Good Neighborhood," for instance, he compares a group of boys and girls to "figures held in some glass ball, / One of those in which, when shaken, snowstorms occur; / But this one is not yet shaken." Yet the youngsters are fated to go the way of all flesh; in a striking image, Justice describes them, running in their bright sweaters,

Bruce Bawer. "The Poetry in Things Past and Passing." *Washington Post Book World* (January 3, 1988): 4.

as "a little swirl of colors, / Like the leaves already blazing and falling farther north." Time holds them green and dying, though they sing in their chains like the sea.

Poems with titles like "Young Girls Growing Up (1911)" thus coexist in *The Sunset Maker* with poems entitled "Purgatory" and "Cemetery"; the poet shifts easily—or rather, with a sad unease—from images of innocent youth to reflections upon death and decrepitude. In several poems he elegizes loved ones, including (in "Psalm and Lament") his mother, after whose passing "the yard chairs look empty, the sky looks empty, / The sky looks vast and empty." The quietly insistent repetition is characteristic of the poems in this book, and seems designed to reflect the repetitiousness of the daily routines and natural events (e.g., sunsets) which persist despite a loved one's death:

> Out on Red Road the traffic continues; everything
> continues.
> Nor does memory sleep; it goes on.
>
> Out spring the butterflies of recollection,
> And I think that for the first time I understand
>
> The beautiful ordinary light of this patio
> And even perhaps the dark rich earth of a heart. . . .
>
> Let summer come now with its schoolboy trumpets and
> fountains.
> But the years are gone, the years are finally over.

His mother's passing, then, has turned the poet's own existence into a sort of death-in-life. Yet this state is not without its consolations, bittersweet though they may be. For one thing, he now has a deeper understanding of life and a more profound appreciation of the simple beauties around him. He also has nature, which—even as it seems to mock his mortality or, alternately, to grow old and weary itself—can, with its ever-returning spring, awaken his long-dormant memories of other, happier springs. Finally, he has his art, by means of which he—the sunset maker, the God-mimic—can bring his affections, his memories, and his very self to life for those who choose to read him.

This is presuming, of course, that he continues to be read—a score on which Justice is less sanguine than Emily Dickinson, who boasted in one famous poem that she could fashion two sunsets to the Almighty's one, and who ridiculed publication as "the Auction / Of the Mind of Man." Unlike Dickinson, Justice considers an audience necessary to the artist. In one elegy, he memorializes "the Unknown Poet, Robert Boardman Vaughn"; in the title poem and a pendant story, "Little Elegy for Cello and Piano," the speaker notes that nobody but he remembers the works of his late composer friend Eugene Bestor—and since he recalls only one six-note cello phrase from the entire oeuvre, he thinks of Eugene "as surviving through this fragment." He reflects that after his own death, "nobody will recall the sound / These six notes made once," and then Eugene will be truly dead. Unless, of course, the poem and story (in both of which those notes are preserved) continue to be read.

Music occupies an important place alongside poetry in this book; several poems, as well as the memoir, "Piano Lessons," recall Justice's boyhood music teachers. Two of the poems are subtitled "A Song," and indeed, whether Justice writes in prose, free verse, or form (this book includes two villanelles and several sonnets), his work has a manifest musical quality. Justice's ear is perfect: Much of one's joy in his poetry derives from his consistently delicate patterning of sounds, particularly from the wonderful half-rhymes that fill poem after poem— for example, "Villanelle at Sundown"—with a multitude of similar sounds that echo softly off each other:

> Turn your head. Look. The light is turning yellow.
> The river seems enriched thereby, not to say deepened.
> Why this is, I'll never be able to tell you.

> Or are Americans half in love with failure?
> One used to say so, reading Fitzgerald, as it happened.
> (That Viking Portable, all water-spotted and
> yellow—
>
> Remember?) Or does mere distance lend a value
> To things?—false, it may be, but the view is hardly
> cheapened.
> Why this is, I'll never be able to tell you.

Justice's work is memorable not only for its music, though, but for its visual imagery. It does not seem to be a mere coincidence that the title poem mentions a painting by Bonnard, for many a Justice poem—dense with words like "diaphanous," "vague," "wisps," "misty," "ghostly," "blurred," "hints," "glimmerings"—sets a soft-focus, pastel-colored, Bonnard-like canvas before the mind's eye. Justice is a verse Impressionist, an Intimist of the written word.

If one has any reservations about *The Sunset Maker*, it is that the stories and memoir are not up to the poetry. Though it is interesting to see Justice rework a poem's material into prose (something he does twice in this book), it is very much a poet's prose: fastidiously composed and exquisitely contemplative, but structurally weak and short on action and conflict. Yet this is a minor cavil. On the whole, *The Sunset Maker* is a deeply affecting volume—a beautiful, powerful meditation by a modern master upon the themes of aging, lost innocence, and the unalterable, terrifying pastness of the past.

Review

Laurence Donovan

Speaking at the Miami Book Fair a few years ago after receiving the Pulitzer Prize for his *Selected Poems,* Donald Justice remarked, "I miss Miami when I'm away," and then added, after a pause, "and I miss Miami when I'm here." This sense of loss, of promise unfulfilled and beauty trammeled by the barbarism of progress, has been at the center of Justice's life-long poetic meditation, delicately expressed in a craft and diction resistant, in its traditional manner, to the aggressive yawpery of Ginsberg or the fashionable experimentation of the Merrills, Dickeys, and Ashberys. True to the sad dream of a lost America, echoing the eloquence of Stevens and the directness and simplicity of Rilke, he has often returned in thought to the Miami of his childhood, that sunny, quickly-to-be-tarnished dream of the Merricks and Flaglers—"And sometimes, / Where the city halts, the cracked sidewalks / Lead to a coral archway still spanning / The entrance to some wilderness of palmetto— / Forlorn suburbs, but with golden names!"

The Sunset Maker, his current volume, provides a poignant elegiac coda to these concerns. (The musical metaphor is appropriate since the book is thematically arranged around a brief prose memoir of early piano lessons and a group of poems repeating and transforming the same material.) *The Sunset Maker* is even more personal than the preceding always-autobiographical work: it contains many memorial poems and memoirs, compounded of Yeatsian wonder and regret, addressed to relatives and friends who

Laurence Donovan. "Review." *South Florida Poetry Review* 5, no. 2 (winter 1988): 49–51.

have meant much to the poet. Among them are Mrs. Snow and Mrs. K., his early piano teachers, types of impoverished but genteel martyrs to their callings not to be found today, and cameoed in the poet's memory; Carl Ruggles, who instructed him in composition; his grandmother; and Robert Boardman Vaughn and John Lenox, poet and musician, the one who lived a life of bohemian risk, writing little and courting ruin with his search for the ideal, and the other whose eloquence was also in his spoken words and who stood—massively and myopically—for Bach and Mozart and against the bulldozers and merchants who were slowly destroying his Edenic Coconut Grove—grand eccentrics the two of them, and continual catalysts in the poet's conscience.

Of Lenox he writes:

> One winter he was the best
> Contrabassoonist south
> Of Washington, D.C.—
> The only one. Lonely
>
> In eminence he sat,
> Like some lost island king,
> High on a second-story porch
> Overlooking the bay . . .
>
> ■ ■ ■
>
> Here, if you care, the bay
> Is printed with many boats now,
> Thick as trash; that high porch is gone,
> Gone up in the smoke of money, money;
>
> The barbarians . . .
> But enough.
> You are missed. Across the way,
> Someone is practicing sonatas,
> And the sea air smells again of good gin.

Of Vaughn, a drunken and desolate sacrifice to dreams, beaten to death in New York City:

> Lately he had wandered between St. Mark's Place and the
>   Bowery,
> Already half a spirit, mumbling and muttering sadly.
> O the boredom, and the horror, and the glory!
>
> All done now. But I remember the fiery
> Hypnotic eye and the raised voice blazing with poetry.
> It was his story and would always be his story—
> The boredom, and the horror, and the glory.

The spare, understated style of the first poem and the traditional format of the second allow Justice to avoid the sentimental trap and the subject afflatus that are the risks of autobiographical poetry, into which tasteless mire Sylvia Plath falls continually and which Robert Lowell barely skirts.

The concluding piece in *The Sunset Maker*—a story: "The Artificial Moonlight," is set in the fine old house overlooking the bay in Coconut Grove, where John Lenox lived upstairs and I and my first wife lived downstairs. (It has long since been replaced by a dreadful structure called "Sailboat Bay," first harbinger of the Grove's decline into condominiums and boutiques.) It is a nostalgic story of one symbolic night in the lives of old friends and acquaintances who had not yet marked out their separate paths to failure, and ends with the narrator/observer thinking back years later on the eventual destinies of the group. A sort of memorial musing on the past, presented in Justice's clean, unrhetorical manner, it is the perfect sunset for the collection.

The characters in "The Artificial Moonlight," I might add, are, with the slightest of masks, based upon me and my friends. The portraits, although not wholly flattering, seem true enough to be unobjectionable, although I believe my sexual prowess is somewhat exaggerated. At any rate, I am happy not to have qualified for an elegy.

From Best Rhymes with Zest
John Lucas

I'm afraid that this [that his language "feels ultimately derivative"] is equally true of Donald Justice, a poet whom I've
much admired in the past but whose new collection *The
Sunset Maker* amounts to not much more than a form of
sonorous whingeing. Yes, he is immensely skilled, but why
so many dying falls, why the darkness without extended
wings? One way of answering this question is to point out
that Justice is in thrall to a particularly damaging convention
of American letters which takes melancholy as a synonym for
cultural fastidiousness.

A different, less enchanted answer might involve stating
that what Justice lacks is that "thunder" without which saying "no" becomes little more than a self-pitying refusal to
rejoice.

John Lucas. "Best Rhymes with Zest." *New Statesman* 115, no. 2976
(April 8, 1988): 28.

Mythical Childhoods
David Hartnett

Donald Justice has always been a poet for whom memory and art are manifestations of the same haunting. Like his contemporaries Anthony Hecht and James Merrill, he has remained faithful to the Stevensian notion of a "Supreme Fiction" while avoiding the more extreme cerebralism of Stevens's own poetry. The mood of *The Sunset Maker,* his fourth collection, is characteristically elegiac; but nostalgia and sadness are continually being filtered through an almost bouyant sense of creative renewal.

"October: A Song" seems straightforwardly wistful: "Summer, goodbye. / The days grow shorter. / Cranes walk the fairway now / In careless order." But, as the first line's courtly apostrophe suggests, this poem is as much about a poetic subject as a scene. In "Nostalgia and Complaint of the Grandparents," the lament for time past is grounded in self-awareness. The dead talk as though their lives had always been posthumous:

> Eternity resembles
> One long Sunday afternoon.
> No traffic passes; the cigar smoke
> Coils in a blue cocoon.
> Children, have you nothing
>   For our cold sakes?
> No tea? No little tea cakes?

Their repetitious petulance may make these Hardyesque wraiths more human, but it also fixes them as voices within

---

David Hartnett. "Mythical Childhoods." *TLS* no. 4437 (April 15–21, 1988): 420.

an artifice. Even the knowingly artless refrain, "The dead don't get around much anymore," is continually undergoing permutation by enjambment.

This poem's Proustian feeling for time as a product of and yet a threat to the imagination reminds us that Justice has consistently elegized childhood and youth. *The Sunset Maker* contains a series of poems and prose sketches about the poet's own early musical education in Miami, but these lack intensity. More memorable are those poems conceived in the shadow of masters such as Hart Crane and Rimbaud, whom Justice himself has called "poets of a mythical childhood." The phantasmagoric "Nostalgia of the Lakefronts" draws on *Les Illuminations*, but the way the random processes of recall are counterpointed against the ghostly wreckage of a sestina is entirely original. "Manhattan Dawn (1945)" evokes visionary adolescence in an idiom which pays delicate homage to "The Harbour Dawn" section of Crane's *The Bridge* yet develops an idiosyncratic feel for time becoming art: "There is a smoke of memory / That curls about these chimneys / . . . that lifts, / Diaphanous, from sleep / To lead you down some alleyway perhaps . . ." When, in the sequence "My South," Justice shows the act of memory turning into an act of composition, Crane's "Van Winkle" is a liberating presence: "She [the poet's mother] stands this way for a long time . . . / And then a / Slow blacksnake, lazy with long sunning, slides / Down from its slab. . . ." In the mimetic labour of these lines time itself undergoes a marmoreal transformation.

A Donald Justice Reader (1992)

A Poet's Poet
Dana Gioia

In 1975 I took a course at Harvard from Elizabeth Bishop. Her general popularity at that moment can be measured by the size of her class; enrollment totaled five students. Although Bishop had won the Pulitzer Prize and the National Book Award, she was considered a "poet's poet," a writer treasured by fellow artists but not much noted by critics, and hardly known at all by the common reader. Today Bishop's reputation stands as high as that of any American poet of the last forty years. She is perhaps the only major poet of her generation on whom academic critics and non-specialists can enthusiastically agree. But back then a coterie sustained her modest *succès d'estime*.

Today Donald Justice occupies a similar position in American poetry. He is our most notable "poet's poet," with all the ambiguities that bittersweet honorific implies. He has won most of the major awards—the Lamont, the Pulitzer, the Bollingen. His work appears in all the anthologies edited by poets, but it remains conspicuously absent in most of those compiled by professors. He is widely regarded as the most influential poetry-writing teacher now alive. His former students from Iowa, Syracuse, Gainesville, and Bread Loaf constitute a *Who's Who* of American poetry. They include writers in every aesthetic camp. Since his didactic emphasis has been on craft, concentration, and precision, he has founded no school of poetry. Consequently, his work has attracted almost

Dana Gioia. "A Poet's Poet." *New Criterion* 10, no. 9 (May 1992): 68–71.

no attention from academic critics. Yet he is one of the few living writers whose verses American poets are likely to quote from memory.

A Donald Justice Reader presents the author's own selection from the work of four decades. Two general observations must be made about this superb volume. First, it is surely notable that so much of Justice's best work can fit into such a modest-sized book. His published oeuvre is remarkably—indeed regrettably—small. Second, it is equally notable how substantial this thin volume seems. His work gives the impression of weight, breadth, and variety. How does Justice manage this paradoxical accomplishment? Like Bishop (or Larkin, to cross the Atlantic for a parallel), he writes on such a consistently high level that he makes every poem, story, or essay matter.

Rereading the poems, one grows so lost in admiration for what they do well that it is easy to forget how much they do not attempt. There are no long poems in the Justice canon— not only no epics but also no narratives of even moderate length, extended meditations, verse memoirs, or dramas. There is not even a lyric sequence longer than a few pages. His medium is the short poem, usually of forty lines or less. One might say that he has spent his life perfecting that medium, but his mastery was there from the beginning. In his first book, *The Summer Anniversaries* (1960), one finds a dozen poems as exquisite as "On the Death of Friends in Childhood," a six-line wonder:

> We shall not ever meet them bearded in heaven,
> Nor sunning themselves among the bald of hell;
> If anywhere, in the deserted schoolyard at twilight,
> Forming a ring, perhaps, or joining hands
> In games whose very names we have forgotten.
> Come, memory, let us seek them there in the shadows.

Within the medium of the short poem, however, Justice has explored an extraordinary range of possibilities. The seventy-six poems gathered in *A Donald Justice Reader* constitute an encyclopedia of literary form and style. It is remarkable enough to find sonnets, villanelles, couplets, and sestinas coexisting in the same volume as surreal odes and aleatory "sonatinas"—not to mention poems based on blues lyrics and nursery rhymes. But surely it *is* unique to find all these styles handled with equal mastery, to see the same author use such apparently contradictory procedures to produce convincing poems. Whereas another writer might have borrowed an unfamiliar style to try something different in a new poem, Justice somehow managed to reinvent each manner from within. He created poems that were both strikingly different and yet recognizably his own.

Born in 1925, Justice began—like most of his generation's best poets—by writing formal verse. His early work rings with traditional music. It sometimes sounds as if Yeats had been transplanted to the American South. Listen to the opening of "Ladies by Their Windows":

> They lean upon their windows. It is late.
> Already it is twilight in the house;
> Autumn is in their eyes. Twilit, autumnal—
> Thus they regard themselves. What vanities!
> As if all nature were a looking-glass
> To publish the small features of their ruin!

Some readers have never forgiven Justice for abandoning this sonorous style, and one can understand their disappointment. (They will be further disappointed to learn this much-anthologized poem has been omitted from the *Reader*.) These early poems gorgeously demonstrate the magic of the old meters. But in the 1960s Justice—once again with most poets of his generation—discarded rhyme and meter for free verse. But whereas his contemporaries generally began writing autobiographical poems, Justice became a serious experimentalist. He not only discarded traditional form but also, eventually, conventional notions of genre, sequential exposition, originality, and even authorial control. "Experimental" poetry is usually a name given to an interesting artistic mess, the critical equivalent of an "A for effort." But Justice's experiments virtually all succeed. To each new method, he brought an extraordinary control, a *formal* tightness one rarely associates with experimental verse, especially the sort which displays no overt principles of organization. Much of Justice's innovative work is expansive and surreal, but sometimes it achieves an epiphanic minimalism, as in "The Thin Man" (quoted in full):

> I indulge myself
> In rich refusals.
> Nothing suffices.
>
> I hone myself to
> This edge. Asleep, I
> Am a horizon.

The careful reader will notice that this poem is written in syllabics. Gradually, Justice was working his way back to closed forms. By 1980 he was once again working primarily in meter, though his poems now addressed the autobiographical subjects that they had scrupulously avoided in the past.

The shape of Justice's poetic development may be interesting, but it is decidedly not what the author wants to communicate in *A Donald Justice Reader*. He has deliberately mixed his poems to hide their chronology. Instead he has arranged them loosely in thematic groups, as if to emphasize the consistency of his concerns across the different phases of his career. This decision suggests the author's sympathies lie not with critics, who find questions of overall artistic and stylistic growth paramount, but with the common reader, who cares mostly about the human content of individual poems.

A Donald Justice Reader ends with fifty-odd pages of prose—a memoir of childhood piano lessons in Depression-era Miami, two short stories, and three brief literary essays. I knew all of these pieces previously, but, rereading them with the special savor for design and detail that a second or third viewing allows, I felt a keen and unexpected disappointment. I wasn't disappointed with the selections. No, every one was perfect of its kind. My chagrin was with Justice. Why had someone this good written so little prose?

Perhaps the secret of Justice's reticence in prose is also the key to his skill. His prose is almost as concentrated as his verse. Every sentence carries a noticeable weight. Of course, the prose of poets is legendary for its density of local effect, especially in richness of description. Justice's special accomplishment is to have made his packed prose style both relaxed and immensely readable. One doesn't notice how much was said (or implied) until one looks at it carefully. Justice's story "Little Elegy for Cello and Piano," for instance, is only five pages long. The narrator remembers attending an afternoon concert at the Phillips Collection in Washington with his brother-in-law, a moderately well-known composer, who will die a few months later. Simple, intimate, and, yes, elegiac, the story is almost over before it begins. Yet how much we learn about the three main characters! Every detail discloses some crucial fact, sometimes about both the narrator and his subjects. This story is a joy to read, but what agony it must have been to write and re-write. It is, however, futile to speculate on what Justice might have written, especially in the presence of all he has created. *A Donald Justice Reader* should be an occasion for celebration, not complaint. Anyone who worries that enduring poems are no longer being written should read this singularly impressive collection.

Refined Craftsman
David Kirby

The most accessible door to Donald Justice's mind is his extraordinary short essay entitled "The Invention of Free Verse." Justice proposes that a commemorative tablet be erected in Crawfordsville, Indiana, "somewhere in the environs of Wabash College," with the year 1907 clearly marked. In that year Ezra Pound wrote this line: "Lips, words, and you snare them." The two stressed syllables followed by the two unstressed is the so-called ionic or double foot thought to have been used by the Ionians of Asia Minor in their orgiastic worship of Dionysus and Cybele. That's vintage Pound, then; if anyone in this century raided ancient cultures and used their artifacts as though they had just been invented, it was Uncle Ez.

But, says Justice, Pound adds a history-making line to his original: "Lips, words, and you snare them, / Dream, words, and they are as jewels." To Justice the repetitious second line is an astonished confirmation of the first ("For Pound himself the experience must have been like what the scientist undergoes in his laboratory, not altogether sure yet what he has or whether he has anything at all"). This confirmation leads to more variations. "Eyes, dreams, lips, and the night goes"—if you can start a line with two stressed syllables, why not with three?

In 1907 in Crawfordsville, then, "the iamb was first broken in a way decisive for twentieth-century poetry." Now how many contemporary poets think their free verse represents even an awareness of, much less a struggle against, the

David Kirby. "Refined Craftsman." *American Book Review* 15, no. 1 (April/May 1993): 26.

iamb? And how many exam-writing Ph.D. students would have seen in Pound's rearrangement of stressed and unstressed syllables the invention of contemporary free verse? Almost anyone asked to compose a short history of modern poetics would give most of the credit to Whitman or the French Symbolists. But Justice sees it differently.

If Justice's viewpoint is idiosyncratic, so is his entire argument. He doesn't seem particularly interested in developing his point; the essay proper runs to just over two pages and is followed by a one-page end note consisting mainly of quotations from Tennyson, Hopkins, and others to show how Pound differed from his predecessors. Too, Justice's style is indolent, almost apologetic. It is easy to imagine one of today's turbo-charged New Historicist critics devoting an entire book to a recreation of turn-of-the-century Crawfordsville and Pound's secret, anarchic ignition of the fuse of the modernism, the lighting of a bomb that would explode deafeningly a few years later and thousands of miles to the east with the publication of *The Waste Land*. But it is as though Justice can't be bothered, as though he is saying, "Okay, so I rewrote literary history. Time to call it a day."

Justice's poetry has this same curious doubleness to it. His poems are ingenious yet lethargic, beautiful and weary. Reviewers of his work (and these include many of the most acclaimed poets and critics of recent years) often use the conjunction "but" to deliver a double-edged compliment. Thus Thom Gunn: "Mr. Justice is a gentle poet, and in his best poems the gentleness has its own firm clear strength, but sometimes there is a possibility that the gentleness may deteriorate to a mere wistfulness." And Charles Molesworth: "Mr. Justice is capable of wit, but it is often the wit of the defeated."

If Justice's poetry has a single locus, it is the world before television. A short poem, "Time and the Weather," best exemplifies this world even if it does not show the poet at the height of his powers:

Time and the weather wear away
The houses that our fathers built.
Their ghostly furniture remains—
All the sad sofas we have stained
With tears of boredom and of guilt,

The fraying mottoes, the stopped clocks . . .
And still sometimes these tired shapes
Haunt the damp parlors of the heart.
What Sunday prisons they recall!
And what miraculous escapes!

Such words as "sad," "damp," "bored," and their equivalents recur throughout. More often than not, the speaker is a boy with a lot of time on his hands. Too, he is an indoor and bookish boy aware of the promise and denial of life in the American South. A stunning poem sequence entitled simply "South" begins with an epigraph by Faulkner's Quentin Compson ("I dont! I dont hate it! I dont hate it!") and describes the boy-persona's alternation between heroic imaginings and sheer anesthetic boredom. The words "Some promise of romance those Southern nights / Never entirely kept" loom large, not only in this poem but elsewhere. Who has not felt defeated by nature? Who, even (or especially) among Southerners, has not been struck dumb with rage at the South?

"South" in particular and these poems in general recall a Stephen Crane sketch entitled "Mr. Binks' Day Off," in which New Yorker Binks and his family visit his aunt in the New Jersey countryside. The Binkses are bored and irritated with the slow pace of country life yet exalted and purified by the trees and fields. Mainly, though, they are speechless, and the sketch ends with Binks stretching forth his arm "in a wondering gesture" and saying, "I wonder why the dickens it— why it—why—." Justice is as relentless as Crane in taking language as far as it can go and then admitting that there are ideas and feelings that simply cannot be expressed in words.

Thus there is in these poems what Freud would have called an "eternal recurrence of the same" (*ewige Wiederkehr des Gleichen*—the phrase is Nietzsche's). We are born, we age, we die, we are born again, though how or why is never quite certain. No wonder, then, that critics like Gunn and Molesworth find Justice's poetry wistful and defeated, whereas other readers might find it simply intellectually honest.

If there is an absolute good in Justice's world view, though, a contrast to all the entropy and inarticulateness, it is art. The title of a memoir in this collection called "Piano Lessons" suggests simultaneously both the sadness and boredom of childhood and their antidote. Here Justice ponders death (a friend down the street died of rheumatic fever, and the neighborhood boys served as pallbearers) and stalled marriages (most of his piano teachers were women who supported mysterious, silent men suffering from alcoholism or tuberculosis or shellshock). Mainly, though, he ponders the piano lessons themselves, the irritation and ennui and then the breathtaking sublimity. Over and over again, art overcomes death and failed love. But then they overcome it. Then it overcomes them, and so on.

A story called "Little Elegy for Cello and Piano," collected here, also deals with music in a way that illuminates Justice's conception of the relation of art and life and the fragility of each. Typically, the emphasis is on inexpression. The elegy of the title is described as "Ten or twelve minutes of music, no more, but hardly to be improved upon—sad, regretful, complete." The narrator's favorite phrase from this piece is "A brief inhaling and exhaling, a somewhat drawn-out deep gasp or sigh," about which he admits, "I do not of course know what it means."

In a way, each Justice poem is a "deep gasp or sigh" that defies meaning. He admits in an "Author's Note" (typically, not an "Introduction" or "Preface" or even "Foreword" but simply an "Author's Note") that his works are, in fact, short, though "the truth is I would have written novels and five-act tragedies if I could have." He cites a favorite writer here—

not W. H. Auden or John Crowe Ransom or Mark Strand, three poets to whose work Justice's invites comparison, but, curiously, at least at first, Sherwood Anderson. On reflection, though, Anderson is the perfect comparison; his works, too, are short, his characters similarly perplexed, fumbling, dazed.

There is an enormous difference, though, between the formlessness of Justice's characters and the formal perfection of his art. The difference is so great, as a matter of fact, as to call the reader's attention constantly to the fact that, as the memoir† "Piano Lessons" reveals, life and art are quite separate. One of his finest lyrics, titled, with typical modesty, simply "Poem," begins:

> This poem is not addressed to you.
> You may come into it briefly,
> But no one will find you here, no one.
> You will have changed before the poem will.

And so on through seven quatrains that sometimes recall Wallace Stevens, that other poet of aesthetic distance ("O bleached mirrors! Oceans of the drowned!") to conclude with the line with which the poem began.

Some poets render their subjects marmoreal—Ransom comes to mind here, in poems like "Bells for John Whiteside's Daughter"—but not Justice. In Justice's poems, the poetry itself is made of marble; it is the subjects that decay. Always there is the interplay between life and art that ends with speechlessness, as in a poem like "In the Attic," where a child hears the "drowsy aria of the flies" as he settles his chin "onto palms above / Numbed elbows propped on rotting sills."

Ultimately, this is a poetry that encourages not passion or enthusiasm but something more like connoisseurship, a highly cultivated, world-weary awareness that appreciates equally the gasp-making redolence of a ripe Stilton and the moldering elegance of cities like New Orleans and Venice. That is to

---

† *text:* story

say, Justice's is a sensibility that produces poems that will dismay most erstwhile readers of poetry yet enthrall at least some of the inveterate. Earlier I cited Thom Gunn and Charles Molesworth as representing those readers inclined to praise Justice with faint damns. But other readers, such as Vernon Young, reverse the Gunn/Molesworth he's-good-but formula in such utterances as this: "I doubt if there are six poems [by Justice] which could be claimed for the public sensibility. But Justice has written a dozen lyrics I'd call virtually incomparable."

If that makes Donald Justice a minor author, then perhaps "minor author" is a term that should fall from use. Certainly Justice is a type, though, that of the refined craftsman, seemingly a little dejected that he chose not to erect skyscrapers or compose symphonies. To think about Donald Justice is to recall Reconstruction author Grace King's description of another writer of that time, George Washington Cable. Cable was well along in years when King saw him and he had suffered much; she remembered him in a way that suits the Donald Justice who emerges from these poems, as one who is "very picturesque, very sad, with beautiful manners."

Intimations of Inadequacy

Robert Richman

Donald Justice is one of our most reticent poets. He may very well be the most reticent poet of his generation—the generation of Richard Wilbur, Anthony Hecht, Louis Simpson, Adrienne Rich, and the late Howard Nemerov. For Justice is even more sparing in output than the notoriously slow-working and slow-to-publish Hecht. "I'm not all that much for increasing the world's population of poems," Justice once said in an interview. Of his four books of all original material—*The Summer Anniversaries* (1960), *Night Light* (1967), *Departures* (1973), and *The Sunset Maker* (1987)—two were fifty-two pages or less. (A 137-page *Selected Poems*, containing seventeen new poems, came out in 1979.) No wonder Justice's 171-page *Reader*, which has seven previously uncollected poems, is as slender as it is.

Justice has been equally restrained with his prose. This too sets him apart from the poets of his generation, who are, for the most part, a critically garrulous bunch. Justice's lone prose volume, *Platonic Scripts* (1984), contains six essays, seven interviews, and ten pages of extracts from a notebook. The *Reader* doesn't exactly ameliorate the situation. The book's prose selections—three essays, two stories, and a memoir of Justice's Miami childhood—are superb, but one yearns for more.

One essay omitted from the *Reader* is the one on his late friend, Henri Coulette. This essay, which was co-written by Robert Mezey, served as an introduction to the 1990 edition of Coulette's *Collected Poems*. This omission is unfortunate because Justice and Coulette are kindred spirits. Both poets,

Robert Richman. "Intimations of Inadequacy." *Poetry* 162, no. 3 (June 1993): 160–66.

as Justice said about himself in a 1970 interview, seek to "displace the self from the poem—not to remove it entirely, but to displace it, in some degree." In Coulette's work, the displaced self gives way to other selves—actors, double agents, and Jews destined for death camps—who speak for the absent poet. In Justice's case, the standbys are writers, mostly poets.

The writers on whom Justice relies, however, seldom speak in monologues, as do the selves in Coulette's poems. Instead, the words Justice borrows are assimilated into poems that seem to be spoken in Justice's voice. His borrowings from César Vallejo, Weldon Kees, Wallace Stevens, Rilke, Catullus, Baudelaire, Mallarmé, Thomas Wolfe, Henry James, Somerset Maugham, and others are openly acknowledged in titles, epigraphs, and notes.

Justice once observed in an interview that when reading Robert Browning, the master of the dramatic monologue, "you know, clearly and definitely, it's not Browning talking, and the poem is the better for that . . . [nowadays there is an] unacknowledged confusion of a poet with narrator." Justice continued:

> Aren't you surprised at how easy it seems to be to assimilate a great multitude and variety of experience which others have spared us the necessity of acquiring for ourselves, and not only to assimilate but to write about. . . . [I]f you develop . . . a great affection for Chekhov, say . . . then you can invent for yourself Chekhovian characters and situations or even borrow passages from things he wrote and treat them as if they were your own, almost your own. . . . [Y]ou could feel that way about a hundred others, too, and master their experience as well simply by turning the pages.

Even though Justice abjures dramatic monologues that imaginatively freed poets like Browning and Coulette, the writers' words that Justice "treats as his own" are needed for the same reason: to unchain his imagination. Justice admits his handicap: "neither suffering nor exaltation . . . leads to poetry, at least not for me," Justice writes in the essay "Bus Stop: Or, Fear and Loneliness on Potrero Hill." Or, as he writes in "Variations on a Text by Vallejo": "When I took out this paper and began to write, / Never before had anything looked so blank, / My life, these words, the paper, the gray Sunday."

None of this is meant to imply that Justice isn't moved by the things of the world. Hardly; but when it comes to consigning those emotions to the page, he often needs the bits and scraps of perfected language to get him going. No doubt there are times when Justice responds without assistance to reality's often paralyzing realm, but if the poems are any proof—"Sestina on Six Words by Weldon Kees," "Variations on a Theme from James," "After a Phrase Abandoned by Wallace Stevens," "Homage to the Memory of Wallace Stevens" (in which he writes: "Now all quotations from the text apply, / Including the laughter, including the offstage thunder, / Including even this almost human cry")—he'd just as soon rely on books. Much the way Virgil led Dante, Justice likes to be guided, by his many literary betters, through the inferno of the poem.

Justice, who usually writes in meter and rhyme, claims that his main interest in poetry is form. Although subject-matter is not unimportant, it is a secondary consideration. This would make Justice an Old rather than a New Formalist, since poets of the latter camp emphasize subject-matter over form. "Sincerity," he writes in an essay on Baudelaire, "is saying what the form obliges you to say regardless of whether or not you believe in it." No wonder, as Justice notes in the same piece, that a poet's "pose" may paradoxically "be sincere." The sincere poet, Justice writes, "becomes a performer, a charlatan, a great pretender; art is artifice. What he has to be sincere about is his art." Justice would agree with Picasso's remark, "We all know that art is not truth. Art is a lie that makes us realize truth."

It comes as no surprise to learn that as a young man Justice studied the most abstract of the arts, music. From the beginning Justice has been skeptical of a naively mimetic poetry. The difference between poetry and music, of course, is that music is quite forthright about its inability to reproduce physical reality. Poetry, on the other hand, with its seemingly referential statements and images, suggests a closer relationship to reality than it actually possesses.

Justice likes to remind readers of the distance between poetry and life. One way he does this is to write artificially—to use meters. "Like the odd mustaches and baggy pants of the old comedians," Justice writes in the essay "Meters and Memory," meters "put us on notice that we are at a certain distance from the normal rules and expectations of life." Another way to point out the poem's distance from reality is to divulge its literary origins. One more way to show how far poems are from life is to use imagery that suggests it. Justice isn't above a flagrantly self-reflexive remark, like "the *the* has become an *a*" (in "Homage to the Memory of Wallace Stevens"). Usually, though, Justice's poems live a double life—as a commentary on life, and as a commentary on the poem's status as a nettlesome aesthetic object.

One poem that leads this kind of double life is "Children Walking Home from School through Good Neighborhood." It seems, at any rate, that the "good neighborhood" through which the children walk exists not only in the real cities and towns of our experience, but on the page, as well: a tranquil aesthetic "neighborhood" that is even more serene than the one it evokes:

> They are like figures held in some glass ball,
> One of those in which, when shaken, snowstorms occur;
> But this one is not yet shaken.
>
> And they go unaccompanied still,
> Out along this walkway between two worlds,
> This almost swaying bridge.

October sunlight checkers their path;
It frets their cheeks and bare arms now with shadow
Almost too pure to signify itself.
And they progress slowly, somewhat lingeringly,
Independent, yet moving all together,
Like polyphonic voices that crisscross
In short-lived harmonies.

Today, a few stragglers.
One, a girl, stands there with hands spaced out, so—
A gesture in a story. Someone's school notebook spills,
And they bend down to gather up the loose pages.
(Bright sweaters knotted at the waist; solemn expressions.)
Not that they would shrink or hold back from what may
come,
For now they all at once run to meet it, a little swirl of
colors,
Like the leaves already blazing and falling farther north.

This poem is the last word in formal polish and grace, but how well does its image of quiet tranquility reflect reality? Not all that well, at least not in Justice's view. Hence his wish to self-reflexively question the mimetic accuracy of an image that appears to be a by-product of the search for formal perfection. The questioning starts with the first line's *held,* which here means, not just *borne,* but *imprisoned;* aptly, for what is being held hostage in the poem's beautiful but inanimate prison is a group of living children. It would appear, at any rate, that the first stage of this poem's composition involved formally following through the initial motivation or spark, and the second stage involved disavowing the posing-as-real images that the heedless aesthetic imagination had wrought.

Not all of the poem's self-reflexive images are so critical of the poem's mimetic claims. For instance, the lines, "And they go unaccompanied still, / Out along this walkway between two worlds," appear to suggest that the children move, not only between the "two worlds" of childhood and adulthood, but between the "two worlds" of art and life, as well. Also not overtly critical are the lines, "Independent, yet moving all together, / Like polyphonic voices that crisscross / In short-lived harmonies," which could conceivably describe both the children and the lines of the poem. Also uncritical is the image of the girl whose movement is described as "A gesture in a story." (Her gesture exists in two stories: Justice's and hers.) Although none of these images casts a shadow on the poem's ability to reflect reality the way *held* does, they do remind us that poetry is as much on Justice's mind as reality.

Also curious is the image of the snowstorm that doesn't occur because the glass ball "is not yet shaken." This seems to suggest that it is wrong to grant the reality's "storms," especially its emotional storms, access into the poem. For allowing these "storms" into posing-as-real poems diminishes and dilutes them. "First Death," a poem about the death of the poet's grandmother, is stripped of strong emotions, one senses, because Justice doesn't want them taking part in the counterfeit life of the poem. It is this counterfeit life that Justice wants to keep us apprised of by means of the self-reflexive images.

Once one knows to keep an eye out for them, Justice's self-reflexive cues pop up everywhere. When he writes, in "Sonnet to My Father," that he is "Leaving this likeness only in [his dead father's] place," it is unclear whether "likeness" refers to the poet or to the poem. And in "Poem," Justice writes that the poem in question is "not sad, really, only empty." And in the first section of "American Scenes (1904–1905)" (which Justice tells us is culled from James's *Notebooks*), the poet writes: "Each fanlight, each veranda, each good address, / All a mere paint and pasteboard paltriness!" These self-reflexive images are much like the admissions of borrowings in other poems: intimations of inadequacy that this intensely conscientious poet must impart.

In "Thinking about the Past," the poet chides himself for attempting to preserve those moments of the past that will, as he writes, "never change, nor stop being." For to seize the past in verse reduces its vanished abundance to words, all "fixed into place now," as Justice writes, "all rhyming with each other":

> Certain moments will never change, nor stop being—
> My mother's face all smiles, all wrinkles soon;
> The rock wall building, built, collapsed then, fallen;
> Our upright loosening downward slowly out of tune—
> All fixed into place now, all rhyming with each other.
> That red-haired girl with wide mouth—Eleanor—
> Forgotten thirty years—her freckled shoulders, hands.
> The breast of Mary Something, freed from a white
> swimsuit,
> Damp, sandy, warm; or Margery's, a small, caught bird—
> Darkness they rise from, darkness they sink back toward.
> O marvellous early cigarettes! O bitter smoke, Benton . . .
> And Kenny in wartime whites, crisp, cocky,
> Time a bow bent with his certain failure.
> Dusks, dawns; waves; the ends of songs . . .

In "Cinema and Ballad of the Great Depression," meanwhile, Justice likens the economic indignity of men with the indignity of having been transformed into a lifeless aesthetic object: "We had become a line somehow," gripes the poem's speaker.

In "Mrs. Snow," however, the memory is vivid, the poetic rendering doesn't vex Justice all that much, and the poem is free of self-reflexive omens:

> Busts of the great composers glimmered in niches,
> Pale stars. Poor Mrs. Snow, who could forget her,
> Counting the time out in that hushed falsetto?
> (How early we begin to grasp what kitsch is!)

But when she loomed above us like an alp,
We little towns below could feel her shadow.
Somehow her nods of approval seemed to matter
More than the stray flakes drifting from her scalp.
Her etchings of ruins, her mass-production Mings
Were our first culture: she put us in awe of things.
And once, with her help, I composed a waltz,
Too innocent to be completely false,
Perhaps, but full of marvellous clichés.
She beamed and softened then.

                         Ah, those were the days.

But just as often the past is fading from view, not coming into
focus.

And yet, as alert as Justice is to the representational failings of poetry, and as much as this reticent poet seems to flirt
at times with total silence, he never quite washes his hands of
poetry. One reason, certainly, as he himself has suggested, is
the many formal rewards of verse. It could be argued, in fact,
that each poem is a kind of hopeful formal rejoinder to the
painful knowledge, expressed in the content, of its many representational shortcomings:

We shall not ever meet them bearded in heaven,
Nor sunning themselves among the bald of hell;
If anywhere, in the deserted schoolyard at twilight,
Forming a ring, perhaps, or joining hands
In games whose very names we have forgotten.
Come, memory, let us seek them there in the shadows.
                "On the Death of Friends in Childhood"

But beyond the strictly formal excellence of Justice's work,
there is the added marvel of one poet's unrelenting honesty
about the boundaries and limitations of art. Donald Justice is
one of our finest poets.

bibliography

DONALD JUSTICE: A BIBLIOGRAPHICAL CHECKLIST

Compiled by
Michael Peich and Jeffrey Cobb

The compilers wish to thank Ms. Iris Snyder and the staff of Special Collections, Library of the University of Delaware, for their assistance.

SECTION A—PRIMARY PUBLICATIONS

A1 ■ *The Old Bachelor and Other Poems*

[Miami, Fla.]: Pandanus Press, 1951.
Blue wrappers; black stamping on white insert.
Limited to 240 copies.

A2 ■ *The Summer Anniversaries*

a. First edition:
Middletown, Conn.: Wesleyan University Press [1960].
Hardcover edition: Gray cloth, black and yellow stamping; dust wrapper. Paper edition: White stiff wrappers; black, gray, yellow, and purple stamping.
No priority.

b. Revised edition:
Middletown, Conn.: Wesleyan University Press, 1981.
Hardcover edition: Gray cloth, black and green stamping; dust wrapper. Paper edition: White stiff wrappers; green stamping.
No priority.

A3 ▪ *A Local Storm*

Iowa City, Iowa: The Stone Wall Press & The Finial
Press, 1963.
Light green wrappers; black stamping.
Limited to 270 copies.

A4 ▪ *Three Poems*

[Iowa City, Iowa]: [Virginia Piersol] [1966].
Dark blue wrappers, hand sewn.
Privately printed by Virginia Piersol in a workshop taught
by Kim Merker at the University of Iowa.
According to Donald Justice, about half-a-dozen copies
were printed.

Note: Illustrations by Virginia Piersol.

A5 ▪ *Night Light*

a. First edition:

Middletown, Conn.: Wesleyan University Press [1967].
Hardcover edition: Gray cloth, black and red stamping;
dust wrapper. Paper edition: White stiff wrappers; green
and black stamping.
No priority.

b. Revised edition:

Middletown, Conn.: Wesleyan University Press [1981].
Hardcover edition: Gray cloth, black and light orange
stamping; dust wrapper. Paper edition: White stiff wrappers; black, dark gray, and light orange stamping.
No priority.

A6 ▪ *Sixteen Poems*

Iowa City, Iowa: The Stone Wall Press, 1970.
Brown wrappers; black stamping.
Limited to 250 copies.

A7 ■ *From a Notebook*

Iowa City, Iowa: The Seamark Press, 1972.
Olive green cloth, black stamping on white spine label.
Limited to 317 copies.

A8 ■ *L'Homme qui se ferme*
A Poem by Guillevic
The Man Closing Up
A Translation and an Improvisation
by Donald Justice

Iowa City, Iowa: The Stone Wall Press, 1973.
Gray wrappers; black stamping.
Limited to 150 copies.

A9 ■ *Departures*

a. First trade edition:

New York, N.Y.: Atheneum, 1973.
White stiff wrappers; black and brown stamping.

b. First limited edition:

[Iowa City] Iowa: The Penumbra Press/The Stone Wall
Press, 1973.
Tan cloth, red stamping and blind stamping on cover and
red stamping on tan spine label.
Limited to 175 numbered and signed copies.

A10 ■ *Selected Poems*

a. First edition:

New York, N.Y.: Atheneum, 1979.
Hardcover edition: Gray cloth, silver stamping on spine,
blind stamping on front cover; dust wrapper. Paper edition: White stiff wrappers; purple and brown stamping.
No priority.

b. First English edition:

[London]: Anvil Press Poetry, 1980.
White stiff wrappers; black, red, and gold stamping.

A11 ■ *In the Attic*

[West Branch, Iowa]: The Toothpaste Press, 1980.
Broadside, 7⅚" x 10⅞".
Limited to 150 numbered and signed copies.

A12 ■ *Tremayne*
Four Poems by Donald Justice

[Iowa City, Iowa]: The Windhover Press [1984].
Gray paper wrappers; black stamping.
Limited to 210 copies.

Note: Cover drawing by Laurence Donovan.

A13 ■ *Platonic Scripts*

Ann Arbor, Mich.: The University of Michigan Press
[1984].
White stiff wrappers; black and blue-green stamping.

A14 ■ *Men at Forty*

[Colorado Springs, Col.]: [The Press at Colorado College]
[1985].
Broadside, 15" x 20¾".
Limited to 150 numbered and signed copies.

Note: Included in a portfolio of 24 broadsides entitled
"The Printed Poem, The Poem as Print," edited by Dana
Gioia and Alastair Reid.

A15 ■ *The Sunset Maker*
Poems/Stories/A Memoir

a. First edition:

New York, N.Y.: Atheneum, 1987.
Hardcover edition: Black cloth, copper stamping on
spine, blind stamping on front cover; dust wrapper. Paper
edition: White stiff wrappers; black, orange, brown, red,
and blue stamping.
No priority.

b. First English edition:

[London]: Anvil Press Poetry, 1987.
White stiff wrappers; black, orange, brown, red, and blue
stamping.

A16 ■ *The Death of Lincoln*
An Opera by Edwin London
On an Original Libretto by Donald Justice

a. First limited edition:

[Austin, Tex.]: [W. Thomas Taylor] [1988].
Navy blue cloth; dust wrapper.
Limited to 125 numbered copies signed by composer and
Donald Justice.

b. First trade edition:

[Austin, Tex.]: [W. Thomas Taylor] [1988].
Gray paper wrappers; black and red stamping.
Limited to 1100 copies.

A17 ■ *Young Girls Growing Up* (1911)

[Minneapolis, Minn.]: Minnesota Center for the Book
Arts, 1988.
Broadside, 9½" x 14".
Limited to 150 numbered and signed copies.

A18 ■ *A Donald Justice Reader*
Selected Poetry and Prose

a. First edition:

Hanover, N.H.: Middlebury College Press/University
Press of New England [1992].
Red cloth, silver stamping; dust wrapper.
Copyright 1991, but published early the following year.

b. First paper edition:

Hanover, N.H.: Middlebury College Press/University
Press of New England, 1993.
White stiff wrappers; red and black stamping.

A19 ■ *Banjo Dog*
Poems and Linocut Illustrations
by Donald Justice

a. First limited edition:
[Riverside, Calif.]: Thaumatrope Press, 1995.
Navy blue cloth, gold stamping on leather spine label.
Limited to 45 copies signed by the binder, Barbara
Blumenthal, and Donald Justice.

b. First trade edition:
[Riverside, Calif.]: Thaumatrope Press, 1995.
Black die-cut wrappers with yellow-orange paper insert.
Limited to 150 signed copies.

Note: Four linocut illustrations by Donald Justice.

A20 ■ *New & Selected Poems*

a. First edition:

New York, N.Y.: Alfred A. Knopf, 1995.
Maroon cloth, gold stamping on spine, blind stamping on
front cover; dust wrapper.

b. First paper edition:

New York, N.Y.: Alfred A. Knopf, 1997
White stiff wrappers; brown, black, and gray stamping.

SECTION B—BOOKS EDITED
BY DONALD JUSTICE

B1 ■ *The Collected Poems of Weldon Kees*
Edited by Donald Justice

a. First limited edition:

Iowa City, Iowa: The Stone Wall Press, 1960.
Limited to 200 numbered copies, of which 20 (numbered
I to XX) are bound in full black leather, with gold stamping on spine and blind stamping on front cover. Copies
numbers 1–180 are quarter-bound in black leather, with
gray-green paper boards, gold stamping on spine, and
blind stamping on front cover.

Note: Fifteen review copies, in white wrappers, were
issued.

b. First trade edition:

Lincoln, Neb.: University of Nebraska Press [1962].
White stiff wrappers; green stamping.

Note: Preface by Donald Justice. Trade edition includes
six uncollected poems not selected by Justice.

c. Revised trade edition:

Lincoln, Neb.: University of Nebraska Press, 1975.
With a new preface by Donald Justice. Four of the poems
added to the first trade edition omitted.

d. First English edition:

London: Faber and Faber, 1993.
White stiff wrappers; orange and blue patterned stamping
and black stamping.
Contents: same as revised trade edition.

B2 ■ *Contemporary French Poetry*
Fourteen Witnesses of Man's Fate
Edited by Alexander Aspel and Donald Justice

Ann Arbor, Mich.: University of Michigan Press [1965].
White stiff wrappers; black stamping.

Note: Contains "A Note on the Translations" by Donald
Justice and includes translations by Justice and others.

B3 ■ *Syracuse Poems, 1968*
Selected, and with a foreward, by Donald Justice

Syracuse, N.Y.: Department of English, Syracuse
University [1968].
White wrappers; black stamping.
Limited to 1000 copies.

B4 ■ *The Collected Poems of Henri Coulette*
Edited with an introduction by Donald Justice
and Robert Mezey

Fayetteville, Ark.: University of Arkansas Press, 1990.
Black cloth, gold stamping on spine, blind stamping on
front cover; dust wrapper.

B5 ■ *The Comma after Love*
Selected Poems of Raeburn Miller
Edited by Donald Justice

Akron, Ohio: University of Akron Press [1994].
Green cloth, black stamping on spine; dust wrapper.

Note: Introduction by Donald Justice.

INDEX

In the following index, DJ refers to Donald Justice. Cross-references to titles are always to the section of **Works** under the main entry for Donald Justice. Books and anthologies have double entries under author and title, individual poems entries only under author. An author's works are indexed at the end of his entry. When a person or work is referred to but unnamed, there is a subentry headed "referred to." Restaurants, movie theaters, and minor institutions are indexed only under city.